Nightmare Remains

Nightmare Remains

*The Politics of Mourning and
Epistemologies of Disappearance*

◆

Ege Selin Islekel

NORTHWESTERN UNIVERSITY PRESS
EVANSTON, ILLINOIS

Northwestern University Press
www.nupress.northwestern.edu

Copyright © 2024 by Northwestern University. Published 2024 by Northwestern University Press. All rights reserved.

An earlier version of chapter 3 originally appeared as "Building Anew: Spaces of Grief and Memories of Death," Copyright © 2022 Johns Hopkins University Press. This article first appeared in *Theory and Event* 25, no. 1 (January 2022): 25–46.

Printed in the United States of America

10   9   8   7   6   5   4   3   2   1

Library of Congress Cataloging-in-Publication Data

Names: Islekel, Ege Selin, author.
Title: Nightmare remains : the politics of mourning and epistemologies of
    disappearance / Ege Selin Islekel.
Description: Evanston, Illinois : Northwestern University Press, 2024. |
    Includes bibliographical references and index.
Identifiers: LCCN 2024017144 | ISBN 9780810147485 (paperback) |
    ISBN 9780810147492 (cloth) | ISBN 9780810147508 (ebook)
Subjects: LCSH: Burial—Turkey—Philosophy. | Burial—Latin America—
    Philosophy. | Mass burials—Turkey—Philosophy. | Mass burials—Latin
    America—Philosophy. | Death—Turkey. | Death—Latin America.
Classification: LCC GT3273.5.A2 I75 2025 | DDC 155.9/37—dc23/eng/20240610
LC record available at https://lccn.loc.gov/2024017144

CONTENTS

Acknowledgments	*vii*
Prelude	*3*
Introduction	*5*

Part 1. Necrosovereignty

Chapter 1 Absent Death	*25*
Chapter 2 Disappearing Grief	*43*
Chapter 3 Building Anew	*63*
Interlude	*81*

Part 2. Nightmare Knowledges

Chapter 4 The Epistemology of Loss	*91*
Chapter 5 Stories of Nothing	*111*
Chapter 6 Fables That Stir the Mind	*129*
Coda	*145*

Notes	147
Bibliography	165
Index	173

ACKNOWLEDGMENTS

There are many people that this book is indebted to, and much of this debt cannot be paid. First and foremost are the protagonists of this book: the Saturday Mothers, the Mothers of the Plaza de Mayo, the Mothers of Soacha, and all those who do the arduous work of mourning, mourning together, year after year, and day after day. I am thankful to Murat Kocaman, Bilge Demirtaş, and Can Gündüz who, unbeknownst to them, set me on this long road back in 2016 by telling me of a landfill in a town far from my hometown. Every journey has a starting point, and by and large, the documentary they directed, *Ölü ile Diri*, is the starting point of this one. Similarly, I am thankful to those in the Truth, Justice, and Memory Center (Hakikat, Adalet, Hafıza Merkezi) in Turkey, whose work makes up a large portion of the archive that I engage in this project.

Starting points are not easy to pinpoint, and they proliferate when you put them under a microscope. There is another starting point for this book as well, all the way back to 2017 when I wrote the very first article, "Absent Death," presented at the Foucault Circle session of the American Philosophical Association, and published in philoSOPHIA, a version of which became the book's first chapter. I am thankful to Lynne Huffer and Shannon Winnubst, who were the editors of philoSOPHIA back then, who allowed me the freedom to write, think about, and publish on Turkey, a geography that is not so much a part of the imaginary of the contemporary discipline of philosophy in the Global North. The world is indeed small when looked at through the lens of philosophy, and I am thankful to them for inspiring in me the freedom needed to travel across worlds. I am grateful to Banu Bargu, whose work, perhaps unbeknownst to her, has provided me with a lexicon for speaking and writing on power and whose support along the way has meant a lot. María del Rosario Acosta helped me think about how thought travels across the world and how there are dialogues of violence across the peripheries of the world. From her, I learned of the grammars of listening to silences. From Lynne Huffer, I learned that at times murmurs mean more than the words spoken. I am thankful to Miguel Gualdrón, as conversations with him immensely helped me think about the similarities between Turkey and Latin America and how peripheries speak to each other. I am grateful to Nathalia Hernandez, with whom I first thought about the making of the Third World and the way that this making works on a global scale.

vii

I am deeply thankful to the Books in Progress group at Fordham University: Shiloh Whitney, Sam Haddad, and Jeff Flynn have been incredibly generous with their time and thoughts. This book benefited greatly from their careful, and at times line-by-line, reading and comments; I am forever grateful to have had the chance to work with them. Many thanks are also due to Christian Halstead, my former graduate assistant, who read through, proofread, and copyedited earlier versions of the book. I am thankful to Crina Gschwandtner, as her support has been immensely helpful and important to me.

I presented various chapters in several venues; I am especially indebted to audiences at philoSOPHIA: A Feminist Society, SPEP, and the Foucault Circle, where I received helpful feedback. Sections of chapters 2 and 4 were published in *Turkey's Necropolitical Laboratory* (ed. Banu Bargu, 2019); a version of chapter 3 was published in *Theory & Event* (2022); and a version of chapter 5 was published in *Foucault Studies* (2023). I am thankful to the editors and the anonymous reviewers in these venues. Similarly, I am grateful to my anonymous reviewers from Northwestern University Press for their supportive and challenging comments. The ACES Fellowship at Texas A&M University allowed me the time and space to finish this work. My editor at Northwestern University Press, Faith Wilson Stein, shepherded this book to completion and provided support throughout. However much we want, life does not just stop at the time of writing; indeed, much happened throughout the process of finishing this work. I am thankful to Faith for her kindness and support throughout and for reminding me of the importance of being kind to oneself.

Writing is not an easy process, and it is especially difficult when the topic at hand is emotionally taxing, as it was in this case. I could not have written or completed this book if not for the presence in my life of dear friends as I moved across the United States several times. I am grateful to Alison Staudinger and Floyd Wright for sharing with me what home can mean and the joy and strength that can be found therein, even when it is so complicated, so fraught, and at times filled with grief. I am thankful to H Rakes, Sina Kramer, Andrew Dilts, and Marie Draz for our West Coast times together, where the writing process of this book started, and for their incredible friendship over the years. I am grateful to Dilek Huseyinzadegan for being there as a friend, wherever I may be, and always being so generous with her time, thoughts, and guidance. I am immensely grateful to Ece Ekşi. We have walked through various stages of life in the last decade or more, and I am thankful for her constant presence in my life, even though we have not lived in the same city in over a decade. I am thankful to Will Montgomery, Jon Lizarraga, and the entire crew of the Monkey Room for providing a much-needed community in my years in New York. I am also thankful to Konstantinos Karathanasis, Alex Chinchilla Pagano, George Villanueva, Ben Howard, AJ Baginski, and the entire "in flux" crew for their friendship as we all tried to figure out what it means to live in College Station.

Acknowledgments ix

I am forever thankful to my parents, Hatice Dedeler and Zeki İşlekel, for teaching me early on that law and justice do not mean the same thing. From them, I learned the importance of striving for a more just world.

My greatest thanks are due to my life partner, Don Deere, for his immense support throughout the years. Over the course of writing this work, we moved across the continent several times and started over again and again. His conversations, insights, patience, and presence ceaselessly helped me find the strength I needed to continue and finish this book. I am grateful for everything.

Nightmare Remains

PRELUDE

I grew up in a haunted country. Bodies thrown into ditches, or people who disappear never to be seen again, are not exceptional figures in this world. They make up a part of the imaginary: having an aunt or an uncle, a father or a brother, a friend, or a friend who has a father, mother, brother, aunt, who was detained and maybe not heard of again, is not a rare occurrence, shared among too many people. There are silences that interrupt conversations, secrets that everyone knows, memories that are kept by many.

Sitting at a *meyhane* table in my hometown, Izmir, the group across from me is talking about their current project: a documentary they have been working on for multiple years. Recently, the people in the region have grown silent and stopped talking to them. The documentary, *Ölü ile Diri / Mirî û jî sax (The Dead and the Living)*, is about a trash-disposal area at the outskirts of a city in eastern Turkey. Most of the bodies there do not have names, nor were their deaths recorded anywhere. I ask M. how he knows about this. He tells me it is because his uncle is there, in the trash. There are people in the trash.

There is a news flash on TV. On the screen, the picture of an old woman, wearing a white headscarf, and holding up a photograph. Her name is Berfo Kirbayir, and she died at the age of 106. She searched for her son for 36 years, and never closed her windows, and never locked her door. Nobody knows where her son may be, or where he was taken after being detained that one night that she described over and over again. She said she sometimes talks to her son, and she meets with her son every Saturday, at Galatasaray Square. Her dying wish was not to be buried until her son's grave was found, and to be buried next to her son. Her wish could not be fulfilled. She was buried, TV says. Her son has no grave.

I am a kid; the adults are talking. They are talking about someone, they are talking as if the person can come in at any minute; it sounds odd. He is an old friend, they say. I ask, "Where is he? When is he coming back?" They stop talking and notice me. There is silence. Finally, someone says, "We don't know." Silence. "He disappeared." There is silence among the adults. I shiver, feel a ghost passing by. The person they were talking about is one of the thousands of people, who knows how many thousands, who have disappeared. People do not vanish into thin air. Silence is made of flesh and bones.

There is an online map of Turkey in front of me, in blue. Scattered on the blue are red and yellow dots. At top is written: "The Map of Mass Graves in Turkey." Each red dot represents graves confirmed: ditches and caves, bodies found, dates attached. Each yellow dot marks graves suspected: bodies rumored, entry not allowed, sites inaccessible, military-protected lands, tops of mountains, bottoms of wells, riverbeds dried up. The red dots are many, the yellow dots are even more. I stare, and I blink. The next time I look, the website is shut down. "There has been an unexpected error," it says. The map does not exist anymore. Where was the error?

I am reading a small book of poetry by Raúl Zurita. Written on the page is: "We walk between the graves talking: Did you eat me? / Why were you hungry Chilean did you eat me?" Sometimes countries eat people. So many are eaten by the places they love.

♦

Somewhere along this journey, I learned to speak of ghosts, and learned that ghosts travel across the world. I became introduced to ghosts on the other side of the world and also to those who do the work of living with them, in a world that is so bent on continuously forgetting and starting anew. This book is my homage to those who speak to ghosts, those who do the difficult task of mourning; mourning those who are gone but not quite dead, those who relentlessly weave words out of nightmares. This book is my attempt to conjure ghosts, for a split second.

INTRODUCTION

A trash-disposal area next to a city, somehow called a river, that has hosted hundreds of bodies for the last forty years or so, entry prohibited. Everyone in the area knows they are there, yet no one has been able to take them out. It has been over thirty years; the families have remained living in the area to be close to the river.

A mass grave pit, with bodies of young men, fully armed, dressed in uniforms. They were found there, no one knows how they got there, or what happened between the time they left their home and were found in the pit.

A lot in a general cemetery, hundreds of tombstones bearing the letters NN, signifying *no nombre*, "no name." The lot is filled in and emptied of nameless bodies that were there at some point and later taken out, to be thrown out of helicopters. Many know that there were bodies there that are now in the depths of the ocean, or on the tops of mountains; but no one knows who ended up where.

Basements of buildings, torn down by artillery shells, hundreds of people slowly die as they wait for a rescue that was never on its way. They were there, and few know how, or whether they got out.

A freezer in a small town, holding the body of a ten-year-old girl whose family was not able to leave their house to take her body out to bury: they knew how to keep her body, even though they could not get her out.

A street, in the middle of which lies the body of a 57-year-old woman, fatally wounded, in front of her own doorstep, while her family was stuck inside. She was there: they knew how long she was there for, even though they could not bring her in.

This book is about what happens in the absence of death. It is about bodies that do not make it to graves, graves that have been emptied out, people who disappear never to be seen again, ghosts that haunt for decades. Death is far from a simple natural or biological state, but rather is continuously engulfed in operations of power, and is taken up to be molded, shaped, utilized, and weaponized. The undead and the unburied, although often invisible and often unintelligible, are far from exceptional figures of contemporary politics: their invisibility and unintelligibility, rather, lie at the core of its methods.

What is the role of the undead and unburied in politics: within which configurations of power do they emerge, through which orders of discourse do they become known or unknown, in and through what kinds of spaces and temporalities do they become memorable, or forgettable? What follows, as a whole, is an articulation of contemporary politics as a management of the right to death: of what I call "necrosovereignty," a method of power operative in the postcolonial context, which organizes not only how individuals and populations live and die, but also their epistemic and political afterlives, such as what they know about death, how that information is circulated, and what kinds of rationalities uphold and reify such information. Necrosovereignty regulates how bodies are mourned and what kinds of knowledge of death are possible, while designating spaces of impossible mourning, erasing archives, and rebuilding sites, thus actively preventing practices that pertain to mourning. Starting from Turkey and building a South-South dialogue with Latin America, I focus on techniques of improper burial, such as enforced disappearances, mass burials, and burial prohibitions. As a whole, I make the case that necrosovereignty is one of the key mechanisms defining contemporary colonial global politics, through its work on archives, memories, and spaces.

This book is equally about nightmares that remain. Nightmares that keep people awake for decades, realities that make nightmares and become indistinguishable from them, nightmares that open up other spaces, that change what is said and what is sayable, what is done and what is doable. Knowledge does not exist only in relation to categories of objectivity and rationality: the world of necrosovereignty makes these categories of cognitive success nonsensical. There are kinds of knowledge that emerge in the absence of records, and there are archives that challenge norms of rationality. Nightmare knowledges are modes of knowing that challenge the archival and epistemic boundaries of necrosovereignty. They involve practices of mourning, such as burying bodies marked not to be buried, turning regular houses into houses of mourning, assembling at city centers regularly over many years, telling stories of disappeared people that are not verified by archives, challenging dominant modes of knowledge and rationality. Insofar as necrosovereignty is bent on turning death into nothing, mourning serves not only as a mode of political action but as a key form of epistemic resistance, a way of challenging colonial/modern orders of knowledge by producing alternative modes of knowing and remembering.

As a whole, I argue that colonial politics works by targeting the afterlives of death: within this political schema, long durational and collective practices of mourning make up a key tactic of epistemic resistance, which reshapes orders of memory and knowledge. In the narrowest sense, this is about improper burial and archival erasure, and how much and how insistently these two are deployed, and what remains from them. In the broadest sense, this is a book about power and knowledge, politics and resistance, and archives and nightmares.

Introduction

Analytics of Power: Necrosovereignty

Necrosovereignty targets the afterlives of subjects and populations: it impacts what happens to their bodies, what is known of them, how they are remembered, how the spaces of their lives and deaths are constituted, and the archives within which they exist. It is a technology of power that *allows or disallows death* to those who are gone, or it works to disappear death itself. As such, necrosovereignty is an assemblage that works on afterlives, a condition that fits neither in life nor death. Necrosovereignty operates on bodies as much as archives, both in terms of spaces of record-keeping and of lived spaces that are themselves records. What I provide here is the analytics of how this technology operates, what kinds of instrumental modes it deploys, what forms of institutionalization it sustains, and which epistemic and spatial dimensions it works through.

Michel Foucault defines biopolitics as a kind of power invested in the maximization of life, concerned with sustaining and managing life. Whereas sovereignty, as described by traditional theorists such as Jean Bodin, Thomas Hobbes, and Carl Schmitt, works on the juridical level, through laws and the state, biopolitics works through extra-state processes and mechanisms, at the intersection of norms, statistics, and economics. As such, it employs dispersed techniques that work on individual bodies, such as surveillance; reorganizing institutions such as schools, prisons, and the military; and also techniques that work on the population as a whole. As a technology of power, biopolitics works *over* life, to "*foster life* or to *disallow it* to the point of death."[1] The line between life and death, accordingly, is drawn in that fine decision of what/whose life gets fostered through the regulation of extra-state mechanisms, and what/whose life is disallowed (and how). Thus, biopolitics denotes the differential distribution of life chances across the population, and it does so both through work on individual bodies and at the level of social regulation of the population.

The biopolitical technology described by Foucault is ultimately distinct from the phenomena that I discuss here, which involve arbitrary detainment, secret detention centers, executions without orders, the erasure of death, the absence of archives, and the proliferation of improper burials. Indeed, while Foucault extensively discusses techniques such as surveillance, statistical regulation, and the like as key technologies of biopolitics, the questions that mark my focus here are notably absent from his account. These questions especially mark the post-colony and the periphery, and they are much closer to another kind of power that Achille Mbembe calls "necropolitics," which focuses rather on the role of death and its overwhelming presence. Accordingly, as much as the politics of welfare states and later the neoliberalism of the Global North demonstrates an emphasis on the maximization of life across the population, ultimately, "the notion of biopower is insufficient to account for contemporary forms of the subjugation of life to the power of death."[2] Thinking of politics and accounting for its colonial and postcolonial faces requires considering how, as Mbembe says, "the political, under the guise of war, of resistance, or of the fight against terror, makes the murder of the enemy its primary and absolute objective."[3] Necropolitics aims to maximize death, quantitatively and qualitatively.[4]

However, the work of power does not end with death; it continues afterwards, erasing archives, building over destroyed cities, altering the seemingly clear distinctions between life and death, and creating entire populations of those that are gone but not dead. By introducing the term "necrosovereignty," I move toward thinking of the work of power on afterlives, which comprise neither the domain of the living nor the dead. In the aftermath of death, disappearance, or loss, necrosovereignty allows or disallows individuals and groups to be dead. This distribution of the right to death takes place particularly through epistemic methods. How knowledge is produced, how information is distributed, what presents itself as knowable, and the rationality that upholds different objects of knowledge together form not external, but rather key elements of power. As Jacques Derrida writes, "one has to know . . . one has to know who is buried where—and it is necessary to know, to make certain, that in what remains of him [sic], he remains there."[5] Necrosovereignty targets the possibility of knowing, of forming coherent discursive totalities: it targets the status of knowers as knowers and the very epistemic capacities of making connections and verifying information. From the falsification of information, to the erasure of archival records, to the rebuilding of sites of memory, knowing and remembering "who is buried where" is precisely the target of necrosovereignty, not an epiphenomenon: necrosovereignty works on a distinctly epistemic register, targeting the possibilities of sense-making, of creating coherent totalities of information. The world of necrosovereignty is an incoherent world: from people dead but never found, to mobile detention centers, to people who search and then themselves disappear, the things in necrosovereignty do not make sense. Most importantly, this happens not in exceptional sites of power or when power enters a void, but rather, in its regular and sustained operation. As I will make the case throughout this book, even the so-called "states of exception" are not so exceptional, nor are they hollow: they are rather marked by corporeal, spatial, and epistemic exercises of power.

Each exercise of power comes with a series of aims and objectives. The method I pursue throughout can best be described as an "analytics," exploring how this technology operates and what it *does*. This means, by and large, bracketing off questions of "what" and "why" in order to prioritize questions around exercises, methods, instruments, institutionalization, objectives. How is necrosovereignty's technology mobilized, and with what aims and objectives? Within which system of differentiation is it situated, where does it work, and through which discourses does it operate? How does it differ from other technologies, such as biopolitics, with which it coexists? What forms

Introduction 9

of institutionalization sustain it? Most importantly, what are the modes of struggle against this technology? In analyzing these, I pursue the goal of destabilizing necrosovereignty, rather than excavating its origins or analyzing its nature. In doing so, my goal is to take away the sense of necessity from necrosovereignty, this work of power on the epistemic afterlives of the dead: a key conviction that I pursue throughout the book is that *it could be otherwise*, that resistance to necrosovereignty is not just a possibility, but it is rather performed consistently and continuously. I thus bracket the ontological and the transhistorical questions, not because they are not important, but because my goal here is to focus on necrosovereignty's points of pressure and condensation. In doing so, I join Foucault in attempting to provide "tactical pointers" of struggle, describing the techniques through which necrosovereignty operates, and the points by which it is resisted.

Moreover, as analytics of power, the account provided here is decidedly descriptive, rather than normative. Whereas normative approaches provide analyses of how a given conceptual object should work in accordance with a given goal, descriptive approaches focus on relations of power in their present tense, as Verena Erlenbusch-Anderson argues.[6] In this sense, normative approaches work similarly to what Charles Mills describes as "ideal theory," accounting for the ideal conditions within which categories such as rights, freedom, or democracy would be meaningful and effective.[7] Non-ideal theory describes the inner logics operative under social conditions that are decidedly not ideal: rather than providing prescriptive conclusions, non-ideal theory provides a diagnostics of conditions that make up categories such as rights, freedom, and resistance in their existing shape and form. I align my work here with non-ideal theory in descriptively analyzing the political technology of turning death into nothing by organizing epistemic afterlives, rather than attempting to prescribe how politics should deal with death.

Take, for example, my analysis of improper burial as a key technique of necrosovereignty. Here, techniques of improper burial denote the corporeal methods through which mourning is sent awry. It is a technique which specifically targets the possibility of mourning on the basis of the body. There may be no body to be found to place in a grave, as in the case of the enforced disappearances that have marked the histories of Latin America and Turkey in the twentieth and twenty-first centuries. There may be no grave in which to place the body, as in the case of Turkey's extended curfews in the 1990s and again from 2015 onward. There may be no names attached to the graves, such as the various "NN" (*no nombre*) graves of Chile.[8] There may be no records of the person, such as in the case of the piles of bodies that are found in rivers or mountainous areas in Colombia and Argentina. Or there may be no graves and no bodies to be found whatsoever, such as the bottoms of the ocean across the Americas or the mountainous zones in Turkey, where bodies have been air-dropped, without any way of identifying exactly where or who has been dropped there. Improper burial happens when bodies are targeted to regulate or prohibit practices of mourning.

Analyzing improper burial as a technique is distinct from a prescription of a "proper burial." Of course, rituals are important in designating the boundaries of political citizenship and subjectivity, in shaping the orders of discourse, in marking humanity. As Valérie Loichot says, "since rituals are practiced by all societies, they are understood as a defining mark of humanity."[9] Moreover, burial rituals seem to have a specific function in creating a relationship with the dead, and creating an entire historical and social organization on the basis of this relationship. Thomas Lacquer, for example, demonstrates that the dead perform a collective work and thus they even "make civilization." In this sense, the dead are "active agents in history" insofar as "the concern for and care of the dead makes up a fundamental part of social organization."[10] Hans Ruin, in his work *Being with the Dead*, expertly makes the case that human community is constituted on the basis of forming, and sustaining, a close relationship with the dead. Rituals, accordingly, play the particular function of building community and sustaining it, not only among the living, but between the living and the dead.[11]

Nevertheless, within the framework of an analytics of power, my task is neither to investigate the historical (or transhistorical) importance of funerary rites, nor to prescribe the proper way of mourning. Rather, my questions are aimed at improper burial as it pertains to its forms of institutionalization, objectives, and instrumental modes. Thus, throughout the book, I treat improper burial as a technique that is often deployed by state and extra-state organizations (such as the paramilitary, the prison-industrial complex, or state-sanctioned extralegal activity), and often times extrajudicially. Improper burial takes place in contexts that are distinct from each other, but it produces surprisingly similar results in making the sound of violence echo across the globe. From the disappearance of the political criminals of Turkey, to those of randomly targeted working-class youth in Colombia taken away to boost body counts in the military's fight against Revolutionary Armed Forces of Colombia (FARC), it does not have a specific group of addressees, save for its frequent occurrence across geographies. Improper burial often takes place not as a singular method but alongside others, such as arbitrary detentions, extralegal executions, regional and national states of emergency, the operations of the "war on terror," the erasure of archives, and the rebuilding of sites of violence in processes of gentrification. Moreover, it appears to have certain goals: it erases entire groups of people from records, and it manages who counts as a member of the "population." In this sense, improper burial is a technique, "a way in which certain actions may structure the field of other possible actions."[12] Throughout the book, I describe and diagnose the ways in which improper burial intervenes in the field of other actions, as well those actions that emerge from, in response to, or in opposition to improper burial. What I provide is an account of power, in order to destabilize it.

Introduction

Diagnostics of Resistance: Nightmare Knowledges

The exercise of power is always connected with practices of resistance.[13] Indeed, insofar as necrosovereignty is invested in organizing and regulating mourning, it is accompanied by practices of resistance, particularly those that politicize mourning. From producing spectacles of organized mourning in prominent city centers, to transforming regular houses into funeral homes, the aftermath of improper burial attests over and over again that mourning does not only exist in the exercise of power, but in and through resistances to it. Focusing on these resistances, moreover, shows us much about how knowledge formation works in relation to power, and how entire epistemologies can be mobilized in the face of necrosovereignty.

José Medina discusses epistemic resistance as a cognitive relationality formed as a response to epistemic injustice: working in both oppositional and non-oppositional forms, resistant epistemologies are built on the premise that the subjects of epistemic injustice are endowed with the capacity to resist, build relations, and deploy other imaginations.[14] Resistant epistemologies are built through establishing different types of cognitive attitudes toward what presents itself as knowable or verifiable. In the context of continuous epistemic injustice, categories that otherwise would be seen as epistemic impasses, such as dreams, nightmares, and perplexities, can be mobilized to put into question what appears to be clear, concrete, or lucid.

The kinds of knowledge that I call "nightmare knowledges" are the unofficial and local knowledges formed in the context of necrosovereignty. Insofar as necrosovereignty targets the possibility of sense-making and creating a coherent whole out of the epistemic sources, nightmare knowledges challenge dominant rationalities by mobilizing so-called "epistemic impasses." For example, the names of those dumped in mass graves are not registered, and the inscription of memory related to mass graves is recorded mostly in the memory of the local population. In the insufficiency of the written archive, collective memory works productively: rather than attempting to verify information through records, it creates and tells stories, shares dreams and nightmares, and organizes political action through these stories, dreams, and nightmares. These kinds of resistances highlight the impossibility of coherent narratives in the context of necrosovereignty: they work by challenging the supposed transparency offered by necrosovereignty, they mobilize opacity, weaponizing nightmares against assumptions of lucidity, and they tell stories of nothing in order to highlight the ways in which necrosovereignty does not "make sense." By analyzing specific epistemic practices that are deployed in the "mothers' movements," such as telling stories in weekly meetings, holding regular demonstrations in public squares, and challenging supposedly clear narratives by appealing to dreams and nightmares, I contend that the local knowledges established in the context of improper burial demonstrate insurrectionary capacities: they challenge not only what is recorded, said, or known, but what is knowable, sayable, or intelligible. As such, these knowledges transform the spaces within which they emerge, along with the subjects of those spaces.

Importantly, the diagnostic approach that I take here applies not only to power but also to resistance. When it comes to movements that politicize mourning, normative approaches come with a myriad of questions about the effectiveness and durability of movements and well-being of the actors. These questions usually have a disqualifying tone: according to them, the Mothers of the Plaza de Mayo and the Saturday Mothers have been engaged in a desperately ineffective method of activism, one that is doomed to end without any real consequences. Similarly, issues around mental well-being are raised on the psychological level, suggesting that the mothers' particular long-durational practices of mourning demonstrate psychic processes that have gone awry, and thus their prolongation makes the mothers' recovery from grief more difficult. Often, these criticisms end up in a highly patronizing tone with respect to these movements, judging whether mourning is good for these actors, what they should do instead, and so on. A fundamental commitment that I pursue here is the goal of taking the mothers as political actors, and I do not seek to prescribe how their modes of resistance should take shape, nor do I seek to disqualify their very difficult task of mourning.

Instead, I problematize the conditions under which collective mourning, and especially, mourning by mobilizing categories that are traditionally excluded from cognitive success, become a part of political organization, while taking into account the choices that are made by subjects as political actors. Throughout, I analyze not whether people should resist through practices of collective and prolonged mourning, nor do I prescribe taking on categories of cognitive impasses such as perplexity or nightmares as main modes of political action. Rather, I describe the conditions under which prolonged mourning presents itself as a viable political action, and the field of relations within which this action becomes intelligible. The simple goal of this book is to pay homage to the members of these movements as political actors and explore the kind of politics within which these actions are inscribed.

Archive and Geography: Weaving a Story of Power

My trajectory finds its footing with modern Turkey and its neglected histories of burials gone awry and enforced disappearances. Yet, it travels across the globe in its archival assemblage, to Latin America. In and through these scenes, what I present here is a periphery-to-periphery dialogue (or a South-South dialogue) among the subjects of necrosovereignty that carves out a space at the borders of the West, highlighting episodes that take place in processes of "westernization," demonstrating the stamp of a kind of power that consists in wielding loss and making death disappear.

Introduction   13

In modern Turkey, that is, the Turkish Republic as a nation-state founded in 1923, improper burial is most commonly associated with the aftermaths of the coup in 1980 and later with the regional "states of exception" declared in the southeastern regions of Turkey in the 1990s, even though these are not the only moments of the country's history that were marked by this phenomenon.[15] The military coup of 1980, the one in the country's history, and its aftermath are infamous as Turkey's own "Dirty War" of sorts. Following a decade of political polarization that took place in the 1970s, and a parliamentary crisis that was accompanied by a deepening economic crisis, the coup d'état of 1980 was declared as a way to put an end to the "terror" of political violence that was taking place on the streets.[16] Indeed, the coup was part of the project of order and progress; it marked a moment in Turkey's long efforts at westernization, its attempts to prove that the Turks, like the westerners, have the "innate ability to modernize."[17] Taking over the government, the military immediately shut down the National Assembly, closed all political parties, confiscated all their assets, and in the process banned all forms of political activism and engagement, banning over 23,000 different political organizations. As the criminalization of political activity rose to unprecedented heights, according to the records, 650,000 people were detained, 230,000 people were prosecuted, and conversely, according to the official records, only about 300 died in prisons or under detention.[18] The unofficial estimates of extralegal detentions are about twice these figures, and there is as of now no concrete number established for those who were extralegally killed (in detention, conflict, or during curfew), just as there is no concrete number established for disappearances.

One of the results of the coup was to create a haunted society.[19] As enforced disappearances started being systematically utilized, the social imaginary of "modern" Turkey became shaped by ghosts of sorts: those who died in detention, those who left never to be seen again, bodies thrown in landfills or ditches, body parts found marked with wounds of unimaginable tortures. The methods of the coup were utilized frequently afterwards, and the undead of Turkey continuously multiplied, especially in the 1990s. Enforced disappearances were most notably used in Turkey's "war on terror" against the Kurdistan Workers' Party (PKK) and reached a peak in the "regional states of exception" declared in the eastern regions of Turkey in the 1990s, especially between 1991 and 1996, that targeted the majority Kurdish population there. The regional states of exception were in operation on and off between 1987 and 2002; they then went into effect again starting with the renewal of the "war on terror" in 2015.[20]

The absence of a grave resembles the absence of an archive, and not surprisingly, the former often coincides with the latter. Tracing what is not there, what has been misplaced and misrecorded, is a work of weaving: weaving together lines and testimonies, weaving graves across locales, or as María Lugones would say, traveling between worlds.[21] Indeed, while techniques of

14   Introduction

improper burial make up much of the social imaginary of Turkey, the phenomenon has been seriously under-studied, with very few theoretical sources in Turkey[22] and almost none in the international field.[23] Within Turkey, partly due to the state's ongoing pressure on movements such as the Saturday Mothers, there have been very few systematic studies, many of which are gathered as part of the work of local nongovernmental organizations (NGOs).[24] The sources that I work with on Turkey consist of the documentation from public announcements of Saturday Mothers' weekly meetings and other searchers' movements, and the direct testimonies found in media sources, news articles, Amnesty International reports, and most importantly, in the ethnographic material prepared by NGOs such as the Truth, Justice, and Memory Center (Hakikat, Adalet, Hafıza Merkezi).

Yet, Turkey is virtually absent from transnational philosophical and theoretical discourses on improper burial, with no current book-length studies on the topic, and Turkey is not commonly included in comparative studies on the topic either. As much as my starting point is "home," theorizing techniques of improper burial in Turkey took me elsewhere, to techniques taking place across the world around the same time period, in other processes of westernization, in Latin America, and more specifically, in Chile and Argentina. Indeed, as few resources as there are on improper burial in Turkey, there is an entire theoretical assemblage of memory and trauma studies from the very long twentieth century of Latin America, where over a hundred coups took place in and across the continent.[25] The use of enforced disappearances in Latin America is assumed to have started in Guatemala in the 1960s, and its systemic use continued afterwards throughout the region, most notably in the 1980s and 1990s, but also continuing still.[26] Out of the nineteen countries in which coups took place, Chile and Argentina earned an awful notoriety with their immense multiplication of the undead and unburied in the 1973 coup d'état in Chile and its aftermath under Pinochet, and with the Dirty War in Argentina, which lasted from 1976 to 1983. As Dulitzky says, "indigenous persons, peasants, community, political and union leaders, students, academics, members of religious communities and priests, military or paramilitary agents (those suspected of collaborating with the enemy), and members of armed opposition groups are among those who were forcibly disappeared."[27] The official numbers of Argentina's Dirty War claim 30,000 people dead or disappeared: these were people officially or unofficially arrested and who were never seen again. In Chile, the coup regime that overthrew Salvador Allende and put Augusto Pinochet in power is estimated to have tortured over 40,000 Chileans and disappeared over 4,000.[28]

Much like in the case of Turkey, none of these numbers is reliable; as I will make the case repeatedly throughout this book, they are instead rough estimates. What they demonstrate, however, is that they have left behind, much like in the case of Turkey, haunted societies, and perhaps unlike Turkey, those who speak of their haunting. Indeed, though it is difficult to gain access to

Introduction 15

sources in Turkey on improper burial, the various Truth and Reconciliation committees in Latin America (and especially the Southern Cone) have made systematic efforts to find the disappeared, archive them, and give a name to the disappeared. Some of these efforts are focused on the legal sphere: for example, the Latin American Federation of the Families of the Disappeared (FEDEFAM) and other organizations have fought since the 1980s to adopt legal mechanisms that would recognize enforced disappearance as an international crime.[29] Many of the efforts of Latin American institutions, such as the Inter-American Court of Human Rights, have had a global impact, so much so that multiple cases in Turkey that made it to the United Nations courts were adjudicated with the courts referring to precedents set by the Inter-American Court of Human Rights.[30] Moreover, the long-durational movements that found their footing in Argentina and Chile, such as the Madres de Plaza de Mayo, explicitly served as inspirations and models to other countries in the Global South. The Saturday Mothers in Turkey is a powerful example of one such organization founded in reference to the *madres* in Argentina.[31]

Thinking about improper burial in Turkey in the absence of an established theoretical discourse thus means making ghosts speak with each other and conjuring them across geographies, weaving different poles from across the globe. The ghosts of Turkey, Chile, and Argentina and the recent ghosts of Soacha in Colombia have much in common with each other. They are, for the most part, contemporaneous, with only a few years separating them in time. The victims lack a common denominator, even when they are called "subversives, terrorists, leftists, or anarchists": many of them were people chosen quite randomly, many of them literally picked up from the side of the road, some of them children, some of them elderly. Their deaths lack records or have too many records that are misleading; their bodies were thrown in ditches or dropped in mountainous areas, but they have also never existed. They emerge as part of the work of progress, the work of order and westernization, in nation-states that are endlessly modernizing.

It is important to distinguish this work from that of the abstract universalizing gaze, which incorporates all it encounters into one body of the same, equating, assimilating, and conflating differences. Improper burial does not make up the inescapable nature of politics, which is to be reinstantiated over time and space. Rather, I weave these experiences together so that they tell the story of a kind of power that aims to make death disappear, the kind of power that aims to wield loss, a power that I call "necrosovereignty." Moreover, this work is countered by a kind of resistance that works by shifting the terms of knowledge and discourse, a kind of resistance that creates new kinds of archives and memories by deploying collective methods of mourning. Thus, in each chapter, I start with one or more scenes: a place, a person, or a story. These scenes lie at the heart of this work, and in many ways, this book as a whole revolves around these scenes. The majority of these scenes are from Turkey, from the cases at the starting points of this research; such as the trash-disposal area known as Newala Qesaba, or from the round-the-clock curfews. Other scenes are from Chile, such as the General Cemetery in Santiago; or from Colombia, such as Soacha, the suburb of Bogotá; or from Argentina, such as the Plaza de Mayo. These are the scenes that I was introduced to along the way. As I start with scenes in each chapter, I provide context, as well as archival information, as limited as the archives are: the number of people reported to be involved, the news reports, if there were any, and the official information, presented locally or internationally, on the context and the background of the scene. Many of these scenes come up repeatedly throughout the book, and thus they appear and disappear in different chapters. Moving between the chapters, these scenes will become familiar to the reader. In each of these spaces, necrosovereignty is not a matter of necessity: in each case, it could have happened otherwise, and it is continuously contested. My hope is that what will become unfamiliar is the work of power in making death disappear.

The Coloniality of Loss

Improper burial and its afterlives indeed echo across the edges of the West. Such echoes emerge from the coloniality of necrosovereignty as a technology of power, one that is both linked to and distinguished from formations of improper burial in the West. Mourning has a long history in the so-called "Western" imaginary, though it takes on a different meaning at the borders of the West. In the imaginary that takes its origin to be ancient Greece, Sophocles's *Antigone* comes forth as the figure of mourning, a stubborn figure who politicizes what it means to mourn: she insists on giving her brother Polyneices a "proper burial" despite the orders of Creon, and disobeys laws in order to properly mourn. Much of the Western imaginary finds its grounding somewhere between this verdict of improper burial and its foundational role in the legitimacy of state-sanctioned violence. For example, Hegel famously argues that the conflict between Antigone and Creon demonstrate a fundamental moment in the relation between family and the State.[32] Hans Ruin argues that Antigone is a "necropolitical heroine" who demonstrates the metaphysical bond between the living and the dead that underlies political community by mobilizing her own life.[33] Through her insistence, Antigone shows that burial has something to do with political membership, and whether or not one receives proper burial is a concern not only for the dead and their kin, but also for politics as a whole. What remains from *Antigone* is the import of mourning, repeated at many moments: a kind of "dead-body politics," as Katherine Verdery calls it, marks many of the moments of the memorialization of corpses, be they saints, political leaders, or unknown soldiers.[34]

As much as the Western imaginary is formed, by and large, on the inscription of proper burial, improper burial marks the project of modernity at

Introduction

the edges of the West. Thus, improper burial takes on a different meaning when considered from a global perspective, considering the abyss that Édouard Glissant talks about: the incalculable loss, not only of people, but of memory, archive, and an entire world, the loss that is the Middle Passage. Sylvia Wynter describes 1492 as the beginning of a new "world order" that marked the emergence not only of a new global politics but also of a radically new redescription of key epistemic categories such as knowledge, truth, and most importantly, what it means to be a subject.[35] For Wynter, the project of the colonization of Africa and the Americas was one of overrepresentation: overrepresentation of the primary subject of politics as a white European male subject, one supposedly capable of understanding the totality of Being, capable of recording and archiving all that exists. Accompanying this overrepresentation was the opening up of the abyss for the Africans: the belly of the boat that swallowed and devoured at once, the sea "pregnant with as many dead as living under sentence of death," the total count of those lost into this abyss and completely absent from archives that are currently knowable to us, a number that moves back and forth by hundreds of thousands on a good day, by millions on other days.[36] The abyssal beginnings of the New World order that Wynter discusses swallowed archives as much as histories, peoples, lands, sufferings, and vociferations. Saidiya Hartman says that the "loss of stories sharpens the hunger for them."[37]

The abyssal archives of slavery and its afterlives break apart the possibilities of analyzing clear records or finding that mighty Truth of all those who were lost. The work of loss, working with loss and in loss, is an all too familiar, if not fundamental part of the afterlives of the abyss: in Sharpe's words, "to be *in* the wake is to occupy and to be occupied by the continuous and changing present of slavery's as yet unresolved unfolding."[38] Nevertheless, the methods that made up the Atlantic slave trade as an economic system are fundamentally different from the phenomena that I focus on here.[39] An equivocation between these would not only be dangerous but also analytically inadequate. Hartman, concerning the Atlantic slave trade, states: "death was not a goal of its own but just a by-product of commerce, which has had the lasting effect of making negligible all the millions of lives lost."[40] In contrast, the techniques of power that make up necrosovereignty are often intentional, and the examples given here have taken place mostly in the twentieth century, often in conjunction with state and extra-state organizations. Loss in necrosovereignty is both an object and objective: it is not a by-product of commerce but an entire political technology, one that is carefully managed.[41]

One of the key convictions that marks the conceptual backdrop of *Nightmare Remains* is Glissant's declaration, which might also be an invitation: "Thought, in reality, spaces itself out in the world."[42] As Wynter and Glissant both show us, the Middle Passage marked the emergence of a kind of loss that can neither be recorded nor recovered, a kind of loss that marks a new world order. To take up Glissant's invitation means accepting the abyss as the beginning of an entire world order: a world order that is built on the abyss, a world order that is bent on wielding loss. Aníbal Quijano discusses this new world order in terms of the "coloniality of power": the global dispersion of power relations that works through the hierarchization and racialization of populations and the rearticulation of the globe as centered in Europe and the West, and the re-formation of entire political mechanisms in accordance with this new worldview. Within this context, a "modern" nation-state is a very specific phenomenon: a colonial phenomenon built on the dream of a centralized power over a delineated territory in a homogenous society, one where homogenization marks one of the key techniques of state organization.[43] However, the very operations of power that make up coloniality take on different shapes globally, in the "West" and at its edges.[44]

As María Lugones says, the coloniality of power impacts the "light" side of modernity differently from the "dark side." Their repetitions of power across the globe take place in a house of horrors, with twisted instantiations, each resembling one another, but at the same time unbearably different. Accordingly, the "modern" nation-state in Europe and the Global North has taken on forms that are both very similar and quite different from those at the edges of the West. Within Europe and European empires, one encounters nation-states founded on histories of internal colonization, a "culture-specific internal domination" inside territories "real or imagined," as Alexander Etkind defines it. This involved the domination of people of different identities within spaces of internal domination or in territories imagined as close to the territory or seen as places that "should be" a part of the national territory.[45] This kind of internal colonization is akin to the "boomerang effect" of colonialism discussed by Hannah Arendt, Foucault, and Aimé Césaire, where methods of power and violence that were born in the colonies made their way back to Europe. The dark side of modernity, on the other hand, has a different relationship to power, violence, and death.

The geographies that I discuss here are located at the borders of the West, where they are both linked to and distinguished from the West. None of them are "outside" of the West, inasmuch as they inhabit nation-state formations that take part in the project of modernization and westernization. Modernization and westernization operate as "a distorted mirror," as Quijano says: what we see is "not completely chimerical," since we possess so many traits that are historically Western, but we are also "profoundly different."[46] Yet, as Quijano says, "the tragedy is that we have all been led, knowingly or not, wanting it or not, to see and accept that image as our own and belonging to us alone."[47] However the West might define us, our self-view is one that is Western through and through. The house of horrors of modernity/coloniality creates heroes and monsters, in reality and in fiction, so much so that the very distinctions between the real and the imaginary become fuzzy. Constructing a nation-state "à la Europea" in the periphery involves particular methods of homogenization and control, ones that are both too similar and

Introduction   *19*

too distinct from those in the Global North. We at the peripheries "continue being what we are not," endlessly modernizing through twisted and distorted projects:[48] each of the geographies that are discussed here is marked by this project of modernity. In the aftermaths of the abyss, becoming "modern" in the periphery means practicing and perfecting how to target both death and its afterlives, learning how to strive for a homogenous society, learning how to engage with and perfect projects of racialization. Thus, in the contexts of Latin America, in Chile and Argentina, one can speak directly of the impact of colonial histories and the formal processes of decolonization from the imperial rule of Spain. But in the context of Turkey, where formal colonization did not take place, one can still speak of the formation of (post)colonial processes of racialization in the formation of discursive and political devices around Kurdish identity, and similarly, the formation of a Turkish identity around a Westernized elite, thus "exalting homogenous nation-statehood as the criteria for 'Western-ness,' in the process othering the ethno-religious diversity of the country as defining 'orientalness.' "[49] While homogenization and racialization thus become the method of modernization in the periphery—loved ones taken away and never to be seen again, supposedly complete archives that erase thousands of people, piles of bodies rotting in trash-disposal areas, mountainous zones filled with countless bodies thrown, and places of massacre that yield their sites to city development projects—all these mark moments of modernization in the Global South. As Nelson Maldonado Torres writes: "the lived experience of racialized people is deeply touched by the encounter with misanthropic skepticism and by the constant encounter with violence and death. The language that they use has also already been shaped by an understanding of the world as a battlefield in which they are permanently vanquished."[50] Within the periphery, the phenomenon of improper burial takes place as westward-tending projections, and necrosovereignty emerges on the periphery's route to the center.

Necrosovereignty is a colonial/modern power, and the modes of resistance that emerge with respect to it in the periphery are both linked and distinguished from Western imaginaries. While the Antigone of the West, as a "necropolitical heroine," splits herself from her reproductive destiny and performs resistance by refusing her reproductive role by refusing to be a mother, those at the borders of the West perform motherhood, often in tension with its traditional script, and at times, as Diana Taylor says, as a trap. For the Mothers of the Plaza de Mayo, the Saturday Mothers, and the Mothers of Soacha, deploying motherhood paradoxically entails renouncing familiar roles: traveling between cities and towns, organizing with different groups, telling stories about themselves, their lost ones, and the stories of others. It is a life filled with the risk of harassment, abduction, arrest, and murder.[51] From the Mothers of the Plaza de Mayo in Argentina, to the Saturday Mothers in Turkey and the Mothers of Soacha in Colombia, the Antigones of the borders of the West are not solitary figures; rather, they form multifarious movements that extend the temporal life of politics beyond death, collectively, and over spans of time. Indeed, these are the best-known and longest-lasting mothers' movements, where the movements have become multigenerational. Between Turkey and Latin America, what echoes is not only the workings of necrosovereignty in making loss disappear but also the resistances that consist in mobilizing loss and creating archives, spaces, and entire worlds that resist the sealed closure of loss.

This is thus a periphery-to-periphery dialogue, between ghosts and the nightmares that remain, giving the analytics of a power that emerges in the periphery and its efforts to find the center: a power that works by making death absent, by erasing archives, by taking sense away from death, by building spaces anew. More importantly, this is a periphery-to-periphery dialogue across resistances that emerge in mobilizing against this power; these resistances fabulate archives in the absence of records, makes sense out of nightmares, and create spaces of mourning in the midst of cities.

Flow and Break

Nightmare Remains consists of two main parts, developed in six chapters in total. The first part, "Necrosovereignty," develops mourning as a key component in a contemporary politics of death that produces specific archives, memories, and knowledges around death. The second part, "Nightmare Knowledges," investigates how the same kinds of knowledge are mobilized and politicized resistantly. While the chapters in the first part focus on the politics of mourning, the latter focus on the politicization of mourning: each of the chapters in the latter part mirrors those of the former, emphasizing the coexistence of power and resistance.

The first chapter, "Absent Death," develops the idea of the "tactics of mourning" that are drawn around death: necrosovereign power not only deals with how and where death takes place but also with the regulation of practices of grief. This chapter explicates why and how politics is invested in mourning, and specifically, what the import of improper burial practices is from the perspective of life and death. "Absent Death" presents some of the key sites of improper burial that are repeatedly revisited throughout the book, such as Newala Qesaba, Patio 29 of the General Cemetery in Santiago, Chile, and the regional "states of exception" in Turkey. The term "necrosovereignty" is introduced here to designate the investment of politics in regulating the right to death and allowing or disallowing individuals and groups to be dead. The techniques of improper burial create haunted spaces, where the distinctions between dead and alive are systematically obfuscated, and the limbo of life and death opens up when those who are gone are not allowed to be dead.

Having established the notion of necrosovereignty, the second chapter, "Disappearing Grief," moves on to the epistemic techniques that produce

Introduction   21

the limbo of necrosovereignty. Necrosovereignty works through methods of knowledge production: erasing archives that pertain to the existence of the disappeared and their disappearance, disqualifying the testimony of relatives and witnesses, and targeting the coherence of narratives and memory. These are all methods of epistemic injustice of sorts, targeting what is known and what is knowable of death. This chapter demonstrates that targeting what is known and knowable of death is a key part of the contemporary politics of mourning. "Disappearing Grief" overall provides a typography of epistemic injustices that make up this assemblage. The epistemic injustices such as gendered hysterization, invisibilization, and archival erasure that take place in necrosovereign contexts target the temporal and logical coherence of memory, narrative, and testimony.

Knowledge does not take place in abstraction from concrete spaces: power/knowledge assemblages work on spatial levels; they organize cities, distribute borders, and regulate circulation. The third chapter, "Building Anew," focuses on the relation between the memory politics of necrosovereignty and its spatial politics. The zones where round-the-clock curfews are declared for extended time periods, so that those who leave their homes are either detained or shot, provide examples of spaces within which life and the living are subsumed under death. This chapter works on the aftermaths of curfew zones in Turkey, wherein sites of violence are destroyed and built anew, ceding their place to urban redevelopment projects, and the traces of death are not only erased but also built over. Focusing on the relation between space and memory, this chapter shows that the spatial methods of necropolitics, such as bulldozing, infrastructural warfare, and the urban redevelopment of sites of violence, work on collective memory on both the involuntary and traumatic levels. Spatial reorganization implies the replacement of sensuous data, wherein the memories of violence are replaced by absences and short-term memories. What is left behind are haunted memories, that is, collective memories shaped by oblivion and absence. Critical engagement with the work of necrosovereignty on memory requires not tracing the traumas but rather engaging with another kind of archive that resides in counter-memories.

The second half of the book, "Nightmare Knowledges," moves from power to resistance. All the chapters here function on the wager that not only power, but also resistance works on epistemic levels, and it is necessary to consider resistance/knowledge assemblages as much as one considers those of power/knowledge. Just as power works through knowledge production methods, archival techniques, and narrative methods, so does resistance, in developing interplays with archive, narrative, memory, and spatial politics. The fourth chapter, "The Epistemology of Loss," develops the notion of "epistemic resistance" as presented by José Medina, and provides an account of the epistemic resistances deployed in contexts of necrosovereignty. The active deployment of mourning is a mode of resistance that produces counter-knowledges and counter-discourses that work through other modes of intelligibility, made up by specific epistemic practices, such as the use of nightmares, active memory, and the prolongation of collective grief. Overall, this chapter shows that these counter-discourses, which I call "nightmare knowledges," constitute instances of collective epistemic agency, where mourning is mobilized against necrosovereignty.

The fifth chapter, "Stories of Nothing," focuses specifically on the collective storytelling practices that are deployed by the relatives and loved ones of the disappeared, such as telling the stories of the day they disappeared, when they heard about the remains in mass graves, or when they had dreams of the disappeared returning and nightmares of them returning dead. These are stories that exist in dreams, nightmares, and erased memories. Thus, this chapter works on fabulation, and specifically "critical fabulation," as Hartman calls it, the kind of fabulation that works in the absence of archives, and is deployed as a collective practice rather than an academic one. This kind of practice is an example of a collective epistemic resistance that is deployed to mobilize nightmare knowledges. Such mobilization plays into the dramaturgy of the real: these stories turn disappearance into a non-event, shift the actors of it from the state to the disappeared and their remnants, and shift the temporality of disappearance from the past to an ongoing present. In the assemblages of necrosovereignty, which erase records, disqualify testimonies, and rebuild spaces anew, fabulations of nothing function as a mode of resistance that can shift the meanings of events and archives, and produce lives and deaths out of limbo.

The final chapter, "Fables That Stir the Mind," titled after a Sylvia Wynter essay, returns to the relations between space and resistance in practices of fabulation. Formulated as the mirror to chapter 3, "Building Anew," this chapter considers reinvention against building anew, and analyzes how spaces are taken up not only through power but also through resistance. Thus, the focus of this chapter is the other spaces of necrosovereignty, the ones that coexist with death-worlds, spaces such as the city squares that regularly become spaces of meeting, or the funeral homes that become spaces of organization. Dwelling on Wynter's analyses of the spatial and epistemic politics of fables, this chapter demonstrates that spatial reinvention is an inseparable form of epistemic resistance, which creates new memory spaces. Against the spaces of violence that become haunted ordinary spaces in building anew, spatial reinventions reconstrue ordinary spaces as spaces of memory, spaces to conjure the ghosts of necrosovereignty. This spatial reinvention, moreover, is one that resides in the emergence of other spaces, as well as other subjects, and other modes of knowing, understanding, and remembering. Thus, "Fables That Stir the Mind" makes up the last chapter of the book by performing what *Nightmare Remains* has set out to do: showing that contemporary politics is invested in organizing and shaping practices of mourning, and that mourning, nevertheless, is politicized to produce other modalities of knowing and remembering.

Part 1

✦

Necrosovereignty

Chapter 1

Absent Death

In Siirt, a town in eastern Turkey, there is a trash-disposal area called Newala Qesaba, the "River of Butchers."[52] Around 1988, the families of more than eighty people were notified that the remains of their children were there. There was a brief investigation, which ended when the journalist covering the issue, Günay Arslan, was detained in 1990. Between 1984 and 1991, during the height of the "fight against terror," the River of Butchers was used to dispose of not only trash but also bodies, most commonly, the bodies of the disappeared. For a long time, the area was protected by the military, and now it is open to the construction of condominiums by a company called War Construction.[53] There have been no official exhumations possible, and the families who were notified are not allowed to retrieve the remains there. The number of bodies that are in Newala Qesaba is estimated to be more than 300. Newala Qesaba is one of the 253 identified and confirmed mass gravesites in Turkey, which are considered to host 3,485 sets of human remains in total.[54] The number of the "disappeared," however, is much higher than this number, although an exact report on the disappeared in Turkey is still nonexistent.[55]

The fates of mass graves and the disappeared coincide not only in Turkey: Argentina and Chile are also notorious for their disappeared. In the General Cemetery of Santiago there is a separate lot, bearing the name "Patio 29." Here, the graves are marked by crosses bearing only the initials "N.N." (*ningún nombre, no nombre, nomen nescios*, "no name"). Patio 29 was one of the three mass graves in the Santiago area (there is also one in Lonquén and another one in Yumbel) that received much publicity in 1978 and 1979, when exhumations and work to find the bodies of the disappeared reached a peak. During the investigation, it was learned that Patio 29 had received more than 300 bodies in a three-month period, sometimes with more than one body crammed into the same coffin.[56] These mass graves received so much attention that the Chilean military decided to empty them out, including Patio 29: the solution found was to surreptitiously make a number of the dead "disappear" once again, this time by digging them up and then air-dropping the remains at sea or over mountainous regions.

25

Finally, there are examples of improper burial resulting from a regional "state of exception." Regional states of exception have a different history than national states of exception; in them, practices such as curfews or cease-and-desist orders are declared only in a specific region or area.[57] A common practice of the regional states of exception that have been ongoing in eastern Turkey since 2015 has been to implement a round-the-clock curfew, during which time the residents of the areas are not allowed to leave their homes. In September 2015, a ten-year-old girl called Cemile was shot by the military in front of her house, steps away from the door. Her family was able to drag her body in, and yet was not allowed to go out to bury her: the dead body of Cemile was kept in a freezer in her family's house for over nine days before it was taken from the house.[58]

The question at the heart of this chapter is how politics is invested in practices of mourning and, specifically, what the import of techniques of improper burial is from a perspective that takes into account the relationship between politics and life and death. What kind of power is at stake in such examples of power invested in mourning? In answering these questions, we will visit the biopolitical framework of Foucault's corpus throughout and first briefly elaborate the role of death in biopolitics in relation to necropolitics. We will then analyze these accounts in relation to techniques of improper burial in order to problematize the role of mourning in the work of these technologies of power. The final section of the chapter focuses on the question of mourning and the political practices of mourning. Here, we will touch on readings of *Antigone* and Judith Butler's discussion of grievable lives as two possible articulations of the relationship between politics and practices of mourning. Last, we will return to the cases of Newala Qesaba mentioned earlier and question the relationship between death and mourning, articulated from a perspective that works on death not as a natural category but as an element of power. Overall, this chapter demonstrates that the regulation of grief is a specific technology of power, which is here called a "necrosovereign" technology. As such, it makes the reach of biopolitics on death and the dead possible. The question at the heart of biopolitics, which Foucault states as "make live or let die," is coupled with a necrosovereign element of *making* die, that is, actively allowing or disallowing individuals and groups to be dead.

Biopolitics of Death and Necropolitics of the Dead

Famously in *History of Sexuality, Volume 1,* as well as in the lecture courses entitled *Society Must Be Defended,* Michel Foucault argues that modern politics is shaped by a concern with life. Somewhere in the eighteenth century, the primary technique of power ceased to be that of the power to take life that is characteristic of sovereignty; instead, power invested itself with a full apparatus that takes life as its object. This model of power, which he calls

Absent Death

biopolitics, "infuses life and aims to ensure, sustain and multiply life."[59] Such a shift in the primary mode of power, in Foucault's account, took place not only in the relation between power and life and death, but also in juridical power and normative power and the ways in which power takes up and deals with the subject in general.

Sovereignty is a specific model of power that works on the juridical level, through laws and the state. It is a discontinuous form of power that takes territory and the law as its objects, rather than the subjects populating the territory or obeying the laws: the relation between the sovereign and the subjects is established through sporadic encounters, such as ceremonies, the laws, and taxation on the basis of land. Hence, the sovereign encounters the subject only in the moments when the laws are broken, taxes are not paid, or the borders of the territory are crossed. For this reason, Foucault calls the sovereign power a "negative" exercise of power that is not concerned with the subject as such. All these encounters heighten the singularity of the sovereign, while dis-individualizing the subjects: subjects constitute a mass that is relevant to the sovereign only insofar as they fall inside or outside the laws and the borders. The height and the limit of sovereignty, for Foucault, is not so much the type of effect it has on the lives of the subjects but much more so on the question of *whether or not* it has any effect on their lives: as a negative exercise, the only type of impact the sovereign has is in terms of negating their lives. In Foucault's words, "sovereign power's effect on life is exercised only when the sovereign can kill."[60] The sovereign, in this sense, is the one who can "*take* life or *let* live."[61] The assumption of the act of sovereignty, in this sense, is that the subjects' lives do not have any qualitative determinants for the sovereign unless the sovereign intervenes. As much as it is invested in the moment of killing, however, sovereignty makes a spectacle of death as an attestation of the might of the sovereign. Foucault's *Discipline and Punish*, for example, famously begins with a torture scene, where Damiens, the regicide, is quartered, dismembered, and torched, all in front of the eyes of the public, in order to make an example of the power of sovereignty. For Foucault, such an act of public torture demonstrates the investment of power in prolonging the moment of death in order to prolong its threat of death: the very spectacle performs the function of demonstrating sovereign power, where the audience and the regicide at once are reminded of the power of the sovereign to kill.

Inasmuch as sovereignty is decidedly a "juridical" mode of power attached to the state and state mechanisms, Foucault suggests that in contemporary politics, it is accompanied by another technology of power. Unlike sovereignty, this other technology, "biopower," does not approach life negatively and express itself in the moment of ending it; instead, biopower infuses life and aims to "ensure, sustain and multiply life."[62] This new form of power works both on the level of individuals and on the population. In the first volume of *History of Sexuality*, Foucault divides the two functions that are both part of this technology. On the one hand, disciplinary power (i.e., anatomo-politics) works on the mechanics of the body: it categorizes, classifies, hierarchizes, examines, and, in so doing, it normalizes and individualizes subjects.[63] The distribution of bodies along the axes of space and time makes up the primary scope of this disciplinary power: by categorizing, organizing, and distributing individual bodies, it aims to extract the maximum amount of energy from them in the least costly way possible. To this end, it applies surveillance, categorization, and the classification of bodies so that they form a multiplicity consisting of individuals. Biopolitics, on the other hand, works through extra-state organisms, at the intersection of norms, mores, and also economics. Its scope is specifically the population, and it is concerned neither with the relations between a sovereign and the people, nor with the disciplining of individual bodies: its concerns involve the relation between this mass and its environment, the livelihood of this mass and the continuation of its health. Hence, biopolitics deals not with surveillance techniques, timetables, and the allocation of individual bodies like disciplinary power does, but instead with rates of reproduction, mortality rates, biological disabilities, the effects of the environment on the health of population, and the risk factors for the health of the population. Instead of ruling over a territory, biopolitics is concerned with the "well-being" of populations and deploys various technologies to ensure life and longevity. Switching from the sovereign capacity to "take lives," biopolitics works to "*foster life* or to *disallow it* to the point of death,"[64] or in other words, to "make live or let die."[65] In biopolitics, life seamlessly becomes dependent on mechanisms of power, which target the mass of the population and take life as an object to be "optimized."[66]

This characterization of a "shift" in the models of power has led to criticism of it in various accounts. Jacques Derrida, for example, in his *The Death Penalty* seminars, questions whether such a periodization is actually viable, or whether there are such semantic distinctions in the first place.[67] Derrida questions whether the distinction that Foucault makes between "taking life" as a juridical and sovereign phenomenon, and "letting die" as a specifically contemporary phenomenon, can be made so easily. He asks: "what if taking life and letting die were the same thing?"[68] On a similar point of critique, Judith Butler famously calls Foucault's account a "wishful construction" in which "death is effectively expelled from Western modernity, cast *behind* it as a historical possibility, surpassed or cast *outside* it as a non-Western phenomenon."[69] Much of Foucault's account, however, works not on the replacement model, but rather on the permeation model: the account he describes is less one wherein a given model of power, say biopolitics, arises and eliminates all traces of its predecessor, in this case, sovereignty; he cautions that "we should not see things as the replacement of sovereignty by a society of discipline, and then of a society of discipline by a society, say, of government."[70] Rather, Foucault's account is much more concerned with the "infiltration" or "permeation" of one model of power by another one: biopower *permeates* sovereignty, so that the mechanisms of sovereignty work alongside and in the service of biopolitical regulation. Law becomes a tactic of management; surveillance becomes a method of border control: different technologies start enforcing and supporting each other through time, and there is not a clear semantic separation between different models of power.

Even though Foucault does not argue that the shift from sovereignty to biopolitics is a clear semantic one, there remains something unsettling about the argument that the predominant mode of power in contemporary politics works to optimize life. Achille Mbembe argues: "The notion of biopower does not suffice to account for the contemporary ways in which the political, under the disguise of war, of resistance, or of fights against terror, makes the murder of its enemy its primary and absolute objective."[71] Mbembe argues that there is yet another apparatus that dovetails with biopolitics, what he calls "necropolitics," which deals with the production and regulation of death through the production of "death-worlds."[72] Necropolitics, in Mbembe's account, works where the sovereign right to kill takes on a normative ground and entire populations are positioned as akin to death. The regional state of exception during which Cemile died would be an example of the necropolitical production of death-worlds. The populations in areas of southeast Turkey where the states of exception are announced and curfews are declared are, in this sense, made into a die-able population, for it is assumed to already have an intimate relationship to death. As one of the ministers of the Turkish Republic stated in early 2016, one "should not be surprised about death" in these areas, since it is a routine part of life.

To a certain extent, this emphasis on death exists in Foucault's own account. The regional states of exception or Newala Qesaba, given that they target the regions primarily inhabited by the Kurdish population of Turkey, could be considered in relation to what Foucault discusses as state racism in his 1976 lecture courses titled *Society Must Be Defended*. Here, Foucault argues that the death function of biopolitics is fulfilled by state racism, which is "primarily a way of introducing a break into the domain of life that is under power's control: the break between what must live and what must die."[73] State racism creates a positive relationship between the right to kill and the assurance of life, forming a moment of intersection of sovereign power and biopolitics in the discourse of social defense: the main argument of state racism is to say, "the more you kill, the more you will live."[74] As Erlenbusch-Anderson helpfully notes, the account of racism that Foucault offers is a "functional account of racism" that differs from ethnic racism: by "state racism," Foucault means "not a mode of oppression directed against other races external to the social body, but 'a principle of exclusion and segregation' deployed to protect the health of the population."[75] As such, he uses this term as a biological operation that is performed in the name of the health and well-being of the population, as what Erlenbusch-Anderson calls a *mechanism of social defense*, that works by bringing together discourses such as abnormality, enmity, and terror. Such an account is helpful, for, given that all of the instances mentioned so far have taken place in the "fight against terror," the lives and deaths at stake testify to this racism of a state against its own members in an effort of biological warfare that works on entire populations, in a kind of "cleansing" operation undertaken by the state.

And yet, what strikes one with regard to regional states of exception and mass graves is the strangeness of the entire situation, such that it does not seem to fit within the models offered by Foucault. For one thing, as much as the Foucauldian formulation of sovereignty is to be understood through the sovereign order to take lives, the extrajudicial killings we have discussed take place outside the purview of sovereignty. Even though these are often called "state killings," there are no death penalties issued and no juridical processes that take place. The killings are related to the sovereign, and yet they do not present a spectacle of the sovereign's power in the way that the death penalty or the traditional right to take life does: the moment of death is missing from all memory that could be established. In one moment, persons are alive and in the next, disappeared. The moment of death—the spectacle of it, which is what Foucault articulates as the height of sovereignty—is precisely what is missing.

Moreover, enforced disappearances and other techniques of improper burial work on different registers than that of killing or taking lives. Even though death is intimately tied to disappearance, disappearance does not equate to death. Rather, disappearance is a complex technology involving the state and the mechanisms of abduction, together with mechanisms that would involve the relatives and those who are close to the disappeared, and the memory of the disappeared altogether. According to the UN International Convention for the Protection of All Persons from Enforced Disappearance, the term "enforced disappearance" expresses "the arrest, detention, abduction or any other form of deprivation of liberty by agents of the State or by persons or groups of persons acting with the authorization, support or acquiescence of the state, followed by a refusal to acknowledge the deprivation of liberty or by the concealment of the fate or whereabouts of the disappeared person, which place such a person outside the protection of the law."[76] These state-initiated abductions usually take individuals to secret or unofficial detention centers for unforeseeable time periods, and the disappeared and the relatives of the disappeared are either not informed or actively misinformed about their fate and whereabouts. As Bargu puts it, "Given the secrecy and uncertainty, enforced disappearance works as a violation that has no temporal end, except for the production of a body, dead or alive."[77] Within such temporal uncertainty, the threat of death and its spectacle—which are both key elements of sovereignty in Foucault's account—lose their force, giving their place to various ambiguities instead. Although endlessly mixing into each other, death and disappearance are not the same thing, nor can sovereign killing be equated with these extrajudicial processes of disappearance or the extrajudicial places of burial. In this sense, as Gordon puts

Absent Death 31

it, disappearance is not just another name for execution; it is, rather, a "thing in itself"[78] that demonstrates another kind of investment of power in bodies and life and death than the juridical modes of killing or taking lives per se.

However, this investment in techniques of improper burial does not quite fit within the working procedures of the biopolitical apparatus either, for the very technologies that are commonly identified with the work of biopolitics appear to encounter barriers when it comes to these techniques. In Foucault's account, inasmuch as biopolitics works on and through the population, much of its operation takes place through record-keeping and information-gathering, accompanied by statistical regulation in accordance with such records. In *Society Must Be Defended*, for example, Foucault asserts that biopower's field of intervention involves "the birth rate, the mortality rate, various biological disabilities, the effects of the environment, and so on."[79] These tasks of biopolitical regulation of "health" and "well-being," in other words, take place through gathering data and information, keeping track of records, and observing variations. In the case of techniques of improper burial, on the other hand, what is notable is precisely the absence of such data or records, for the information of the mass graves or those who die during regional states of exception is very poorly, if at all, recorded. If biopolitics is the kind of power that works through statistical regulation, in the cases at hand, the statistical archive is quite difficult to access and much of the information has vanished, either due to direct secrecy or simple neglect. Unlike the conventional technologies of biopolitics that work through intensive surveillance, tracking, and statistical regulation, there is very little surveillance involved and little or no tracking maintained, so there is hardly enough information that would lend itself to any kind of regulation. As said at the beginning of this chapter, a concrete report on the exact number of those who have disappeared in Turkey still does not exist, even though the question has been studied by a variety of human rights organizations. In Argentina, the difference in the accounted numbers is drastic: for example, the Argentine National Commission on the Disappeared reports the number to be 9,000, whereas Colonel Ramón Campos, police chief for the province of Buenos Aires, claims that the number is more than 45,000. The Mothers of the Plaza de Mayo, on the other hand, assume the number to be around 30,000.[80] As a counterpart to the disappeared, mass graves divide into identified ones and the unidentified ones: in Chile and Argentina, Gordon states, "virtually every cemetery had its *no nombre* grave. Getting rid of corpses was a problem for a country that denied that there were any."[81] Yet, even though these are marked graves, the numbers they hold are quite difficult to know, insofar as most of them contain multiple bodies crammed into a single coffin, and moreover, burial itself was accompanied by other methods such as air-dropping. In Turkey, mass graves are at mostly random and arbitrary places, where finding them is almost entirely dependent on some coincidental encounter. Hence, Newala Qesaba is a trash-disposal area, and many other mass graves are in sites such as wells, caves, or holes dug in mountainous areas. With such unstable quantitative data, the very functioning of biopolitics along the lines of statistical regulation appears to be compromised at each and every step.

Techniques of improper burial thus cannot be fully characterized by sovereignty, but not by biopolitics either. Bargu argues that when considering the intersections of biopolitics and sovereignty, especially in the moments where the state coincides with biological warfare, "neither sovereignty, nor discipline, nor security singly defines the contemporary characteristics of the contemporary power regime."[82] For Bargu, contemporary politics testifies to a profound shift in the apparatuses of the Foucauldian models of power, where what we see is now neither biopolitics nor sovereignty, but what she calls "bio-sovereignty." Bio-sovereignty exists as a mode of power in which "sovereignty persists, but it is permeated and transformed, not only with the invasive diffusion but with the conscious, voluntary and rational adoption and incorporation of disciplinary and governmental techniques."[83] Moreover, much of the state violence does not stop with the killing itself: the apparatuses of the bio-sovereign state target the body as much as the life of the individual, actively using the dead in order to reach the living. Hence, Bargu uses the term "necropolitical violence" to denote those acts that target the dead bodies of those killed in armed conflict, by way of their mutilation, dismemberment, denuding, desecration, dragging, and public display; the destruction of local cemeteries and other sacred spaces that are designated for communication with and commemoration of the dead; the delay, interruption, or suspension of the conduct of funerary rituals; the imposition of mass or anonymous internment; the pressure for clandestine internment; and the repression and dispersion of funeral processions for the newly dead.[84] For Bargu, various practices that target the dead body aim at, as she says, a "utilization of the dead" in order to reach the living, in order to subdue, terrorize, and control the living.[85]

There is much to be said about the effects of targeting the body of the dead on the living. However, in the case of techniques of improper burial, not only the politics of living but also the politics of mourning, referring to both the practices and possibilities of mourning, become issues at stake. After all, if necropolitical practices on the body of the dead can be utilized in order to reach the living, this is possible through targeting practices of mourning as well. The notions of biopolitics, sovereignty, and necropolitics all need to be complicated in order to be able to account for the investment of these kinds of politics in mourning, in the sense of its possibility and its practices, the way it is recognized and understood, the way it makes itself knowable, recognizable, and understandable. Rather than focusing on what power does to the living through techniques of improper burial practices, this book focuses on what it does to the ones that are gone, their lives and afterlives. What I call "necrosovereignty" is the kind of power that consists not only in taking lives or making live, but the kind of power that consists in *letting die*

Absent Death

33

or *prohibiting death*. Relatedly, "necrosovereign assemblages" refers to the conjunction of biopolitics, necropolitics, and sovereignty in order to point to the infusion of the work on life and death into the practices of mourning. The rest of this chapter takes death in a structure of necrosovereign assemblages that work to create death and death-worlds. I argue by the end of the chapter that just as the mode of power that is operative here fits into the categories of neither sovereignty nor biopolitics, the death that is produced through this structure is also dissimilar to sovereign killing or biopolitical mortality.

Ölü ile Diri / Mîrî û jî sax / The Dead and the Living

There appears to be an element of "exceptionality" involved in the cases of techniques of improper burial, an active carving-out of a space outside the law. In Turkey, Chile, and Argentina, the histories of mass graves and disappearances are tightly linked to the histories of a variety of states of exception. For traditional theorists of sovereignty, the state of exception is not outside the purview of sovereignty but is precisely the exemplary site of sovereign power. Jean Bodin defines sovereignty as the power to "make and annul laws," where that moment of annulling is inscribed in the juridical character of sovereignty.[86] Carl Schmitt situates sovereignty in the moment of the state of exception, in the power to declare the state of exception and suspend all law.[87] The exception is that space in which sovereignty is manifested par excellence, where the entirety of the juridical order is lifted. Giorgio Agamben asserts that the state of exception is a "zone of indistinction" where the juridical order is suspended and the legal order is hollowed out to leave in its place a void.[88] Agamben makes the argument that this zone of indistinction is the regular state of affairs within the contemporary political order: life loses its formal quality, and all life becomes "bare life."

Nevertheless, in the case of techniques of improper burial, one of the defining elements of the technique itself is precisely the vastness of its frequency, its repetition, and also, its geographic variety. Indeed, enforced disappearance as a technique has a history that is not geographically specific; despite the common association of the technique with Latin America, there is mounting evidence that it has been used by a variety of states across different continents. Much of the activism and investigation regarding enforced disappearances focus indeed on their wide geographic occurrence. According to the UN Working Group on Enforced or Involuntary Disappearances, the cases that remain under "active consideration" extend over a total of eighty-four states,[89] including not only Turkey and those in Latin America, but also countries in the Middle East, Europe, Africa, and Asia,[90] as well as the United States, specifically with respect to its own "war on terror."[91] While these studies have mostly investigated "active" cases, broadening one's scope of analysis to include the mass disappearances of the first half of the twentieth century—including the Spanish Civil War and Nazi practices during World War II—demonstrates that enforced disappearance as a phenomenon is far from an occasional occurrence in times of crisis but is rather a frequently used tactic. The techniques of what are called "improper burial," moreover, include not only enforced disappearance but also methods of targeting the body in order to regulate and organize the practices, and even the possibilities, of mourning: as such, they have an even larger extension in both their geography and frequency. Valérie Loichot, for example, discusses the investment in making bodies unable to be mourned in terms of the "unritual," which she argues is at stake in the watery graves of the slaves that were dumped in the ocean during the transatlantic slave trade, specifically in the Middle Passage and beyond.[92] The language of "exceptionality," in the sense of marking any kind of rarity, thus is not helpful in understanding the techniques of improper burial. Rather, as Bargu says, improper burial appears as "one among many tactics" that are deployed in reaching the living and the dead, and is tightly implicated in the emergence of the modern state and its apparatus.[93]

The language of hollowness and indistinction that is prevalent in Agamben's conception of "states of exception" resonates to some extent with the experience of improper burial. In cases of enforced disappearance, the person "disappears into thin air" as it is reported often by the relatives, or as it is said in Turkish, "becomes a bird and flies." The secrecy involved in the process, together with the absence of both the body and the records of the person, open up a gap indeed. However, unlike Agamben's description of life in the state of exception, the experience of disappearance is not hollow, nor is it void. It is rather a complicated web consisting of unforgotten knowledges, unsaid statements, inaccessible mass graves, unreturned bones, and undead deaths. Those who remain know, more than anything else, that there is an existence to those who are put in a trash-disposal area, despite the lack of official information or acknowledgment, despite the lack of personal testimony. Apart from the denials, the lack of evidence, and the lack of records, the knowledge of disappearance becomes a thing in itself. Erasure works not as a complete impossibilization, nor does it work as the complete destruction of knowledge. In *Mîrî û jî sax* Günay Aslan says: "You believe people when they tell you that they see dogs carrying human body parts, or they tell you that odd cargo comes to Newala Qesaba," despite the absence of photographs, despite the river being covered with snow, despite the area being part of a banned military zone where no permits of exhumation have been given.[94] In improper burial, rather than the hollowness of existence that Agamben describes, there is instead a proliferation of what Lynne Huffer calls the "murmur": a kind of "background noise" on the politics of improper burial, constituted by muffled sounds and rumors, interlocutions between state officials and residents, dreams, desires, nightmares, stories, pleasures that have little room in ordinary speech, and that nevertheless signify a limbo between presence and absence, or life and death.[95]

Moreover, this murmur is constituted not only by the living that remain, but by the ones that are gone as well, for there are both official and personal ways in which they become un-dead. For one thing, there are the official ways: the families left behind are not qualified for state support, for example, for those who have disappeared and those in mass graves who are still not "officially dead," even years and years after their disappearance, even when there is more than sufficient reason to believe that they are dead.[96] The state's recognition of death is a contested issue for a variety of reasons, including using the disappeared as a tactical instrument to subdue or terrorize the living, and also, paradoxically, utilizing the disappeared as a negotiating tool between the state and human rights organizations. Chile has a long history of ebbs and tides in the cases of the disappeared, declaring them dead, annulling this declaration, then returning some of the bones, and then admitting to having returned the wrong bones. For example, after the exhumations in 1979 in Patio 29, a group of people received bones that were supposedly those of their relatives. Much later, in January 2001, the armed forces, in a reconciliatory initiative, revealed the fate of 200 disappearances, and admitted that 130 of the remains at the site had subsequently been air-dropped into the ocean. "Many people who had received remains of relatives buried in Patio 29 were shocked to find that their names were on the list of 130 disappeared thrown into the sea," so the bones they had received did not belong to their relatives.[97] The state recognizing the disappeared as "dead" thus often comes at a high price; and yet, the absence of such recognition also becomes a tool for reaching the living through the disappeared.

The cases of unofficial deaths and disappearances and the techniques of improper burial do not point to a void, a lawless and formless life: in the absence of death, they form a limbo that is filled with knowledges and memories, together with official and intrapersonal practices of undoing death. In marking their relationship to sovereignty and sovereign authority, thus, it is important to consider states of exception not as abyssal spaces where all meaning vanishes.[98] These are rather spaces that work as breaches to other technologies of power, other methods of a relationship to life and death that are intimately tied to the possibility of grief. Rather than focusing on their void, one must thus listen to their murmur, watch what is there and not there, what is said and not said in the coming and going of the dead, the disappeared, and the living, and pay attention not to the way in which power hollows out, but the way it fills in, proliferates, and regulates. Mass graves and disappearances are thus spaces that are not defined by absence or void. They function not only to destroy evidence or to obscure massacres but to deny the relatives their mourning, to create sites of impossible mourning: they are examples not only of killing but of a tactics of mourning, of obstructing, delaying, or foreclosing mourning. Together with death one must consider mourning as a political category, as a technique employed within necrosovereign assemblages.

36   Chapter 1

Unmourned Death: Antigone and Grievable Lives

In many ways, Sophocles's *Antigone* can be read in parallel to the story of
Cemile. The state appears in Creon's prohibition of the burial of Polyneices,
whose corpse is to be left to rot on the streets after he died in battle, per an
edict of the victor Creon. Antigone refuses to obey this edict of Creon and
plans a secret burial for her brother. Antigone emerges as a figure who stands
at the clash between kinship and the state in her attempt to give her brother a
proper burial. The play revolves around the question of the relations between
the state and the family, between burial practices and political membership,
between gendered practices of mourning and legal sanctions on mourning. As
Hans Ruin says, *Antigone* shows the ways in which the relation with the dead
is crucial for human sociality.[99] With her relentless insistence on giving her
brother a proper burial, Antigone has occupied Western thought and imagination for over 2,000 years, and she has been construed as a heroic model by
some and a victim by others. For some readers, Antigone represents a figure
of feminine disobedience in her insistence on giving her brother a proper
burial and her defiance of Creon's edict, whereas for others she represents
the role of the family as opposed to state sanctions and therefore fulfills her
role in the economy of politics that is founded upon a division between the
feminine family/home and the masculine state.[100]

Throughout, however, one thing remains persistent: mourning and burial
are political practices, practices that have something to do with the laws and
the state. Bonnie Honig notes that the sanction on Polyneices's burial by Creon
mimics the legislation of Solon, which restrained public lamentation and particularly targeted expressions of grief (mostly voiced by women), especially
over those who have died in battle. The practice of banning or restricting
public manifestations of grief has been employed in a variety of societies
from Athens to modern Europe.[101] Hegel, in his reading of Antigone, suggests
that the question of burial is tied to the question of membership in the city-
state: in burial practices, the individual death of the person becomes complete
through the recognition of his death by the state and culture. As Hans Ruin
reads Hegel's point, rituals, accordingly, play the function of building community and sustaining it, not only among the living but between the living
and the dead.[102] In the absence of mourning practices, the risk that awaits the
individual is thus that of a second death, of a death that is not quite a death,
an unrecognized and unmourned death. But through mourning practices and
burial, life in the state becomes a complete whole, preserving concrete individuals and concretizing itself through their individuality.[103] Thus, as Cecilia
Sjöholm states, "only those that count as members of that state are allowed
the recognition of the burial," and the fact that Polyneices does not receive
a burial speaks of a constitutive relationship between the restriction of grief
by certain members and the construction of the citizen's identity in a city-
state.[104] In the banishment of Polyneices's body from the meanings of culture,

Absent Death

citizenship, and ethical life, one can see a parallel to the banishing of Cemile's body from meaningful citizenship, and even a meaningful life.

There is a political connection between lives that are grieved and those that are considered to be meaningful or worthy ones. In *Frames of War*, Judith Butler suggests that the political and epistemological conditions of life and its apprehension as life are interwoven with the politics of grief: "In ordinary language, grief attends to life that has already been lived, and presupposes that life as having already ended. But, according to the future anterior, grievability is a condition of a life's emergence and sustenance."[105] Grief is conditioned by the apprehension and recognition of life, and is also the condition for such apprehension. This apprehension, on the other hand, is dependent on the production of life in accordance with the norms and political structures that qualify life as life. That this life is one that can end, that it is exposed to death and remains in opposition to death, can only be recognized if it is apprehended as life in the first place. Life is not a biological category that is immediately present. In order to count as life, it has to be recognized as such and be realized through the structures that it is embedded in. This necessity for recognition is also the mark of the distinction between grievable lives and ungrievable lives, lives that count as life and those that fall short of the normative meaning structures. "An ungrievable life is one that cannot be mourned because it has never lived, that is, it has never counted as a life at all."[106] The question of techniques of improper burial we have at hand seems to testify to the ungrievability of these lives: because the necropolitics of the lives of Cemile, the Chilean disappeared, and the residents of Newala Qesaba are lives situated as already akin to death, they are precisely *not* apprehended as lives that are exposed to death. The ends of these lives are thus unapprehended, since such life already never existed.

Unlike Polyneices, who occupies, by and large, a foundational role in the imaginary of the West, Cemile and the Chilean disappeared occupy places that are at the edges of the West. Improper burial takes on a different meaning when considering the shift in the global world order, or what Glissant calls "the abyss," that is, the innumerable loss that was the Middle Passage, where the millions that were lost in the slave trade remain unnamed and incalculable. Christina Sharpe says that to be "in the wake" when considering the abyss is a particular kind of work. Thus, as she says, "wakes are processes; they are rituals through which to enact grief and memory"; but at the same time, "wakes are also the track on the water's surface by a ship, the disturbance caused by a body swimming, or one that is moved, in water."[107] Being in the wake, in the aftermath of the abyss that Glissant talks about, is a form of consciousness that has an intimacy with death. Or alternatively, being in the wake is a form of consciousness in the afterlives of what Orlando Patterson calls "social death," a kind of death that goes beyond corporeal death but exists primarily in the absence of social recognition, which is replicated on the existential and ontological levels.[108] Calvin Warren calls this

38   Chapter 1

operation that marks Blackness in the afterlives of slavery an "ontological terror," the reduction of one's being to the status of *nothing* precisely through the operation of social death.[109]

The subjects of this chapter—Cemile, many of the Chilean disappeared, and the inhabitants of Newala Qesaba—do not occupy Blackness any more than they occupy the role of Polyneices, one of the foundational corpses of the dead-body politics of Western Europe. Nevertheless, it is important to note that life and the apprehension of life are categories that are interwoven with grief and practices of mourning. The political nature of the regulation or prohibition of funerary practices can be analyzed as one of regulating membership to, and inclusion in, political structures. Throughout, life emerges not as a natural process but rather as a process conditioned by normative, political, and epistemological conditions of recognition. In discussing the politics of grief, it is crucial to think of life as a non-natural category, one bound up with the meanings that it attains. The absence of what Christina Sharpe calls "wake work," in this sense, pertains to the reduction of the life of the person to nothing.[110]

However, unofficial deaths and mass graves come with an aftermath that at times deals with the dead more than with the living, and specifically with what happens to their deaths, more than their lives, either in the present or in the future. In the insistence of the Chilean military on making the remains buried in Patio 29 "disappear" more than once, what is at stake is not just a politics of the living that functions in ontological and existential registers, but a politics of the dead that deploys specific technologies to regulate or organize mourning and its practices. Organized technologies such as secret detention centers, enforced disappearances, and air-dropped bodies refer to a specific investment of power that is incumbent not only upon life and its qualifications, but also on the dead, their deaths, and their afterlives. It is thus necessary to complicate the category not only of life, but that of death, as a category that is subject to the interplay of power and recognition, shaped in relation to power.

Unnatural Death

When describing sovereign power, Foucault points to the paradoxical relationship between power and life that becomes apparent in the sovereign right to kill. He states that "the right to life and death is a strange right," since it suggests that life and death are not phenomena that are immediately present. "To say that the sovereign has a right of life and death means he can, basically, either have people put to death or let them live, or in any case that life and death are not natural or immediate phenomena which are primal and radical, and which fall outside the field of power."[111] Rather, in the sovereign right to kill, life and death emerge as effects of power, as interwoven with the techniques and technologies of power. "In terms of his relationship with the sovereign, the subject is, by rights, neither dead nor alive. From the viewpoint of life and death, the subject is neutral, and it is thanks to the sovereign that the subject has the right to be alive or, possibly, the right to be dead."[112] In this sense, power, in the mode of sovereign power, does not intervene in the natural processes of life and death. Rather, both become produced through the work of power, through the intervention of sovereignty.

This relationship between power and death may be why power does not deal with death in a singular fashion, that there is not one death. After all, "there are many ways of dying."[113] While "social death" in Patterson's sense refers to the absence of recognition of life that creates a semblance of death in existential or ontological registers, one can also consider different kinds of death produced in various power formations. For example, in punitive systems based on exclusion, where the primary task of the sovereign is to keep threatening elements away from the social organization, death can take place as actively eliminating those threats or abandoning them outside the city. Indeed, one can point to various examples of this: the expulsion of the "mad" in the fourteenth and fifteenth centuries in Europe, or the capital punishment of criminals, would be about such an impulse of elimination and exclusion. In "societies of confinement," however, death within the walls of prison is understood as "absolute security," or the "absolute closure" of such threats. In societies based on debt relations, punishment becomes a method of retribution, where the criminal "pays his debt" to society by serving a term of imprisonment.[114] There are thus different kinds of death, produced or reproduced in relation to specific technologies of power. If power can actually relate to death not only quantitatively, impacting whether or not or how many people die, but also qualitatively, where the very shape of death changes, then the question at the heart of techniques of improper burial becomes that of the *kind* of death that is produced through these techniques.

What kind of death, though, is produced in the new amalgamations of power formulated as necrosovereignty? Foucault argues that with the introduction of biopolitics into the technologies of sovereign power, death takes on a different shape, where it no longer symbolizes the spectacular manifestation of sovereign power but rather becomes a constant element of a life that works to perpetually diminish it. If biopolitics is primarily a power *over* life, the appearance or the spectacle of the end of life becomes the risk that biopolitics faces as a power that aims to "optimize" life, and death itself "becomes shameful."[115] As a result, the visibility of death becomes a threat to power: death becomes a private affair and becomes "the moment when the individual escapes all power, falls back on himself and retreats, so to speak, into his own privacy."[116] This does not imply that death disappears from the scene of history, nor does it mean that power now aims to eradicate death or works against it. As we have seen in the previous sections, death is present and no less intertwined with power. This time, however, this occurs through a different kind of technology, that of privatizing death itself through the interplay of its recognition and its absence. Hence, as Foucault says, "power no longer recognizes death" and it "literally ignores death."[117] In the cases of Newala Qesaba, or Patio 29, what is at stake is not so much the question of the presence or absence of death as such: what is not recognized is not life, but rather, death.

The absence of the recognition of death, or the privatization of death, does not imply the renaturalization of death or the return of death to its pre-political, immediate existence. After all, neither sovereignty nor biopolitics ever abandons the spheres of life or death: instead, they amalgamate into each other and therefore are transformed into monstrous formations. Thus, if death becomes private, this occurs through the privatization of the sovereign right of death and its dispersion among the population: death becomes a private individual right, encompassed in practices that aim to withdraw the effects of power over death, practices that would make it private.[118] Through this privatization of death, necrosovereignty turns the sovereign right to kill into the distribution and regulation of the right to die,[119] which is disproportionately distributed throughout the population. Necrosovereign assemblages exist precisely in relation to this privatization of death and the regulation and distribution of the right to die. Rituals can thus be seen as precisely the practices of making an individual death: rather than making the death of the individual into a public experience, on the contrary, they make the death of an individual into an apolitical and private experience.

Nonetheless, the disappeared do not fit into these categories of private deaths, either with graves that are marked and known, or with names attached to their bodies; their absence is not that private death that is legible and acceptable, or digestible for biopolitics. Rather, the rituals pertaining to them take place much farther from their bodies, since their graves are as absent as their remains, and their names are infinitely farther from the ditches and lots in which the bodies may be found. The absence of such practices creates another kind of limbo, a limbo that opens up in the absence of a "life," a grievable life or a life that can be governed, and in the absence of death as well, for the death itself becomes unrecognizable. As Gordon states, "death exists in the past tense, disappearance is in the present."[120] If the mothers of those in Newala Qesaba still state that their children might one day just "walk through the door," it is precisely due to the fact of how present the limbo of their children is, how absent both life *and* death are.[121] The emphasis on the absence of death becomes even clearer in the demand of the mothers of the disappeared in Argentina: *Aparición con vida*, "Bring them back alive."[122] This statement might indeed appear contradictory when there is such a high probability of death in the case of disappearance, and even more compelling when this statement is used in conjunction with mass graves where there are indisputably the remains of people who are dead. However, the demand speaks precisely to the impossibility of pointing to

Absent Death 41

life or death in the context of a bio-sovereign assemblage that recognizes
death only when it is a de-politicized and private death. The techniques of
improper burial work to create a kind of death that does not belong to the
sphere of either life or death in biopolitics. This is a kind of death that occurs
in the absence of the right to die, a kind of death that is absent; it is a kind of
death that cannot be made private, or a kind of dead body that does not fit
into either empty graves or old photographs. The "literal ignorance" on the
side of power toward death does not imply the banishment or avoidance of
death, nor does it work to keep death at bay; rather, it is an active method
of necrosovereignty that regulates the right to die by organizing, regulating,
and systematically erasing the practices of mourning. It is a method deployed
on the dead body, to render death absent. Much like life, death is not just a
natural category, nor is it simply a primal or biological one: it is a political
category through and through. Disallowing death is much more than killing
or letting die, and it goes much further than neglect and ignorance: it is the
making of a death that does not fit into the categories of an intelligible death,
the making of a death that one cannot say is "mine" or "ours."

Erasing Grief, Absent Death

Mass graves and techniques of improper burial point to an interest in power
that goes beyond the dichotomy between life and death, between taking life
and letting live, or making live and letting die. In these cases, what is at stake
is not killing, but it is not exactly letting-die either: there is rather an erasing
and rendering absent of life and death. Mass graves and improper burials
open up spaces where there is no life and there is no death: there is neither
a life that can be put under surveillance and regulated, nor a death that can
make the power of the sovereign spectacular, neither a life that can be witnessed, nor a death that can be mourned. They open a different kind of space,
an extrajudicial and extra-political space that consists of knowledges of horror and memory, as well as official and unofficial methods of obstruction of
the recognition of death and of mourning.

Neither life nor death are simply natural or biological categories. They
are often bound up with power and recognition: together with the question
of whether life is apprehended as life, there is also the question of whether
or not it is possible for death to be apprehended as death. The absence of
recognition of death opens up another kind of death, a space where both
life and death are unrecognized and unrecognizable. This absence forms the
basis of necrosovereign assemblages, where death is produced and distributed throughout the population by means of the distribution and regulation
of the right to die. Necrosovereign assemblages work to *make* such death
by making a private death into a right that is to be distributed throughout
the population: on the other side of this death is nothing, a vast absence

filled with silences, where many who may no longer be alive reside. Improper burial, mass graves, and disappearance as a method are those of the *literal ignorance* of certain kinds of deaths, the making of the flesh and bones of this absence: this literal ignorance is of deaths that do not fit into categories of private death, that do not fit into empty graves, erased archives, or bodies that are made invisible.

Allowing or disallowing people to be dead is part of the work of power. If the grief for the inhabitants of Newala Qesaba, the former residents of Patio 29, and Cemile and others in Cizre and surrounding areas is made impossible, it is precisely by creating a kind of death that is not a death—not the kind of death that is legible and understandable, not the private death of bio-sovereignty. Regulation of the practices of mourning is a necrosovereign technique, making and unmaking the dead, together with their deaths. Considering the *how* of necrosovereignty invites us to pay attention to the dead that did not die, the kinds of deaths that exist in the absence of private deaths. After all, if the death of necrosovereignty is *not* a private affair, then it is important to investigate what such technologies do on the level of political and epistemic subjectivity: how these technologies shape what is done to mourning, what is remembered about death, how it is remembered, and how it is organized. In order to investigate necrosovereignty as the contemporary politics of mourning, one must turn to the technologies that target the knowledge and memory of death. The next chapter focuses on the epistemic techniques of necrosovereignty, which target knowers as much as knowledge.

Chapter 2

✦

Disappearing Grief

The Saturday Mothers, as the mothers of the disappeared in Turkey have come to be known, have been meeting on Istiklal Street in İstanbul on Saturdays for the last 806 weeks at the time of writing this chapter. The oldest member of the Saturday Mothers, Berfo Kırbayır, died at the age of 106, after over thirty years spent looking for her son. Her son, Cemil Kırbayır, was detained in 1980. The day after her son's detention, Berfo Kırbayır went to the police station to look for him. She was told that there were no records of her son. In fact, according to their records, she never had a son: her son does not exist. In her years of searching for her son, Berfo Kırbayır worked more than she probably ever thought she would on proving that she had a son, and that the son had disappeared. In those years, Berfo Kırbayır also learned and unlearned many things that may or may not have happened to that son, all of which existed in some parts of records at some point: according to some records, he had died of torture within days after his detention; according to others, he had escaped, whereas other traces suggested he had been moved between various detention centers before disappearing from the records of any of those centers. No records included what may have ultimately happened to his body.

There are many gaps in the record when it comes to techniques of improper burial, and indeed, sometimes those gaps are produced by the proliferation of records. Instead of none, sometimes there are too many records, too many things said, and too many things done. The "false positives" in Colombia are an example of this. In 2008, the *Washington Post* reported that the corpses of at least eleven young men and boys from Soacha, a suburb of Bogotá, had been found thousands of miles away from that suburb, bruised with marks of torture and combat, armed with weapons, and dressed in uniforms belonging to the Revolutionary Armed Forces of Colombia (FARC).[1] Later, it was revealed that this was a much more common occurrence than just the eleven that had disappeared from Soacha, and there were many more that have first disappeared and were later found with weapons on their bodies. According to the records of the military, each of these persons had been killed "in combat."[2] But the families of over 3,000 identified bodies claim that what got those bodies there was not their involvement in any guerrilla activity.[3] Human rights organizations claim that the bodies from Soacha were "false positives"—that is, civilians who were kidnapped and murdered, and then reported as "combat kills" by the Colombian armed forces in order to boost the body count of guerrillas in their own version of the "war against terror."[4] While the number of "false positives" is estimated at around 10,000, the exact number is unknown and any official record of the orders to boost body counts is missing.[5]

As Mbembe says, "sometimes, after you die, power is not done with you."[6] This chapter works on the afterlives of death, on what happens to what is known of death in necrosovereignty. The question at the heart of this chapter pertains to the *how* of death in necrosovereignty: how it works, what is known about it, what is said of it, and last, what is left of it. The chapter consists of three parts: the first part analyzes the relation between necrosovereignty and knowledge production and suggests that necrosovereign techniques on memory and testimony are epistemic techniques. The second section investigates archival erasure as a method of knowledge production, or rather as a method of subjugating knowledge. The last section focuses on the techniques of knowledge production that work not on the official record but on the mnemonic and epistemic capacities of the subjects who inhabit spaces of necrosovereignty. I will call these techniques "necro-epistemic" methods as they target the temporal and logical coherence of memory in death-worlds, producing "irrational" rationalities in relation to a knowledge of death.

The Power/Knowledge of Death

Not only death but also the right to death is distributed and redistributed. Necrosovereignty regulates mourning to create limbos of disallowed death. Rather than "making live" or "letting die," necrosovereignty works by letting or not letting individuals and populations die, by infiltrating the space of death with techniques of improper burial, by disappearing the body, by mass burying, by replacing death with presences and absences at once. This work, however, is inseparable from questions pertaining to knowledge and its production: how knowledge is produced, how information is distributed and the normative frames through which it is made available, the kinds of logics that are used, and the value of truth attributed to knowledge all become important questions. Much of mourning, after all, takes place through arranging, organizing, and regulating what is known of death. Questions regarding the knowledge of death, its surroundings, and its conditions involve information on the whereabouts of the lost one, their last actions, the last people they saw, why they did what they did, how they died, what happened after they died, who knows about their aftermath, how they acquired such knowledge, and how credible these people are. Investigating necrosovereignty in this

Disappearing Grief

45

sense requires paying attention to these knowledge production mechanisms around death.

However, power and knowledge never work too far from each other: mechanisms of power work not only by ordering and arranging institutions, people, and things; they also work on what is known and what is knowable. Indeed, the working of power in relation to and on knowledge is a complex web. Foucault refers to power/knowledge, wherein "the exercise of power perpetually creates knowledge and, conversely, knowledge constantly induces effects of power. . . . It is not possible for power to be exercised without knowledge; it is impossible for knowledge not to engender power."[7] Technologies of power are inseparable from the methods deployed in the field of knowledge. Relations of power that traverse the social body are "indissociable from a discourse of truth, and they can neither be established nor function unless a true discourse is produced, accumulated, put into circulation, and set to work."[8] Power/knowledge refers to this inextricable relation between mechanisms of power and the discourses of truth and epistemic methods that are involved in the veridiction of truth.

Foucault's account of power/knowledge (*pouvoir/savoir*) has produced a large body of knowledge of its own. Rabinow and Dreyfus famously call this conception "the most radical element in Foucault's work."[9] It is important to discuss this conception not only in order to investigate the intricacies of Foucault's account, but also to analyze the implications of such a conception in the context of necrosovereignty. For one thing, to argue that power and knowledge are inseparable implies that they not only intensify each other, but they also produce the scope and objects of each other. In this sense, it is not only the case that a given object of knowledge is also an object of power: new objects of knowledge can be produced in accordance with mechanisms of power, and vice versa; new mechanisms of power can be deployed in accordance with the emergence of new or other objects of knowledge. The famous figures that Foucault discusses, such as the "criminal," the "pervert," and the "monster," are born simultaneously as both objects of power and of knowledge: what is known and knowable of each figure is entangled with a whole amalgamation of power relations, each one sustaining and upholding the very existence of the figure.[10] For example, the emergence of the penitentiary as an apparatus of power took place through the emergence of the "criminal" as a dangerous individual to be studied by both legal and psychiatric systems; whereas the emergence of the "pervert" as an individual to be studied has taken place through the emergence of sexuality as a mechanism of power. As Foucault says, "it is not possible for power to be exercised without knowledge, [and] it is not possible for knowledge not to engender power."[11] Power and knowledge not only go hand in hand with each other, they also invent and reproduce each other. At the heart of power/knowledge assemblages that Foucault discusses is a simultaneous production: in each mechanism of power, as Mary Beth Mader says, what is at hand is "simultaneously the

46 Chapter 2

creation of knowledge and the *form of power*."[12] In turn, both ends of the assemblage, the object of knowledge and the mechanism of power, produce each other insofar as they both play a part in the emergence of the ensemble that upholds them together.

Second, power/knowledge assemblages are active mechanisms rather than concrete wholes. Discussing knowledge in assemblage with power means investigating not only objects of knowledge but also investigating what knowledge and knowledge production *do* in the first place. In this sense, knowledge does not constitute a concrete block, whose only correlate is truth or falsity: knowledge has various forms and methods, and these methods can do different things, know different things, and organize those things differently. The question at the heart of this analysis is not the distinction between knowledge and ignorance, or the presence of knowledge or the absence thereof, but rather the techniques of knowledge that are operative in presences and absences of knowledge, or the "general semblance of things" that produces presences and absences. The issue in investigating knowledge is not to bring to light what is hidden by power or to make known what is commonly ignored, but rather to analyze the techniques of knowledge that are operative, taking knowledge first and foremost as an active category that does things.

The mechanisms involved in power and knowledge are not identical to each other, nor do they produce a general semblance of a totality. Take *Discipline and Punish*, described as "The Birth of the Prison" in its subtitle. While prison emerges as a mechanism of power connected to various objects of knowledge (the criminal, the inmate, confession, innocence, the value of penitentiary labor, etc.), it traverses various practices. As Colin Koopman helpfully lists, these include the "ritualized temporal ordering in monasteries, spatial ordering as instantiated in military encampments, spatial partitioning techniques developed in architecture, mechanisms of narration and confession in religious practice, surveillance strategies . . . planning strategies . . . medical techniques . . . practices of examination."[13] The mechanisms of power that are deployed, such as spatial ordering and partitioning, take place simultaneously through epistemic practices such as narration, confession, or examination. The variety of practices that are deployed on the level of both power and knowledge primarily mark the separation between these registers, as opposed to their parallel or identical relationship. Indeed, power and knowledge can deploy disparate techniques and technologies in their assemblages. For example, power mechanisms around sovereignty work not only through discourses involving enmity: there can be different kinds of objects deployed in relation to certain power-effects, where discourses about threats, even when not attached to specific persons, can function in relation to instantiations of sovereignty. As Koopman says, "the entire point of the co-production idea is to open up a space for inquiry into the interactive relationship between knowledge and power."[14] This interactive relationship

Disappearing Grief 47

between power and knowledge consists of an amalgamation of practices, techniques, and technologies through which objects of power come to be known, or objects of knowledge come to be exercised upon. Investigating modes of power as factors in power/knowledge assemblages thus means not investigating how they produce a standpoint through which information is distributed but rather the modes of knowledge that interact with these mechanisms of power. In Foucault's words, "relations of power/knowledge are not static forms of distribution, they are matrices of transformation."[15]

When considering necrosovereignty and its nightmarish productions, understanding knowledge in opposition to ignorance, and as shaped by processes of information-gathering and archive-building, becomes particularly insufficient. Nevertheless, bringing the insights of power/knowledge into our analyses of necrosovereignty has several implications. First, insofar as necrosovereignty works on death and the dead, this work occurs not only through organizing bodies, lives, and deaths but also through the forms of knowledge that emerge in relation to such bodies, lives, and deaths. Understanding necrosovereignty as a power/knowledge assemblage means not only investigating what it does at the level of bodies through techniques of improper burial but also the kinds of knowledge that accompany those techniques, and the mechanisms of knowledge that are played out, produced, practiced, or distributed around techniques of improper burial. Second, these mechanisms of knowledge are neither identical nor reducible to technologies of power operative on the bodies: in this sense, the dumping, immolating, or disappearing of bodies does not have a clean-cut parallel to the modes of knowledge that are produced around improper burial. Last, investigating necrosovereignty as a power/knowledge mechanism does not mean analyzing whether any knowledge of the lost ones is actually present or not, nor is it a quest to bring to light what is hidden or concealed in necrosovereignty. Rather, it is a question of what is done on the level of knowledges, investigating the technologies of knowledge that interact with the mechanisms of necrosovereignty. In short, it means investigating not only the modes of power connected to death and grief but also what is known of death and grief and how it is known.

Invaluable work has been produced on normative knowledge production and information distribution around death through the production of discursive objects and figures. Jasbir Puar, for example, argues that discourses such as the "war on terror" attest to how necropolitics hides itself by promoting the kinds of life that are normatively deemed standard and acceptable.[16] In this sense, the contemporary politics of death produces discourses that would distinguish healthy or normal lives, while discursive objects such as the "terrorist" would justify the ways in which certain lives and people easily slip off to death. Objects of knowledge such as "terrorists" thus directly do the work of necropolitics, marking off the bodies of individuals and populations as essentially "killable" bodies. The work of death, in this sense, would be an object of knowledge only in cases where lives that are deemed as normal and acceptable are endangered; promoting the well-being of these kinds of lives would entail actively hiding the work of death. In order to function in this way, necropolitics produces discourses and discursive objects that delineate threats to health and well-being: discourses on terror, with the discursive object of the "terrorist," are a production of this kind, in which the terrorist is marked as that figure who is a threat to the objects of health and well-being. The specific work of death—involving both killing and causing death, the method, process, or action through which death takes place—would thus become accidental information, a side element of the discourses on health, well-being, or of discourses on terror. These discourses would thus function similar to what Erlenbusch-Anderson calls "grids of intelligibility" or what Butler calls "frames," insofar as they provide a general coherence for events that would otherwise be unrelated or incoherent:[17] people disappearing from their hometowns in order to be killed miles away and buried with weapons placed beside them become meaningful as an example of terrorist activity, where the "war on terror" attains explanatory power to provide coherence for the object of perception. Similarly, it is this framing that also destroys certain objects of knowledge, keeps them from making sense together, or obstructs any form of access to them altogether.

Much of the analysis of the epistemic dimensions of biopolitics and necropolitics thus focuses on the grids of intelligibility, frames, or discourses that tie various objects of knowledge together. Such an approach requires a certain amount of distancing, a way of looking at such discourses "from afar"; this distance involves either temporal or historical separation, wherein the analyst looks back or yonder at moments in the archive of past times or distant geographies, and the research focuses on how a certain object of knowledge is represented elsewhere. For example, Butler's account in *Frames of War* focuses on the photos of Abu Ghraib prison as they were published in the United States, where the question of the grievability of such lives was a question asked from the position of the US public and the specific race politics of the United States. The positioning of the analysis as distant to the object analyzed is not a rare attitude, and this attitude marks Foucault's own account as well. After all, if mechanisms of power interact simultaneously with entire regimes of knowledge that produce various discursive objects, does it always require a "looking back" to diagnose assemblages of power/knowledge? Does one have to have a distance in order to discuss the present?[18] Foucault says in *The Archeology of Knowledge* that "it is not possible for us to describe our own archive."[19] Is it necessarily the case that analyzing power/knowledge always requires a "detour," either a detour "elsewhere" to another geography, or a "detour through the past"?[20] Moreover, as Amy Allen asks in the case of Foucault and his relationship to his work, "from what perspective can he claim access to these conditions? Does not the claim that he can have access to them require Foucault to jump over his own shadow?"[21]

Disappearing Grief 49

This is primarily a question of method, or a question of positionality in analyzing power/knowledge. The complications of the question involve not only how one analyzes the power/knowledge assemblages within which one lives but also what one does with this analysis as well, the goal or aim of the analysis. A fundamental wager that I pursue here is that the knowledge of death is not limited to how it is reflected "outside" of necrosovereignty, or to what people living distant to the worlds of necrosovereignty know about death. The world of necrosovereignty is not a hollow world that can only exist in the form of its representations to the outside. Similarly, rather than determining whether lives and deaths are grievable in an abstract place of dislocation (which often refers to geographies of the Global North), necrosovereignty works on the concrete political and epistemic practices that are involved in mourning and grief. Analyzing the epistemic practices that interact with necrosovereignty therefore requires investigating what is registered, remembered, archived, or told: once again, not from the position of a discursive, geographic, or temporal distance, but rather from within existing spaces of necrosovereignty. Thus, if we are to take the question of knowledge in necrosovereignty seriously, it is necessary to discuss not only the knowledge *of* necrosovereignty, but also the knowledge produced *in* necrosovereignty, the kinds of knowledge that accompany the techniques of improper burial, and the epistemic methods involved in the regulation and organization of mourning. This would require investigating the practices of knowledge production that are deployed, where the inhabitants of death-worlds not only constitute objects of knowledge, but are also subjects of that knowledge; they are epistemic and political subjects who partake and participate in necrosovereign assemblages.

Archival Disappearances and Subjugated Knowledges

One term given by Foucault to this local analysis of knowledges—a mode of study that focuses on what people know at the local level—is "genealogy." In the lecture courses *Society Must Be Defended*, Foucault discusses genealogy as a method of interacting with what he calls "subjugated knowledges," knowledges that emerge from out of people's interactions with power. Genealogy, he says, is an "insurrection of knowledges," the kinds of knowledge that take place on the local level, the local discursivities, and most importantly, their "desubjugation."[22] There are two modes of subjugated knowledge that he discusses: the first are the knowledges whose contents have been actively disguised or erased, knowledge that has been "buried and disguised in a functionalist coherence or formal systematization," and the second mode is "the kinds of knowledges that have been disqualified from counting as knowledge."[23] In sum, he describes genealogy as a story of "the buried and the disguised," a historical knowledge of "struggles" first and foremost, a knowledge that gives a story of struggles, and also a story of struggles against the subjugation of knowledge.[24] In attempting to give an account of knowledge in necrosovereignty, it would be a question of these struggles, and the question of diagnosing the subjugation of knowledges in the context of mourning and death.

The first of the subjugated knowledges that Foucault discusses, what he calls "the buried," are the kinds of knowledge that do not coincide with official or dominant discourses. These are, in other words, the kinds of knowledge that encounter active dismissal and denial, the knowledges that are buried deep within the archive, and that may never see daylight. Enforced disappearances and the erasure of their records are an example of this first kind of subjugation of knowledge, and these occur not necessarily in the past, but rather simultaneously with the work of necrosovereignty. On the level of archival records, the disappearance takes place as a form of erasure of the disappeared and the knowledge regarding them. The latter information— about the aftermath of disappearance, such as information on bodies that were air-dropped (sometimes as they were alive), or about the ocean floor being covered with human remains along the shores of Argentina—attains a poetic quality in the face of archival disappearance; these details become both irrational and rational, both forgettable and impossible to forget at once. Within this poetics of surrounding events, both the disappearances and the disappeared are erased, leaving behind first and foremost a gap in the archive, in which the whereabouts of the bodies are buried deep, even if the bodies themselves are not. Sometimes, those who have remained disappear later on, as in the case of Kemal Birlik: when he was discharged from his sentence of over two years, his two relatives went to pick him up. That was the last time anyone saw him, or his two relatives. Other times, if the person was detained publicly prior to their disappearance, some of the witnesses can themselves disappear, as well as the records of those witnesses. Thus, as Gordon put it, "a terrifying constituent feature of the disappearance is that the *desaparecidos* have disappeared and so too all public and official knowledge of them."[25] In cases of disappearance, the technique works to disappear the memory of the person as well as their physical existence, along with any records that would attest to their existence. Antonius Robben states: "the anonymous burial of the executed and the disappeared entails their physical, social, political, legal and spiritual eradication."[26] This erasing act of enforced disappearance targets not just the body but also the memory and the archival records of the person. In Gordon's words, "a key aspect of state-sanctioned disappearance is precisely the elaborate suppression and elimination of what conventionally constitutes the proof of someone's whereabouts. The disappeared have lost all social and political identity: no bureaucratic records, no funerals, no memorials, no bodies, nobody."[27] What is lost and what is disappeared, in the cases of enforced disappearances, goes beyond instances of detention, or how and where a person was detained or disappeared, to

Disappearing Grief

include the elimination of all proof that could point to the whereabouts of the disappeared at any given time. The identity of the disappeared vanishes when there are no bureaucratic records, no funerals, no memorials left behind. As a whole, there is "no person" to disappear from the records, for all corroborating evidence regarding the possibility of disappearance has been erased, taking the disappeared and their social, political, and spiritual existence with them. The continued absence of records on the detention of the disappeared is echoed and reinforced by the erasure of the individuals themselves from public records. In most cases of disappearance, there are no records of the person who has disappeared: no records of a death or funeral, but also no records of detention, court orders, and, in many cases, no records of birth either. The name of the disappeared may become a forbidden subject, since uttering the name in public might put the speaker at risk of detention.[28] As Banu Bargu explains, erasure may involve the eradication of the possibility of remembering, since those who remember can also disappear.[29] In the absence of records, there is no person, no body, no one to disappear in the first place; in the absence of utterances, there is no loss, nothing to grieve, and nothing to remember. Bargu calls this process "invisibilization," which "renders bodies, history, and violence invisible."[30]

Archival erasure works on multiple levels: it erases the person, the world within which the person existed, and the world within which that person has disappeared as well. Between names that were taken in and out of records many times, and those that did not make it to the archives in the first place, the numbers become too vague and shifting, and so piecing out "who/what/where" becomes difficult, if not altogether impossible. The difficulty in piecing out the "who/what/where" attests to the destruction of enforced disappearances as an archive, where the records or testimonies of enforced disappearances cease to function as bearers of information that exist in relation to a series of other things and are therefore meaningful as objects of knowledge. The methods of archival erasure consist of actively erasing the archive or falsifying what is already in the archive. Of the "false positives," for example, about 3,000 of them have been identified through the efforts of the Mothers of Soacha, and only some of them (far from a majority) were provided formal burials after that. On top of the difficulties in obtaining records on how and under what conditions these people were buried, there is the added difficulty of obtaining records even on the purely numerical level. Even though the goal of murdering the "false positives" was apparently to increase the body counts in the "war on terror," not all of the "false positives" were actually counted, nor were they all recorded, so paradoxically, the complete "body counts" are nonexistent. Between the contradictory testimony of the officials who have been prosecuted and the remains that were found, the numbers of "false positives" vary by thousands and, as has been demonstrated, there was very little organization involved in the whole process. Different units disposed of bodies in different locales, and even though these human remains were supplied with weapons, there is no concrete count of how many and where.[31] Although the stated goal of creating "false positives" was to inflate the body count of dead counterinsurgents, what we have is precisely the absence of such a count. As a whole, what remains from these testimonies is an unknown number of human remains in various rural areas, dressed in clothes that are not their own and who are marked with no name, no reference, and no identity, apart from the nameless title of "the enemy."

Invisibilization can also take the shape of the proliferation of records or the displacement of records. The categories of enmity, terror, or subversion have a long history in the case of enforced disappearances: these categories mark precisely that shift from the absence of records to the presence of too many records. In and through the proliferation of such categories, the disappeared often cease to be subjects: the possible ties between the subject and the state, or the subject and the community, become invisible together with the histories of violence, disqualifying claims for the kind of juridical subjectivity attached to sovereignty that would interact with subjects on the basis of rights, on the basis of the right to live or the right to die. In the case of the Dirty War in Argentina, for example, where the Mothers of the Plaza de Mayo have sustained one of the longest-lasting modes of political action for over five decades now, the total number of the disappeared is very far from known, apart from once again the nameless category of the "subversives."[32] This category would point to no concrete entity or concrete group of people; rather, it works not only on the level of political commitments, hence referring to union leaders, activists, students, journalists and writers, but also is used to refer at times to divorce, prostitution, alcoholism, homosexuality, and myriad other identities and acts.[33] In turn, the absence of a coherent definition for who/what counts as subversive would help erase not only those marked as such, but also any mode of violence inflicted upon them. As Diana Taylor writes, "non-human non subjects do not exist in juridical systems,"[34] and any acts that befall them also do not exist as such. As General Ramón Campos once said on the issue of the *desaparecidos:* "it was not people that disappeared, but the subversives."[35] The absence of records on disappearances is countered by the proliferation of records on the subversives: this doubling produces what Foucault calls a "functional ensemble," where the knowledge of the disappeared is buried deep within the archives, precisely in order to enact the task of necrosovereignty: if there are no people, there is no death, and if there is no death, there is nothing to mourn. Instead, there are only "subversives," who do not need to be counted.

Thus, this first mode of subjugated knowledges that Foucault talks about are "blocks of historical knowledges that were present in the functional and systematic ensembles, but which were masked."[36] The task of the archival erasure of both the disappeared and their disappearances is to enact that functional ensemble of necrosovereignty, in which the burial of information would enact the erasure both of people and of the violence done to

Disappearing Grief

them—of histories of violence—all at once. Both knowledge and power *do* things: in the context of necrosovereignty, they produce modes of death beyond natural death; they disappear individuals; they disappear entire histories. Considering necrosovereignty as a power/knowledge assemblage thus requires paying attention to its interactions with knowledge, both in terms of the figures that it produces and in terms of its interactions with the archive, not from the perspective of a detour out and away from the archive, but rather from within the terms of the archive, its presences and absences, its gaps, and holes. Indeed, taking Foucault's description of genealogy as mobilizing local knowledges means looking at what is buried in the functional ensemble of necrosovereignty, the kinds of knowledges that were actively masked. Both enforced disappearance and its archival disappearance can be seen as this first kind of subjugation of knowledge. The information on those who disappeared, their whereabouts, what befell them, what made them subversives—which was once present at some point in the functional ensembles—fell through the cracks of history, becoming buried deep within such ensembles. It requires a task of digging in the archive, quite literally, in order to find the records, the bodies, and the bones that are buried within this functional ensemble. The "erasing violence" of necrosovereignty functions to create gaps in the records, such that the possibility of corroborating not only disappearance but also the existence of the person or any other records that surround the person's life, disappears not only in the archive but also from the archive.

Necro-Epistemic Methods

Although archival erasure is a method for the production of subjugated knowledges, it is not the only method. Power does not work on knowledge solely in the relatively linear modes of eliminating or masking it; rather, it impacts the various connections between different objects of knowledge and the possibility of reaching conclusions by building connections between them. Thus, in Foucault's account, apart from the first set of subjugated knowledges that have been erased or masked, there is a second set of subjugated knowledges; apart from "the buried," there are the "disqualified."[37] This second set of subjugated knowledges is a "whole set of knowledges that have been disqualified as inadequate to their task or insufficiently elaborated."[38] This is a whole set of "localized knowledges" that do not rise to the threshold of official knowledge; they are minor knowledges that contain "raw memory of struggles" that do not attain the status of actual and real knowledge.[39] In this mode of knowledge subjugation, the subjects and their memories are dismissed as "naive" or "hierarchically inferior"[40] and are disqualified from the status of knowers. This kind of subjugation of knowledge is in line with what Miranda Fricker calls "epistemic injustice," where the agent is subjected to games of power that question "their capacity as a knower."[41] These modes of subjugated knowledge suggest that power works on knowledge in more ways than impacting the relation between what is said and how it is recorded, and it involves technologies beyond erasing or masking: indeed, these modes of subjugated knowledge suggest that power works on subjects specifically as knowers, as subjects of knowledge who operate within power/knowledge assemblages.

What are the apparatuses of power/knowledge operative in death-worlds that target the subjects primarily *as knowers*, as subjects of knowledge? These methods, which I refer to here as "necro-epistemic methods," target the temporal and logical coherence of memory by impacting the credibility of the knower and obstructing their lucidity regarding the event. These methods target the coherence of temporality, the erasure of memory, and the gendered hysterization of the relatives of the disappeared. Such methods have epistemic impacts that go beyond the delineation of the limits of the archive, pertaining to how given information (say, about the whereabouts of the person) is recorded and distributed. In the production of such a temporal lag, the question at hand is not about sharing or withdrawing information on the whereabouts of the disappeared. Rather, what is at stake is a certain targeting of the capacity of the searchers specifically *as knowers*, as individuals and groups that have the capacity to grasp, build, and share knowledge. As such, these methods are instances of Fricker's "epistemic injustice," which attests to the work of power upon the epistemic capacities of individuals. For Fricker, epistemic injustice pertains specifically to situations where the person is subjected to the work of power as a subject endowed with epistemic capacities, and where the work of power on knowledge consists precisely in regulating, organizing, or targeting the epistemic capacities of individuals. As such, in Fricker's account, epistemic injustice can take up different shapes, such as testimonial injustice or hermeneutic injustice.

In investigating these methods, it is worth returning to the main characteristics of enforced disappearance, this time to analyze the epistemic dimensions of the experience of this mechanism. One of the earliest descriptions of enforced disappearance, proposed by the UN Working Group on Enforced or Involuntary Disappearances, is helpful insofar as it divides enforced disappearances into three main categories. The first category (A) is "deprivation of liberty against the will of the person concerned," thus involving some version of arrest and forced imprisonment, often in an unknown or secret detention center. The second one, (B), is "involvement of government officials, at least indirectly by acquiescence." Depending on the locale, this involvement can take various forms, from informal conversations with individual officials from the locale in rural areas to unit-level involvements in larger cities. Finally, the third category, (C), is "refusal to acknowledge the detention and to disclose the fate and whereabouts of the person concerned."[42] Since the refusal to acknowledge the detention and the refusal to

Disappearing Grief

disclose the whereabouts of the detained do not always accompany each other, the authorities may acknowledge that the person was detained at some point but still not disclose the whereabouts of the person. Many of the relatives of the disappeared, for example, were at some point told that their loved ones had escaped from prison.

What are the epistemic dimensions of these characteristics of enforced disappearance? In most cases of enforced disappearances, the scenario follows similar characteristics: a person is taken in and never seen again. The refusal to acknowledge the detention of the person is accompanied by the production of a temporal lag between the official account and the experiential one, where those who seek to find the missing person are given varying temporal explanations with no concrete reference to the experiential reality of the event. The case of the three people who disappeared in the Doruklu village of Silopi, Turkey, is a typical example of this. On New Year's Eve, three people drove in their own car to the Silopi District gendarmerie's Central Station in order to bring a turkey to the soldiers, which the soldiers had demanded. When others in the village go to the gendarmerie, having become worried when these three people don't return home, the answer they receive is that "they left ten minutes ago," although those three people were never seen after this point.[43] Most disappearances in Turkey occur at night, when the police or undercover state officials come to the person's house to detain the person. However, they can also take place publicly, when the person is detained walking down the street or waiting in line at the bank or at the pharmacy. In some cases, the person disappears after being called to the station and going there voluntarily. Different modes of temporal variation and lag are produced in relation to modes of detention: if the disappeared person had gone to the government building voluntarily, the answer "they left ten minutes ago" is the most common response, whereas in the cases of public detentions, the temporal lag in the accounts is larger, as those seeking a relative are told the person has been released "a long time ago," even though the person had disappeared just a day before.[44] This temporal lag is often used to situate the testimony of the searchers against the testimonies of the officials: the searchers who are initially met with claims that the person left the gendarmerie station "ten minutes ago" are later told that no such thing happened, and the whereabouts of the person have been unknown for days; or the searchers who claim proof of detention on the basis of the official's testimonies are countered with concrete gaps in the narrative and are thus unable to produce a coherent narrative for their claim.

The experiential temporal lag produced around enforced disappearances is often shaped along the lines of what Fricker calls "testimonial injustice," where the testimonies of the individuals searching for the disappeared are not afforded credibility. In Fricker's words, "the basic idea is that a speaker suffers a testimonial injustice if prejudice on the hearer's part causes him to give the speaker less credibility than he would otherwise have given."[45] In this sense, testimonial injustice is built on what Fricker calls a "prejudicial stereotype," and as Kristie Dotson explains, "prejudice, here, refers to a negative identity-prejudicial stereotype that affects the perception of hearers concerning a speaker's credibility."[46] The credibility of a person is often based on the assessment of their social and political identity as well as their personal history. While bias based on historical oppression can be used to discredit a person, so can the suggestion of former unreliability on that person's part: to think or hear that someone has not been truthful before can discredit the person on the spot, and the suggestion that the testimony of the person is or has been incoherent is similarly discrediting. While the former instance would refer to cases in which bias, such as racial or gender bias, would impact the credibility of person, the latter would note the impact of things such as hearsay regarding the person's character or truthfulness.

In the cases of necro-epistemic methods, the temporal lag produced between the experiential memory of the person and that of the official narrative creates a temporal displacement that facilitates testimonial injustice. The experiential temporality of the searchers is replaced by official temporality, but the replacement does not constitute a coherent whole. Thus, while the searchers are told that the person was released "five minutes ago," this temporality fits neither within the narrative nor the searchers' experience: visiting a gendarmerie station is often an ordeal that lasts many hours, thus the "five minutes ago" often refers in linear time to when the searchers were present in the gendarmerie. But that "five minutes ago" refers not to an exact moment in linear time but to a narrative fiction that works to discredit the later testimony of the searchers: for example, "Five minutes ago from when? If five minutes ago from now, why didn't you see them being released? If they were in the station when you were searching, why didn't you find them there?" This is perhaps most conspicuous in cases of "unofficial public detentions," where the person is detained while in a public place, such as a post office or a patisserie, when they were likely alone, by individuals who look like civilians, who are not in uniforms.[47] While the witnesses describe the situation as "abduction by unknown people," the relatives searching for the disappeared are told that the person was afterward seen here and there, continuing on their rounds. Ramazan Bilir, for example, searched for his brother for three years and pursued a variety of claims made to him by officials about his brother being seen in various cities, until finally he himself disappeared after pursuing someone who'd told him that his brother was in Mardin. Throughout the searching process, Bilir was repeatedly called a "madman" going around, even though much of his search was driven by the information that he was provided by others.[48] Such discordant narratives produce testimonial injustice insofar as their impact is to discredit the testimonies of the relatives or the searchers by crowding their experiential memories with conflicting information and thereby actively producing temporal discontinuities.

Disappearing Grief

It is not only the temporal coherence of testimony that is targeted in necro-epistemic methods, however; it is also the coherence of events. Fricker, discussing epistemic injustice, considers another mode, "hermeneutical injustice," wherein the experiences of the knowers become obscure even to themselves, so that the means of making sense of the experience become unavailable for the knower. In Fricker's words, hermeneutical injustice is an experience one encounters "when a gap in the collective interpretative resources puts someone at an unfair disadvantage when it comes to making sense of their own experience."[49] As a result, the knower is left with a vague series of memories consisting of contradictory experiences, memories, narratives, and silences that do not make sense. In necro-epistemic methods, this gap is often shaped along gendered lines between the relatives of the disappeared and the state. Take, for example, the Saturday Mothers as a specifically gendered group consisting not only of mothers but also the sisters and wives of the disappeared. For many of them, this process involves being both sexualized and hystericized as grieving women. Many of them recall the sexual advances of officials at some point and being told that the disappearance is their own fault, or that their loved ones just abandoned them for no reason. Being told that they are "crazy" for still expecting the relatives to return is a common experience for many, as well as being told that all they need is a husband, a "real man," to keep them in check.[50] Hermeneutical injustice refers to the insufficiency of one's hermeneutical resources to make sense of the events that have unfolded; between silences, requests for sexual favors, various elements of sexual violence, and being held accountable for the continued absence of the disappeared, many of the women indeed refer to "not understanding" what is happening or why it is happening.[51]

The gendered dynamics involved in the case of necro-epistemic methods, however, are not limited to hysterization or hypersexualization: gendered scripts around femininity and masculinity play a role in both the political and epistemic dimensions of the searchers and the disappeared, thus demonstrating the ways in which testimonial injustice and hermeneutical injustice can take place simultaneously and with the very same goal or purpose. In the case of the Dirty War in Argentina, for example, Diana Taylor discusses the double-gendering that occurs, which, on the one hand, feminizes the disappeared in celebration of the masculinity of the State and, on the other hand, traps the searchers in scripts of "bad" femininity. As Taylor explains, this feminization of the disappeared (no matter their gender identity) would take place by rendering the disappeared as passive, weak, or submissive through various methods of torture that might include sexual violence in many forms, as well as the explicit narration of this torture.[52] Concomitantly, many of the relatives remember at some point or another being subjected to jokes made about the scenes of torture, or to the alleged passivity and weakness that their now-disappeared loved ones showed in the face of torture.[53] On the side of the searchers—many of whom (such as the Mothers of the Plaza de Mayo)

58   Chapter 2

identify specifically with womanhood—the feminization of the disappeared would be accompanied by the mothers themselves being told that they are not "properly" feminine, that they are not "woman enough," or that they are "bad women."[54] Attempts at attaining legitimacy for the Mothers of the Plaza de Mayo would thus be delimited in accordance with gendered and, importantly, patriarchal delineations surrounding womanhood and femininity generally, and motherhood more specifically. These gendered spaces of contestation, involving questions about the home (where is your home? what kind of home is it?), domesticity (where do you belong? why aren't you at home?), sexuality (what kind of woman are you?), and motherhood (what kind of a mother are you? whose mother? can you even be a mother if you don't have a child?), all of which are modes of testimonial injustice for discrediting the women, also take on hermeneutical dimensions, actively preventing the mothers from making sense of their interpretative resources.[55] Such double-gendering, both on the side of the strategic feminization of the disappeared and the disqualification of the womanhood of the mothers, attests to the ways in which gendered scripts can be used for what Fricker calls "hermeneutical marginalization," wherein the mothers are asymmetrically participating in collective hermeneutical resources in the sense that their experiences, along with their capacity to make sense of the events, are actively hindered.[56]

It is worth noting at this point, however, that hermeneutical marginalization, or events "not making sense," is not peripheral but is rather a constitutive feature of enforced disappearances. Indeed, many of the elements that make up the organized system called "enforced disappearance" are "unbelievable" in themselves. As Avery Gordon states, "secret arrest, transportation under cover of darkness, the refusal to give information as to the person's whereabouts, and the belief that 'deterring' resistance could be best accomplished by people vanishing 'without a trace' are the elements that refigure the system of repression known as 'disappearance.'"[57] From secret detention centers, to unrecorded torture locations, to random mass burial sites, what makes up the system of enforced disappearance is its implausibility, where the possibility of obtaining information is obstructed at each and every step, and even when it is corroborated and concrete, it doesn't become any less difficult to believe. Thus, the gap in the collective interpretative sources remains even when the relatives do learn something about their disappeared relative's whereabouts. For example, the relatives in Newala Qesaba, some of whom were told at some point that the remains were there in the pile of trash, wake up some mornings utterly convinced that the whole thing "was a dream and nothing more," and still can't believe that it is true.

Moreover, hermeneutical marginalization occurs due to archival disappearance as well. Indeed, the hermeneutical impact of archival disappearance shows itself when those who remain are left with blocks of absences in the epistemological web. Archival disappearance erases not only the person disappeared, but also the world in which the possibility of this person existed and the world to which the person has disappeared, thus leaving gaps and absences in collective interpretative resources. While General Ramón Camps claimed that it was not people who had disappeared, but only subversives, Ahmet Davutoğlu, the prime minister at the time, during the round-the-clock curfews when Cemile died, was arguing that there was "not a single dead civilian" in the towns with curfews.[58] Likewise, the families of Newala Qesaba were repeatedly told that there were only animal bones and random clothes there, because it is a trash-disposal area after all, and the things they saw there were trash, nothing more. Thus, for the relatives who were repeatedly told their loved ones simply did not exist, the information regarding them, regarding their life, arrest, or detention, became incoherent and was reduced to the status of uncorroborated memories that are no different from our memories of dreams or nightmares. María del Rosaria Acosta refers to the "oblivion in collective memory," where the traces of violence can be erased in such a way that the remainders of memory do not make sense beyond inducing horror.[59] Similarly, the cases of enforced disappearances, of bodies thrown into trash-disposal areas where dogs dig up human bones, become tales that are told with little or no supporting evidence, by women who are disqualified as bad women and bad mothers, and by people who may themselves disappear when looking for disappearances, and images of dead bodies that are hard to imagine in the first place and even harder to believe. The subjugation of knowledge involves disqualification: the disqualification of memories from counting as knowledge, the disqualification of the disappeared from counting as people, and the disqualification of mass graves from counting as graves; the knowledge of any of these does not rise to the threshold of real, scientific, or official knowledge.

Power infiltrates knowledge, molds and bends it, and works in and through it. Indeed, rather than a side element to knowledge that works alongside it, power forms an assemblage with knowledge. New objects of knowledge emerge in relation to power and new technologies of power emerge in relation to knowledge. In this sense, knowledge is neither identical to power, nor simply an extension of it: as it interacts with power, knowledge does things, produces objects, deploys techniques. Discussing mechanisms of power, and their relation to life, death, the living, and the dead, thus necessitates talking about the matrices of transformation that take place on the epistemic level.

Insofar as necrosovereignty is a kind of power that works by subsuming life and the living in geographies of grief, this work does not take place without thoroughly investing itself in epistemic methods. As we have said in the previous chapter, necrosovereignty works by actively allowing and disallowing individuals and populations to be dead, continuously producing a kind of death that is not death, a kind of death that is marked by the absence of death. The limbo of impossibilized mourning, where neither death nor life takes place, is not only a political formation, but also an epistemic one. Questions such as what is known and what is knowable of death, what kinds of truth games are played out around death, what kinds of archives are produced around the dead and the disappeared, what kinds of relations are possible with such archives, who is qualified as a credible epistemic agent, and what kinds of interactions are possible among epistemic agents, are not accidental to the work of necrosovereignty. Rather, these questions form fundamental nexuses of interaction with the work of necrosovereignty: investigating necrosovereignty thus requires analyzing the epistemologies that interact with the work of necrosovereignty.

A fundamental question to be reckoned with, however, is what such an analysis might entail, or what the object of this analysis would be. Indeed, knowledges of necrosovereignty do not occur in relation to representations of mourning from the outside, from a standpoint of either temporal or geographic distance. Rather than questions on how, for example, techniques of improper burial are represented elsewhere or afterwards, the epistemological question requires investigating how knowledge is produced within necrosovereign geographies, and the ways in which the subjects of necrosovereignty constitute not only objects of analysis, but also subjects of knowledge. Critical analyses of necrosovereignty, in short, require paying attention to what Foucault calls "subjugated knowledges," the ways in which they work not only on the archive but on the subjects themselves.

The term "necro-epistemic methods" designates the subjugation of knowledge in the context of necrosovereignty, where the knowledge of death and its production forms a fundamental point of interaction with the work of necrosovereignty in producing sites of impossible mourning. These methods involve the production of subjugated knowledges in both senses of Foucault's analysis, producing both buried and disqualified knowledges. Archival erasure is an example of the burying that takes place, where the scenes of violence and the signs of terror disappear from the archive together with the people themselves. These numbers move and shift in the archive: records of birth and death disappear following the physical disappearance of the people, and the traces of both their existence and disappearance become buried in the functional ensemble of necrosovereignty. The collective oblivion that remains, after the disappeared and the buried are gone, is inseparable from the work of necrosovereignty: the invisibilization of people is inseparable from the invisibilization of knowledge, of existence, of death, of disappearance.

This "invisibilization," however, does not constitute the only form of the subjugation of knowledge. Local knowledges involve the disqualified: together with the erasure of the archive, there is the targeting of the sense-making possibilities of the grieving relatives and their communities. Necro-epistemic methods work on the political and epistemic agency of these subjects by targeting their capacities as knowers using methods of epistemic injustice. The encounters with mass graves and enforced disappearances attest to this work of epistemic injustice, where disappearance results in the destabilization of temporal coherence, and gendered hysterization and the erasure of memory result in testimonial injustice. These methods imply both testimonial and hermeneutical injustice insofar as they both rely on the erasure of credible epistemic agents and the targeting of agents' memory. Necro-epistemic methods work on the knowledge of death, and this knowledge consists not only of what is known about death but also of what is knowable and what is thinkable in relation to death.

In the previous chapter, we said that the world of necrosovereignty is neither void nor hollow, that it rather consists of murmurs: indeed, the active production of such murmurs—turning speech into silence, knowers into hysterical women, testimonies into nightmares—is a key element of necrosovereignty. Burying information and erasing archives are both important parts of this work, for sure, but these are inseparable from another kind of work that consists in making non-sense out of grief, actively opening up gaps in entire epistemologies, and producing murmurs out of speech. Genealogy, Foucault says, requires paying attention to such murmurs, paying attention to the raw memory of struggles. The question, then, is one of what remains, of what is erased and what is built anew in necrosovereignty all at once.

Chapter 3

Building Anew

The old walled city called Sur, one of the central districts of the province of Diyarbakir in eastern Turkey, was declared a UNESCO heritage site in 2015.[1] In the years following, between 2015 and 2017, Sur became the site of urban warfare between Kurdish armed groups and Turkish security forces. In the span of these two years that highlighted Turkey's renewed "war on terror" that began in June 2015, after Turkey's governing Justice and Development Party (AKP) had lost its parliamentary majority in the elections, a total of 252 round-the-clock curfews were declared in the eastern regions of Turkey, many of them at Sur, lasting for months at a time.[2] During the curfews, the inhabitants were not allowed to leave their houses, and the curfews were secured with a regular military presence on the streets. When the last curfew was lifted, the face of the area was revealed: the population of the city had been reduced by two-thirds, many of the buildings were destroyed, and the facades of the remaining buildings were marked by bullet holes and graffiti, some with racial slurs reminding passersby of the power of the state, and others with hopeful notes from the insurgents about the change to come in time.[3]

In March 2017, the Turkish Ministry of Environment and Urbanization revealed the new master plan for the city of Sur, a plan whose "high-security service zones" featured new buildings mimicking Diyarbakir's traditional architecture and widened streets that would allow the smooth passage of armed vehicles.[4] In August 2017, the Public Mass Housing Administration (Toplu Konut Idaresi Baskanligi, or TOKI) announced its new program, which consisted of building new condominiums across the old city: over the city's ruins a total of 22,700 new housing residences were planned, most of which were to be occupied by new inhabitants coming from neighboring cities.[5] The advertising campaign of the project stated, "We Are Building Sur Anew."

The impulse to "build anew" is not specific to Sur: in many ways, it was mirrored by another such reconstruction project in the neighboring town of Cizre, in an area that had become known as "Vahşet Bodrumlari," or "the Basements of Atrocity." On January 24, 2016, during the 41st day of one of the round-the-clock curfews in Cizre, the walls of two neighboring apartment buildings were demolished by an artillery shell, and those inside were forced to hide in the basements. In the period between January 24 and February 8, during which those inside were not allowed to leave, the official number of those who died in the basement rose from three on January 27 to seven on January 30, and then to fourteen on February 7. The testimonies of witnesses in the area suggested that the burnt bodies of dozens of people were removed from the building at a later date. Many other testimonies suggest that there might be a much higher number of bodies that were left in the basements, though no official investigations were later undertaken.[6] In June 2017, the lots of the Basements of Atrocity were opened to city redevelopment, and the plans of reconstruction upon the lots were released. The campaign of the project stated nothing less than a promise: "We are giving you your home back."[7]

In the previous chapters we have discussed the erasures of necrosovereignty, the ways in which it produces silences, makes murmurs out of voices, and actively disqualifies knowledges, knowers, and death and the dead. However, necrosovereignty does not consist only in erasure and disqualification: it also produces new knowledges, knowers, spaces, and memories. In this chapter, I turn to the necrosovereign impulse to "build anew," to build and reconstruct new structures, spaces, and knowledges. I focus specifically on why and how necrosovereignty is invested in spatial techniques such as the destruction and reconstruction of space, and what impact these tactics have on the formation of collective memory. The chapter consists of three main sections: the first section is devoted to the relation between necropolitics and space, and examines the function of spatial organization in a kind of power that is invested in regulating death and the dead. In this section, I will discuss Mbembe's account of necropolitics as a spatial formation, one that is involved in methods such as the segregation and fragmentation of space. The second section turns to necrosovereignty specifically and examines the role of memory and spatial organization from the perspective of the necrosovereign tactics of mourning. Here, I articulate the spatial methods of power in relation to methods of creating certain kinds of memories around death. In the third section of the chapter, I will turn to the question of necrosovereign space not only as a site of memory but also an archive, as a site of history. Throughout, I argue that the epistemic methods of necrosovereignty rely on the organization of collective memory, where the spatial techniques of necropolitics organize practices of mourning by targeting the destruction, construction, and reconstruction of collective memory. The archive of necrosovereign space works not as the container of collective memory but rather as the grounds for the possibility of forging counter-memories that challenge necrosovereign methods.

Necropolitics and Space: Problematization

In order to understand the relationship between necrosovereignty and spatial memories, we must first return to necropolitics and space, and discuss what space has to do with death and how the organization of space organizes and regulates death. As discussed above, in Mbembe's account, necropolitics as a technology of power has death as its primary objective: its goal is to regulate and optimize death. This work of the distribution and regulation of death occurs spatially. This spatial work, in Mbembe's account, functions not as a side element of necropolitics but rather as a fundamental part of it. Space, according to Mbembe, is the "raw material" of sovereignty, where the sovereign right to kill operates territorially.[8] The decision about who must live and who must die, the epitome of sovereignty, is a decision that is necessarily carried out within and through space, through its boundaries, borders, and topographies, thus distributing resources and rights within those territories. In necropolitical space, however, there does not need to be the sacred figure of the sovereign in order to distribute the life chances: local commanders can do the killing with impunity, and the space of necropolitics becomes a space of normalized death, where death becomes the defining characteristic. Necropolitics works through the creation of what Mbembe calls "death-worlds," entire "topographies of cruelty."[9] Cizre under its round-the-clock curfew is an example of such a topography, where the inhabitants of the buildings that housed the Basements of Atrocity were killed by an artillery shell that blew up their living room; and yet dying under such conditions could still be a part of the normal organization of things, insofar as death is a part of ordinary affairs under the conditions of round-the-clock curfews.

Even though the necropolitical work of death is necessarily connected to a given space, it is not necessarily geographically locatable or rationalizable. Necropolitical spaces are defined not through their geographic locations but through the methods of power that are deployed in them. What defines a "death-world" is not so much where it is located, but what takes place within a given space. For example, Mbembe asserts that territorial segmentation and segregation are a fundamental part of death-worlds. The fundamental work of the curfew is to limit the inhabitants of a given space to the interior of their residences, nor is it coincidental that towns under curfew could not be reached by any civil or social organization during the period of the curfew. The dynamics of territorial fragmentation, Mbembe asserts, have two objectives: the first is "to render any movement impossible," so that any movement is only possible under surveillance.[10] Indeed, during the curfew, everyone is confined to their homes, and even the most basic forays outside of the home, such as getting groceries or visiting one's neighbors, become restricted ones that mark the affinity between life and death, or the quickness of death's possible arrival.[11] Second, territorial fragmentation "implements separation" between the space of necropolitics and other spaces: thus, the necropolitical space becomes an exceptional space, a space that has its own rules and order and is "divided into a web of intricate internal borders and various isolated cells."[12] The space of necropolitics is highly ordered, where the borders and the cells are not only separated from each other, but each one is surveilled and patrolled. In turn, the order of the town becomes "radically separate" from all other spaces; hence, Sur under curfew and Sur the city can occupy the same geographic location, but what makes the former into a death-world is the ways in which the space is organized and fragmented in order to produce lives within it as akin to death.

The spatial methods of necropolitics involve not only territorial fragmentation but the ordering of the space itself. The space of necropolitics, unlike the space of sovereignty, is not just a horizontal space, such as a territory marked by borders on its periphery. The space of necropolitics is a vertical space as well: the airspace above it and the cellars beneath it, the tunnel and the bridge are all part of the same geography that is shaped by multiple orders of death. Thus, the streets of Cizre under curfew, where the residents were not allowed to walk, function as sites of violence just as much as the underground basements where people died. The town under curfew becomes a multitudinous site of violence; the death basements of Cizre marked the same geography as the ghost town of the streets of the city. Under such conditions, there is no longer any separation between the surface, the underground, and the airspace, insofar as "the underground as well as the airspace are transformed into conflict zones,"[13] where each space is marked by death infiltrating life.

This spatial reorganization across both horizontal and vertical lines, as well as its territorial fragmentation, demonstrate what Mbembe calls "infrastructural warfare."[14] In line with such infrastructural warfare, there is what Mbembe calls "bulldozing." This is a common aspect in necropolitical spatial organization. The examples of "bulldozing" that Mbembe gives are "demolishing houses and cities; uprooting olive trees; riddling water tanks with bullets; bombing and jamming electronic communications; digging up roads; destroying electricity transformers; tearing up airport runways; disabling television and radio transmitters; smashing computers."[15] Bulldozing involves the active destruction of the urban infrastructural network, so that the process of living in the necropolitical space becomes a deadly affair: artillery shells hitting the sides of buildings is a part of such bulldozing, as are the actual bulldozers that regularly entered Sur at the end of the periods covered by regional states of exception.[16] The goal of infrastructural warfare is not only to demonstrate the sovereign threat of taking life but also to mark the affinity between life and death: to show the disposability of the population. What marks a death-world is, after all, not so much the actual dying that takes place, or the number of people who lose their lives: a death-world is where the spatial organization of power blurs the line between life and death so that death is always immanent, if not an immediate part of life. In this sense, the curfewed town is a town not a town of massacre. Rather, it is a town where everyone is living on the brink of death.

Through spatial analysis, we can see the demolition of housing and infrastructure in sites such as Sur and Cizre as a work of necropolitics. The creation of death-worlds entails territorial fragmentation, the vertical multiplication

Building Anew

of sites of violence, and infrastructural warfare. The curfewed town is a segregated space where entrance and exit are not permitted, and where the spatial rules of the town are determined as exceptional and are very different from other spaces. This segregation occurs simultaneously with the reformulation of spaces in the territory as sites of violence, as sites of the "bulldozing" of the facilities for ordinary living, in a reorganization that makes the possibility of death always immanent. In many ways, this attests to the spatiality of power, or how power works by taking space as its object. Or as Foucault asks, "what sovereign did not want to build a bridge over the Bosporus or move mountains?"[17] The aim of working with space and transforming it is shared by various modes of power. Foucault in *Security, Territory, Population* analyzes different techniques of power in relation to their spatial organization: from sovereignty to biopolitics, each model of power works by controlling, reorganizing, and transforming space. In this sense, space is not separate from relations of power: as Foucault says, space is not a natural given, and "we do not live in a kind of void, inside of which we could place individuals and things."[18] Indeed, space is taken up and worked on, articulated and rearticulated in line with relations of power. In short, "we live inside a set of relations that delineates sites which are irreducible to one another and absolutely not superimposable on one another."[19] If necropolitics is invested in such spatial organization, this accounts for the ways in which different locations can be delineated as sites of death, so that the town of Cizre or the district of Sur can be segmented and fragmented, becoming a site of control and a site of terror at the same time. Emphasizing the spatial aspect of power, and specifically of necropolitics, is thus important in understanding what infrastructural warfare can entail under conditions that are shaped by the overwhelming presence of death. Indeed, necropower, as a kind of power that regulates death and the dead, is spatial.

However, unlike Mbembe's description of the spatial work of necropolitics through warfare, destruction, and bulldozing, the aftermath of the city center of Sur and the reconstruction plans for the Basement of Atrocity in Cizre attest to another kind of spatial work of death, the work of regulating mourning and memory in necrosovereignty. This work consists of the reconstruction of the sites of violence: rather than destruction or erasure, it involves building anew and building over necropolitical spaces. But building anew also organizes memory in relation to these given spaces. Whereas bulldozing and demolition maximize death, the impulse of building anew in Sur and Cizre testifies to the work of necrosovereignty on the memory and the meaning of these sites in relation to the possibilities of mourning. In the reconstruction of sites by city development projects on top of the very sites of death, in the bulldozing of spaces where the exact number of bodies lying beneath them is unknown, what is at stake is not only the optimization of death, but also the possibility of what these sites do and can mean, of what is remembered and how it is remembered in and around these spaces.

In this sense, in understanding necrosovereignty by its destruction and demolition of space, it is also important to consider what is built anew in death-worlds, so as to see the ways in which collective memory and grief operate. The rest of this chapter focuses on the relationship between the necrosovereign organization of space and the politics of memory, on the question of what role the spatial organization of death plays in the mnemonic tactics of necropower. I will develop the epistemic methods of necrosovereignty in relation to the organization of collective memory: necrosovereignty, in this sense, works by regulating memories of death through the organizing of space. This spatial organization, moreover, entails developing the necrosovereign space as an archive. A fundamental question at the heart of necrosovereign spatiality, therefore, concerns how to approach this spatial archive.

Memory Assemblages and Mnemonic Tactics

Inasmuch as the curfew town is a necropolitical space, the aftermath of the town does not attest to the work of death by means of destruction. Indeed, Sur and Cizre are both sites of urban redevelopment; they are towns with security zones and widened roads, with new buildings built on top of the ruins of the town's old architecture. If the work of necropolitics is to produce spaces where death is inseparable from life, necrosovereignty is defined by an emphasis on redoing that work, or doing it over, with new buildings and new spaces. The question is, what is the function of building anew in this work of death? What is destroyed and what is built anew, and what does such building anew target? As much as the work of necropolitics consists in maximizing destruction, necrosovereignty works through different techniques that deploy not only the destruction of people and memories but also, on a positive level, the remaking and transformation of spaces and sites, and thus of memories.

As discussed in the first section, techniques such as bulldozing and fragmentation aim for the maximization of death in death-worlds, where life becomes a deadly affair and the death of inhabitants becomes ordinary. However, considering the aftermath of destruction and the building anew of these sites requires analyzing the work of necrosovereignty on memory. The transformation of sites of violence or massacre into novel sites with new buildings or new "city centers" can be understood as a work of reproducing memory, of creating new kinds of memories around the sites of violence. After all, there is something very corporeal about how memories come to be, and the reproduction of a sensible object has much to do with what is remembered and what is forgotten. Much of this sensuous character of memory is familiar from Proust's famous example of eating a madeleine in *In Search of Lost Time*.[20] Here, Proust's narrator realizes that memory works on a sensuous level: the very specific and the simplest of sensations can bring

Building Anew

forth an entirety of memories. The very sensation can open up or close down memory; the smell of the madeleine can bring joy, just as unpaved cobblestones can recall memories of Venice, and torn-down buildings on the streets of Sur can summon memories of warfare and death. In this sense, sensuous data can organize and shape memory, and similarly, memory can impact the ways in which sensuous data is processed. Thus we can say, for example, that building brand-new condos on the grounds of mass graves accomplishes a certain replacement of memory. As the ruins are covered with new buildings, "built in the Seljuk and Ottoman style," as the prime minister of the time proudly declared, the associations of the space are replaced; grief becomes indifference or gives way to other memories and emotions, maybe joy, or even nostalgia for the imperial nation-state.[21]

Of course, what is impacted in the replacement of sensuous data is not really voluntary memory, or even what Bergson would call the "memory-image" of the place, but potentially the involuntary memory. As Alia Al-Saji describes it, a memory-image is a representational image, one that connects our past experience of an object with the present and the future.[22] The memory-image of the site where someone's relative died after being stuck for days, for example, is not something that can be fully erased by erecting new buildings. As the people of Cizre say, they can never forget worrying about their relatives, nor can they forget how the basements smelled once all who were in them were gone. Gilles Deleuze explains voluntary memory in relation to such memory-images of the past, of the concrete presence of the past. As Keith Ansell-Pearson describes it, "voluntary memory proceeds by snapshots and gives us an experience of the past that is as 'shocking,' and as tedious, as looking at photographs."[23] In Deleuze's words, voluntary memory does not relate to "the past's being *as past.*"[24] Indeed, many of the residents of Cizre and Sur state that the memories of the days of curfew are "etched in their minds," and they remember each day "as if it is today."[25] When the past reverberates in the memory in immediate snapshots, the photographic image of the past does not leave our memory: instead, such snapshots retain their place in the memory. In this sense, building sites anew would not replace people's memory-images of such sites because those memory-images remain etched in the minds of the residents. Instead, the replacement of sensuous data and memory would occur not in conscious recollection but in terms of involuntary memory: as the narrator of *In Search of Lost Time* realizes, "the sensations afforded by sensuous signs, such as the uneven paving-stones, the stiffness of the napkin, and the taste of the madeleine, have no connection with what he had attempted to recall."[26] In this sense, the residents of Cizre passing by the sites of the basements of violence and experiencing the sight of the ruins, the smell of destruction and rot, or the emergence of new residences, may make connections distinct from what they would aim to recall. Deleuze suggests that it is often not the voluntary but the involuntary memory that makes meaning out of sensuous signs: the meaning of a site as either a site of violence or a site of security can be shaped through the kinds of sensuous signs that are produced in it and the associations that involuntary memory makes in relation to it.

Yet, perhaps the difficulty in understanding the mnemonic work of necrosovereignty as the work of replacing involuntary memories lies in the multidirectionality of the associations of involuntary memory. As said above, involuntary memory does not work via linear relations, nor can it work through complete replacements. Sensuous data does not have programmable correlations; what is to be remembered walking down a site of memory, of destruction, the absence of the smell of rotting human and animal carcasses might add new sensuous data to the site, but it does not completely replace the past. Instead, each present is, as Al-Saji says, "pregnant with a virtual image," an image of itself as already past, an image that brings forth not singular but a multiplicity of memories, or even the whole of memory.[27] In this sense, no present has a single memory attached to it: for example, the nightclub that is built in the center of Sur for the use of security personnel, with its blue neon sign and increased security surveillance, cannot be enough to produce a singular set of associations. Instead, the neon sign becomes filled with virtual images, which haunt the present; and each present is filled with many memories, of virtual objects that exist in fragments, in halves, "that are found only as lost" and "that exist only as recovered."[28] With the neon blue sign and nightclub, there exist the memories of other nightclubs, other entertainment, together with the sounds of the gunshots, of death, and of grief. Together with the concrete walls of the new buildings, there exist not only the meaning of the new Sur as the site of a new kind of population but also many virtual objects, the traces of the racialized graffiti, or the smell, which comes up in all testimonies. Indeed, if necropolitics works through space, through the undoing of space, through infrastructural warfare and bulldozing, necrosovereignty can be seen as producing another kind of time, another kind of memory, in which life becomes infiltrated by death, and all the signs of life are haunted by virtual images that bring forth death. In this sense, the necrosovereign space would be defined not only by the physical and political proximity of the inhabitants to death but also by the proximity of memory formations to death as well: each memory of life is haunted by the virtual image of death.

Considering involuntary memory in relation to building anew is helpful in understanding the mnemonic function of replacing and rebuilding sites. It is important to note, however, that in the case of the Basements of Atrocity in Cizre or the razed streets of Sur, what is at stake is not only the redoing of any memory, but specifically, traumatic memory, which is bound up with forgetting. As much as involuntary memory produces haunted presences, it is necessary to analyze these mnemonic tactics in relation not only to what is remembered and how it is remembered but also to what is forgotten. In other words, if we are to focus on the mnemonic methods of necrosovereignty in

Building Anew

the production of certain memories, we must also consider these in relation to the production of forgettings, which are specifically tied to the formation of an erased past that is rebuilt and relived over and over again, always in half-measures and never complete.

In effect, insofar as the scenes of violence are erased in the building of condos, this erasure also prescribes a certain impossibility to the past event, where the event becomes wrapped in disbelief and forgetting at once. The residents of Sur, for example, say that they "can't believe what happened to their streets."[29] Many of the people who returned from their forced relocation to find their houses destroyed talk about not understanding what happened. This impossibility of understanding speaks to what Cathy Caruth calls "nonlocatable" experience,[30] a kind of experience that does not have a solid place in memory, that is not situated in a linear succession of events. Traumatic event formation, according to Caruth, is shaped not only by the pain connected to the experience of the event but also by its simultaneous forgetting: there is latency in coming to terms with the event that took place, and this latency occurs because the experience of the event is at once too soon and too late. The impossibility of locating the experience causes the memory to continuously slip into forgetting: what is known about the traumatic experience is thus mixed with what is unknown or forgotten about it. In this sense, the very rebuilding of the city is possible, because the life in death-worlds is already a life that is marked by such forgetting, and because the event of violence, of the artillery shell hitting buildings in Cizre, or the days when Sur were under curfew, is an elusive event, wrapped in trauma.

Forgetting, however, does not mean complete erasure in traumatic event formation. Memory does not simply efface and move on. Instead, the event festers and it keeps coming back: thus, the event becomes both elusive and inescapable, and there is both an absence and an excess of memory pertaining to it. Thus, Caruth writes, "the historical power of the trauma is not just that the experience is repeated after its forgetting, but that it is only in and through its inherent forgetting that it is first experienced at all."[31] Rather than erasing the event, forgetting preserves the event: even though forgotten, the traumatic event is also continuous. Thus, building condos over the uncounted bodies in the Basements of Atrocity can actually turn the violence of the round-the-clock curfew into a permanent violence: if the curfewed town is a death-world, in this sense, the bulldozing and the building anew in the aftermath of the curfew do not erase the memories of it as such but rather preserve the space of the town as a death-world, a space where death infiltrates life even after the curfew has been lifted and the official state of emergency is no longer operative. The effect of such building anew would thus not be the replacement of voluntary memories or the snapshots of violence, but neither would it program the correlations of the involuntary memory. Rather, it is precisely by infiltrating the memory of the sites with forgettings that the haunted presences of necrosovereignty are sustained. In

Maria del Rosario Acosta Lopez's words, erasure can ensure "that the establishment of the original violence is definitive because it is inaccessible."[32] The fundamental element of such mnemonic work is thus sustaining forgettings so that the work of death in necropolitical space becomes a continuous work that moves beyond the temporality of the destruction of sites or the maximization of physical death.

Traumatic event formation and the account of involuntary memory are crucial to understanding the necrosovereign investment of space as an investment in memory, in producing certain kinds of memories and forgettings. Through the account of involuntary memory, we can see the spatial work of necrosovereignty as producing a kind of temporality in which life becomes infiltrated by death: memory is wrapped in sensuous experience, not only in the sense of the conscious recollection of the experience, but in the multiplication of virtual experience, which haunts the experience of the present. The present experience of the new Sur becomes multiplied with its past as a curfewed town, and all signs of life become haunted by the virtual images of death. The account of trauma helps us understand this temporality as particularly a temporality of violence, and a temporality belonging to the death-work of necropolitics: the supposed forgetting that is inscribed in building anew preserves the death-work of necropolitics beyond the temporal limitations of the event of the curfew, where the exceptionality of the necropolitical work can go beyond the limits of the state of exception.

Through both of these accounts, we can come closer to understanding the necrosovereign space as a space where the thin line between memory and forgetting becomes blurred, where memory becomes forgettable, and where forgetting becomes memorable, where the past of the space spirals into its present and its future. Avery Gordon would call such spaces "haunted spaces," spaces that are filled with ghosts. When describing haunting, Gordon suggests that ghosts refer not to events past but to events that continue on into the present and carry on to the future; the experience of facing a ghost does not take the present to the past, but rather ruptures and punctuates the present. Thus, she writes, "to get to the ghost and the ghost's story, it is necessary to understand how the past, even if it is just the past that flickered by a moment before, can be seized in an instant, or how it might seize you first."[33] Haunted spaces are spaces where the virtual is inseparable from the concrete, where the past makes itself known through forgetting and through spiraling involuntary memories. In Gordon's words, "haunting raises specters, and it alters the experience of being in time, the way they separate the past, the present, and the future."[34] As such, the experience of haunting defines a present that is infiltrated by the past and inseparable from it: a "moving present," as Gordon calls it, that moves from the past into the possibilities of the future.[35]

Due to this ordering of the present as filled with the past, the structure of memory in haunting does not work through clear-cut distinctions between memory and forgetting, or between memory and imagination. A haunted space carries the message that "the gap between personal and the social, public and private, objective and subjective, is missing in the first place."[36] In such a haunted space, the past and the present, between mourning and its aftermaths, become just as inseparable as the living are from the dead. The space itself becomes infiltrated both by its past and its future: the space that is built anew becomes a space of bulldozing and reconstruction, of memory and forgetting, or past and present at once. In such spaces, moreover, the very operation of necrosovereignty on memory becomes the spiraling of memory. As Gordon says, living with ghosts is always "leading you elsewhere, it is making you see things that you did not see before, it is making an impact on you; your relation to things that seemed separate or invisible is changing." The work of necrosovereignty is to produce spaces where not only death but also memories of death and memories of grief are inseparable from their own forgetting. In such spaces, "building anew" works not to reproduce memories but to produce the space as a haunted space, where death infiltrates life, and grief infiltrates memory.

It is thus crucial to understand the spatial tactics of necrosovereignty as mnemonic tactics that create haunted memories shaped by death infiltrating life. Unlike the emphasis on destruction and bulldozing that is operative in necropolitics, necrosovereignty does not only produce an affinity between the life and death of the inhabitants through destruction. The work of producing a die-able population is inseparable from the mnemonic work of the production of memories that slip into death, memories that are inseparable from forgettings, and are sustained and erased at once. Yet, memory is not only about remembering, it is about history as well: not only people, but spaces too can remember and bear testimony. Indeed, building anew on sites of memory is in many ways connected to the lives and deaths that those spaces can bear witness to, or the kinds of histories that can emerge from out of such spaces. Similarly, the question of the return of memory is inseparably tied to the question of the archive, the recording of the archive, and the relation between the archive and death.[37] If necrosovereignty works by reorganizing spaces in order to reorganize memories, it is important to question what kind of a history these spaces bear witness to, and what kind of historical approach can emerge in relation to these spaces. The next section will turn to the question of the archive and the question of how to approach an archive that is bulldozed and built anew, or a haunted archive that is shaped more by what is forgotten than by what is remembered.

(Un)Doing the Archive

We can thus say that the spatial methods of necrosovereignty produce not only spaces where life is infiltrated by death but also memories and temporalities of such infiltration: between traumatic event formation and the work of involuntary memory, the spatial methods of necropolitics produce haunted spaces, spaces where memories of life and death become inseparable from each other. Necrosovereignty is invested in mnemonic spatial tactics that produce certain kinds of memories and forgetting surrounding death: the sustaining of the work of death takes place not only through bulldozing and destruction but by rebuilding sites and redoing spaces in order to produce temporalities where memory continuously slips into forgetting; yet the work of necrosovereignty and the affinity it produces with death festers.

Memory, however, is not only the subjective capacity to remember, nor is it simply the process by which the distinction between remembering and forgetting takes place. Memory is also bound up with the question of recording and of remains. As Walter Benjamin says, memory is not an object of exploration, it is rather "the medium of that which is experienced, just as the earth is the medium in which ancient cities lie buried."[38] Exploring memory is not a task of finding something that is buried but is rather a process of going through the material that does the work of burying in the first place. In the case of the collective memory of necrosovereignty, this material ground becomes especially important: the mnemonic work of necropolitics that buries over and redoes memory is inseparable from its spatial work, which buries over and redoes place. Approaching memory requires undertaking the task not only of approaching the formation of memory, but of approaching the site of history. In Benjamin's words, the one "who seeks to approach their own buried past must conduct themselves like a person digging."[39] In this sense, approaching the memory of spaces requires approaching the archive of spaces, or even spaces as archives. In the bulldozing of the basements of violence, in the infrastructural warfare that entailed artillery shells being shot at buildings, in the racialized graffiti that covered the streets of Sur and the security zones that were planted in the center of the city, what gets impacted is not only the space as a site of memory but also the space as an archive: what is built anew is not only how certain sites are remembered but also what remains from those sites.

Mbembe calls these remains "debris," referring to what is left behind in the transactions between the archive and death. Death, he states, "never attacks totally, nor equally successfully, all the properties of the deceased (in either the figurative or the literal sense). There will always remain traces of the deceased, elements that testify that a life did exist, that deeds were enacted, and struggles engaged in or evaded."[40] It is no accident that the memory of death is never fully erased, nor is it ever completely replaced: there remains the debris of death scattered in and around necropolitical spaces. Indeed, if the town center of Sur, despite its widened streets and new buildings, still does not refer only to the memories of life, it is precisely because of such debris that does not leave or abandon the space. Archives, according to Mbembe, are fundamentally aimed at prohibiting the dead "from stirring up disorder in the present," and "the best way to ensure that the dead do not

Building Anew   75

stir up disorder is not only to bury them, but also to bury their 'remains,' the 'debris.' "[41] The aim of building condominiums over the debris is a testimony to this archival work that consists in filling in and burying the remains, where the sites would take on the characteristics of archives that work as forms of interment. The purpose of this kind of interment is not necessarily to lay the debris to rest but rather "to consign elements of that life which could not be destroyed purely and simply" in order to "tame" the debris, to make sure that the dead do not stir up disorder.[42]

What does it mean, however, to approach the necrosovereign space as an archive? What kind of an archive would it be? Derrida discusses the meaning of the archive in relation to *archē*: "the original, the first principle, the primitive." *Archē* designates both "a founding or originating principle" and a place of domiciliation: it was "initially a house, a domicile, an address, the residence of the superior magistrates, the archons, those who commanded."[43] While Derrida focuses on the difficulty of sustaining such a distinction between a domicile and an origin, when it comes to necrosovereign spaces, even maintaining either one of these presents problems. One of the common elements of inhabitant testimonies from the curfew towns upon their return is their surprise at finding the place they left unrecognizable. Many of them say it is hard to believe that the place they returned to is the same place in which they had lived. Indeed, necropolitical space is not a site among others or a place that is merely situated in a given location. If the territorial fragmentation described by Mbembe separates the necropolitical space from its geographic location, the mnemonic tactics of necrosovereignty separate the space from its location in time in relation to its past and present as well. The rebuilt town center of Sur in this sense becomes split from the historical city that had been declared a UNESCO heritage site, but it also becomes distinct from the place where the residents were born and where they lived. The present of the town, as we have seen in the previous section, becomes a haunted present that is stuck between the reverberations of past violence and the productions of the current reality. The sequential ordering of *archē* as the originary becomes impossible since it is wrapped in an order where the former becomes the latter continuously.

Moreover, when it comes to necrosovereign spaces, the sense of *archē* as a space of domiciliation or as an address presents problems. Beyond the spatial tactics of territorial fragmentation that take place for a given time period, what the mnemonic spatial organization of necrosovereignty accomplishes is to separate the town from the curfewed town temporally: in this separation, the latter emerges as what Foucault would call a "non-place," a place that exists solely as a site of confrontation where power's destructive work on things becomes clearer. One of the residents of Sur, for example, describes the status of the town right after the curfew was lifted as an " earthquake zone," whereas others called it a "massive graveyard," but "definitely not a town."[44] The Basements of Atrocity in this sense are not actually in the same place where they were physically located, nor are they locatable as places that have an existence in themselves beyond what happened there. Indeed, the very reason why they are called the "Basements of Atrocity" is because of what occurred in them, and this is why the residents in Cizre say they call those basements by the names of those who died in them. Thus, one of the residents in Cizre says, "We don't know the address. Is there a street to know the address? It is the basement where all those people died."[45] In the work of necropolitics, the space of necropolitics disappears beyond what occurred in it: it becomes a non-place that exists by virtue of the work of necropolitics.

If approaching such a space requires an "excavation of memory," as Benjamin calls it, digging out a non-space is a different task than the historical task of tracing what happened there, or who did what there. The necrosovereign archive does not hold the marks of struggles between equal forces: as an old woman in Sur asked, "We do not know if it was an earthquake or a deluge. Who did what, what is this destruction the punishment for?"[46] Foucault, in *Nietzsche, Genealogy, History*, describes the work of genealogy as paying attention to emergences: the emergence of concepts, relations, species. Approaching the necropolitical archive means approaching the emergence of death-worlds and the state of forces from out of which such emergence occurs. In this confrontation, there is no "closed field offering the spectacle of a struggle among equals."[47] The adversaries, as Foucault says when describing emergences, do not "belong to a common space," nor do they constitute adversaries in the strict sense of term. Infrastructural warfare and bulldozing, and the replacement and undoing of memories, do not occur on a common ground where two or more parties are involved. The space of necropolitics emerges in the work of death. Just as this space is not a "space," the relationship of forces that make up necropolitics is not a "relationship." Rather, the state of forces that marks the necropolitical space "engraves memories on things and even bodies."[48] As one piece of graffiti left by the police on the walls of Sur said, "We are not here to make war, but only to clean up." The space emerges as what the residents of Sur call "a haunted town," an archive of death. Approaching necrosovereign spaces means approaching the work of death, or approaching lives and deaths, as Foucault would call them, "that survive only from the clash of power that wished to annihilate them or at least to obliterate them."[49]

A difficulty in approaching space that has been bulldozed and built anew is that the excavation of the space reveals neither what was hidden there nor the facts of the events. Antoinette Burton discusses the attachment to objectivity with which archives have been synonymous, and the common association of the archivist with the tasks of fact retrieval.[50] When it comes to approaching the archive of necropolitical spaces, however, that assumption of retrieving facts proves to be especially difficult. No official excavations of the Basements of Atrocity were carried out, and given the accounts of bodies that were surreptitiously burned or removed from there, and the lack

Building Anew 77

of official records, the haunted temporality of the basements does not open itself to a disinterested observer who aims to find the facts of the matter or the "origin" of the memories of that space. As the graffiti on the walls of Sur are erased, and the Basements of Atrocity in Cizre are bulldozed to cede their place to brand-new condos, not only does the memory of the residents become shaped by the work of necropolitics, but the archive of necropolitics is also done over and disappears. As one of the residents of Cizre, who believes his brother died in the Basements of Atrocity, but was never able to find his body, says: "He was here and now he is not. The basements too, they were here and now they are not."[51] Other people talk about how the streets have changed, how they can't recognize the streets on which they passed their childhood playing, and others say that they can't find the exact spot on which their relatives died.

The space of necrosovereignty is indeed a non-space that is built anew and built over, over and over again. To read the archive of a non-space is a challenge, for it requires understanding that what is left may never be found in the archive, that there is no truth that can explain all that happened there. The origin of exactly how, why, and how many people died is not hidden in the space of the basements, waiting to be discovered, nor can that information suffice to challenge the work of necropolitics in and of itself. Indeed, between the different accounts of how many people were there in the basements, or why they were there, or people's memories and forgetting of their relatives in and around the spaces, what emerges in such an archive of a non-space is not a list of people who died: what one will find is rather the work of necropolitics, bulldozing the grounds, destroying the infrastructure, erasing memory, and replacing it with new sensuous data.

Even though one might not get to the origin of the matter by approaching such an archive, there are other things one may find. As Kathy Ferguson says, "archives are inexhaustible: they are full of shiny things."[52] The question is how to "marshal those myriad shiny things" from the archive, or how to see and understand them beyond the general order of things from out of which they arise.[53] One may find the gatherings of people from surrounding towns, for example, who go to the city to "visit the dead ones," as an inhabitant says, not because there is a list to be found, but because the city itself has become a graveyard. Saidiya Hartman describes the work of the archive as "entering a mortuary," which "permits one final viewing and allows for a last glimpse of persons about to disappear."[54] If the necropolitical space is an archive, entering such an archive involves catching a glimpse of the ghosts there. What such a glimpse also does is to show moments where non-spaces become actualized, where they become other kinds of spaces beyond the work of necropolitics: the space of the Basements of Atrocity in this sense becomes neither a space of death nor a space of forgetting, neither a space of violence nor a space of new living. Instead, it becomes another kind of space, a space of gathering or a space of remembering, a space of relations that exist beyond its involvement in the violent work of necropolitics. Engaging with the archive means catching a glimpse of ghosts, and as Avery Gordon says, ghosts "always carry a message."[55] This engagement does not so much entail finding the truth of the work of necropolitics, but rather the possibility of another kind of work, another kind of space, or another kind of memory.

Memories are not solid or stable entities: necrosovereignty works in and through them by replacing or repeating them, by erasing or doubling them. Indeed, insofar as necropolitics is a work of death, such work occurs not only through the actual death of inhabitants but through the memory of death and its aftermath as well. Perhaps this is why, when Foucault discusses the kind of historical sense that deals with such an archive, he refers not to the work of memory but rather that of counter-memory: "The historical sense implies a use of history that severs its connection to memory and constructs a counter-memory."[56] Constructing a counter-memory involves working with the archive not in order to find the truth in it, but rather to highlight the separation of this archive from memory, in order to highlight the counter-memories that make up the archive. The residents of Sur say, for example, that they regularly visit the streets, even though the streets have been bulldozed and are now in the process of being remade in the city redevelopment project. Many of them say that they don't visit with the hope of finding their lost ones: as an old woman who visits the lot every day where the basements once stood says, "I don't know whose dead they are, but what does it matter?" Another resident of Cizre says: "We come here because something happened here, and if we don't come here, we ourselves may disappear in history."[57] Entering the archive of necrosovereignty is an act of conjuring ghosts, in a sense, to catch a glimpse of what is about to disappear: not only the lives that make it into the records from their clash with the power that wished to annihilate them, but deaths that survive only in the spaces that are marked by death, and spaces that only survive because of forgettings.

The excavation of memory thus does not involve digging among the ruins of history in order to find what is statically secured there. Memory is not a hidden object of experience whose truth can be securely found by setting aside the work of necropolitics. What is remembered and what is forgotten about the city center of Sur, for example, is not a hidden past that is waiting to be rediscovered beyond the ruins and rubble, or the concrete walls of the new buildings. Instead, memory is a medium of experience that marks bodies and things, infiltrates spaces with meanings, possibilities, and ghosts, and makes the non-spaces of necropolitics into archives. Archives are shaped by their relations to power to a large extent: the necropolitical archive is one where people and buildings disappear and are buried and built over. Approaching such an archive is a task of conjuring the ghosts of a space, catching a glimpse of what is about to disappear, in order to forge counter-memories out of forgettings. If the work of necropolitics is to produce and reproduce memories, the work of necropolitical genealogies is that of severing the ties between memory and history in order to catch a glimpse of what disappears in history, in order to construct counter-memories.

Building Anew

Necropolitics produces death-worlds. It produces worlds in which the conditions of living and dying are inseparable from each other, spaces where life is infiltrated by death, and the lives of the population become akin to death. These death-worlds, moreover, are produced through specifically spatial methods of organization. Through techniques such as territorial fragmentation, infrastructural warfare, and bulldozing, the necropolitical space is what Mbembe calls a "topography of cruelty."[58] The curfew town is an example of such a topography of cruelty: it is separated from its surroundings, and its streets and the spaces above and beneath them become zones of death, so that the actual dying that occurs there is not surprising but is instead a regular part of life in the necropolitical space.

However, the spatial methods of necrosovereignty do not only produce these conditions of living-dying, nor do they consist only of destruction: the curfew town is a space that is built anew, and its entire temporality is shaped through the construction and reconstruction of the memories of spaces. In the rebuilding of the Sur town center or the Basements of Atrocity in Cizre, what is at stake is not only infrastructural warfare or territorial fragmentation, but the reconstruction of spaces as well as memory, the production of a kind of memory where life is continuously infiltrated by death. Through Deleuze's and Bergson's accounts, we can understand this in relation to the sensuous experience of memory: memory is wrapped up in, and is inseparable from, sensuous experience. Moreover, this is the case not only for voluntary memory but for involuntary memory as well. Multiplying the virtual images of spaces that belong to involuntary memory, and reconstructing spaces of memory with completely new sensory data produces haunted presents where the past of violence merges with the present, and death and life coexist contemporaneously. Thus, in such haunted presents, for example, the rebuilt town center exists with the place of atrocity, and the new buildings coexist with racial slurs written on destroyed walls. The temporality of such a haunted present is shaped by violence itself: akin to traumatic temporality, the temporality of necropolitical spaces is fragmented, where the violence of necropolitics festers and is repeated, and the past therefore infiltrates present and future. The spatial methods of necropolitics produce entire temporalities of death.

The work of necrosovereign temporality, however, is a technique not only of memory but one of history. What is built anew in this urban reconstruction is not only how a given space is remembered and forgotten; it is a reconstruction of the space of history, and a reconstruction of space as archive. The death-world is not a space among others that exists in a given location and in a given order with other sites. As it is both spatially and temporally disparate from other spaces, necropolitics produces the death-world as a "non-place," a place that only emerges in its confrontation with force. As such, it is a space that is on its way to disappearance: it exists for the work of necropolitics only, and the tactics of building anew serve to ensure the disappearance of the space itself. In this urban rebuilding, the history of a space is severed from its memory, so that what happened there does not match what is remembered. Thus, for example, between the various accounts of how many people were in the Basements of Atrocity, and the traumatic memories of those who survived, the memories of the basements take on a different shape than the exact information of who was there, how many people were there, or what exactly happened there.

Approaching such an archive on its way to disappearance requires a different historical sense: a non-place does not cover over an origin, nor does it reveal itself only through a careful excavation. In the cases of Sur and Cizre, the space is built anew, basements are covered over with concrete: there is not any "origin" to be found in digging through the space. Entering such an archive can only happen by marking the separation between history and memory, not in order to find out the truth of necropolitics but rather to catch a glimpse of the ghosts of the space, in order to forge counter-memories that do not fit within necropolitical memories. Indeed, if the role of necropolitics is to produce spaces where life is infiltrated by death, contesting that politics means engaging with the other meanings that such spaces can take on, such as a space of gathering, a space of remembering, or a space for organizing. Necrosovereignty construes space as non-space; engaging with such a non-space requires noting what has and what is about to disappear. Entering the archive of a non-space means not only engaging with what is remembered and how much is forgotten. Engaging with these archives also means dealing with the debris in order to weave memories out of forgettings, histories out of disappearances, and lives out of deaths.

INTERLUDE

The words below are not my own. Some are stories told by searchers or by the movements they belong to, some are poems of disappearance, some are names that are not left behind, and all are taken from sources that are publicly available and yet often hard to find. The list reflects the arbitrariness at hand. There is no order, nor is there any categorization; each fragment is very special, and no one is any more special than the next. There are thousands more, whose names are neither provided here, nor in any records. There are too many to be included here, and too many that are still nameless. Each of those below are only fragments, some found in nightmares, some found in memories, of the disappeared that meet with their loved ones weekly. Each belongs to an archive of ghosts, haunted by loss.

Together, they comprise a constellation: a constellation of memories that uphold long-lasting political movements, a constellation of nightmares that speak to each other across the seas. They comprise a constellation of struggles made of flashes of knowledge, that are driven by memory in a world bent on forgetting. Together, they are a story of power, told by resistances.

I will tell, so that it is not forgotten. I will tell, so that everyone knows how the mothers who can't find their children stay upright.

I am one of the first mothers that went to Galatasaray, on May 27, 1995.

My son Hasan Ocak was a teacher. He was a socialist who did not hurt anyone, who would help everyone, whose heart was filled with love for people and nature. He would carry candy or gum with him to hand out to kids that played on the street. On March 21, 1995, he called me. He told me he was going to get fish and cake for my daughter Aysel's birthday. My Hasan never came back home. Wherever we went, they said, "We don't have him." Those who saw him under custody told us he was terribly tortured in detention. They said, "We saw Hasan's name on the detention list, it was written there." That's when I met the families of those who disappeared. I was not the only one who experienced this pain and cruelty.

I appealed to everyone possible. I was in a void; my heart was on fire with the uncertainty of what happened to my son. But I never gave up on searching for my son. I never gave up on my hope of finding my son. After 58 days, my children found photos of his unidentified body in forensic files. He had been tortured, his beautiful face that I could not kiss enough had been torn apart. My children did not show me those photos. My Hasan was not nameless or without family, but they buried him in an anonymous grave so that no one would see the torture he had endured.

We took him out of the anonymous graveyard and buried him in a grave of our own. Then we got together with the other families of the disappeared and decided to sit at Galatasaray Square every Saturday so that no one else would ever disappear. Other families that heard of us started to join us, and we became big together.

I have promised my friends who have left us without having found their loved ones. They are waiting for us all to die without finding our disappeared, but they won't be able to get out of having to give an account. We will not stop until the last disappeared is found, and those who are responsible are brought to justice. I made a promise to my friend Elmas: we will take the photographs of our loved ones to Galatasaray, which is the place of our disappeared.[1]

—*Emine Ocak, the mother of Hasan Ocak*

There are some people, they always keep an eye on the door: their mothers, when they wake up for the morning prayers, their eyes are always on the door, as if their lost ones might return any second. If the disappeared have a spouse or children, they are always there in front of the door, waiting.[2]

—*Interview with A, Unspoken Truth*

Eduardo Alejandro Campos Barra, married, a member of the MIR, was arrested on September 13, 1973, under unknown circumstances. That day, he was seen leaving a building located in the Roosevelt community, Las Barrancas commune (now Pudahuel), in the company of a police lieutenant surnamed Quijada and two other policemen from that institution. At 8:00 p.m. on September 13, he called his sister Silvia Adriana by phone, telling her that he was temporarily in San Bernardo. That was the last communication he had with his family. At the end of September of that year, two detectives went to his wife's house stating that Eduardo Campos had been shot at the San

Interlude

Bernardo Infantry School. His family has carried out innumerable proceedings to the authorities that appear to be responsible for the act, but the authorities have refused to offer any clarification. Moreover, after requesting information from the United Nations Human Rights Commission, the Military Government, in 1974, informed said organization that Eduardo Alejandro Campos Barra "has no legal existence," despite the fact that his birth is duly registered in the Civil Registry, as well as his marriage. His family is still unaware of the fate that befell him at the hands of his captors.[3]

—Memoria Viva, Chile

For ten years my children asked, where is our father? I wonder, what happened? We had a white car back then, and for five years, I stopped whenever I saw a white car, thinking he might come out of it and say, "Where are you going?" Five years passed with that dream; every time the doorbell rang we were scared, thinking it could be bad news. Murdered here, murdered there. We were waiting, we waited for a very long time.[4]

—Interview with S, Unspoken Truth

Nurettin Yedigöl attended the wedding of his cousin in Çağlayan, İstanbul, on April 10, 1981. He left the wedding on his own to go to the house where he was staying together with his friends. The day before, his friends had been detained from this house in İdealtepe. When he went there after leaving the wedding, the police were waiting for him in the house.

Days later, his brother Muzaffer Yedigöl went to the house; unable to find his older brother there, he left a note. Seeing the note, Nurettin Yedigöl's roommate contacted Muzaffer Yedigöl and said that Nurettin had not come home for a long time. He added that he might have fled abroad. Muzaffer Yedigöl and his aunt-in-law went to the police station, the 1st Branch in Gayrettepe, to ask for Nurettin Yedigöl and they left some cigarettes, money, and underwear to be given to him. However, after having taken them first, the police then returned all of these, saying that there was no such person detained.[5]

—Saturday Mothers, in memory of Zeycan Yedigöl,
the mother of Nurettin Yedigöl

84   Interlude

Carlos Gustavo Cortiñas was a state worker at the National Institute of Statistics and Censuses. His responsibility there was to inspect the prices at the municipal fairs. [He was] a student of economic sciences at the University of Buenos Aires and a member of the Peronist University Youth. On April 15, 1977, he was kidnapped on a public road while on the way from his home to his job in the Castelar area (Buenos Aires), in an illegal arrest operation and subsequent forced disappearance. He was 24 years old.

He had begun his work activity on October 6, 1970, under personnel file No. 35,224. Through resolution No. 63, dated May 27, 1976, the resignation that he presented as a result of the persecution to which he'd been subjected was accepted. His file was repaired within the framework of Decree No. 1199/2012 of the National Executive Power, in accordance with the provisions of Joint Resolution 73/2014 and 8/2014 of the Cabinet Secretariat and Administrative Coordination and Human Rights Secretariat of the Nation dated March 14, 2014, and was handed over to his mother Nora Cortiñas from the Mothers of the Plaza de Mayo, on March 25, 2014, in the auditorium of the National Ministry of Economy, in the presence of officials, union leaders, and human rights organizations.[6]

—Comisión de Trabajo por la Reconstruction
de Nuestrá Identidad, Argentina

I am Sehriban Tepeli, the wife of Maksut Tepeli, who was disappeared in custody in 1984. My husband has been disappeared for 36 years. My struggle for justice, my search for my husband, has been continuing for 36 years, and I will continue until I find my husband. We, as the Saturday Mothers, have been continuing this struggle for half a century, and we will always continue, we will continue until we find our disappeared. They have to give us an account of what happened to our disappeared, and those who disappeared them have to give an account. We will continue our struggle.

—Sehriban Tepeli, Saturday Mother

He comes to me in my dreams. Sometimes I see him, he is just sitting there. I see the green nettle trees covering him, he sits below them, they are like a huge umbrella over him. I see him in my sleep. "Ayşe," he calls out to me, I look up, and I see my deceased son next to him,

Interlude   85

too. He asks me, "Ayşe, do your eyes still see?" and "Yes," I reply. "Do you see the white rock over there?" he asks me. "Yes, I do," I reply. "Go there, you will find my clothes," he says. There is a hill, a very high hill. Can I ever forget? Never.[7]

—Interview with A, Unspoken Truth

The Demirkan family lived in Diyarbakir/Baglar with their five children. Their son Mehmet Zafer was preparing to report for mandatory military duty. On September 12, 1995, around 10 p.m., the house of the Demirkan family was raided by 6 or 7 civilian-clothed individuals who introduced themselves as police. They took Mehmet Zafer, saying that "he will be released after his statement is taken," and put him into a white station wagon Renault (Toros). The family went immediately to the police station, but they were told, "We don't have him"; afterwards, they went to all the police stations in Diyarbakir one by one. They always received the same answer: "We don't have him." The family, who have been looking for Mehmet for 26 years, have not reached a conclusion to their efforts. The officials that they appealed to did not take the necessary steps. On our 860th Week, we will join the voice of Behiye Demirkiran, who says, "I will not believe my son is dead until there is a grave by which I can pray. I will continue waiting for him."[8]

—Saturday Mothers, Call for Gathering, 860th Week

Olga Cristina Gonzáles was born on June 9, 1949, in Añatuya, in the province of Santiago del Estero. Maurice [was born] on November 14, 1938, in France. Pablo Jeger was born in 1961, the son of Maurice and his first partner. The couple were activists of the PRT-ERP. They were kidnapped by coordinated forces on the night of July 8, 1975, while they were in their home in San Miguel de Tucumán City. Cristina was four to six months pregnant. Through survivors' testimonials, it is known that Maurice was detained in the CCD "La Escuelita" in Famaillá. The pair and their child due to be born in captivity remain disappeared.[9]

—Abuelas de Plaza de Mayo

86   Interlude

*Your ring is on my finger, Cemil Can. When I come to your mind,
come tell me your troubles, to your mother, Can. My house looks the
same, you can find it easily when you come back, just tell me your
troubles, Cemil Can.*[10]

—Berfo Kirbayir, Saturday Mother

*Hayrettin Eren was taken into custody in Saraçhane, İstanbul, on
November 21, 1980, two months and nine days after the military
coup on September 12, 1980. He was in Saraçhane to meet his friend
Ahmet Öztürk. When his mother, Elmas Eren, asked about her son at
the Karagümrük Police Station, she saw the name of her son among
the names of the detained. People at the police station said that
Hayrettin Eren had been referred to the police station in Gayrettepe.
When Elmas Eren went to Gayrettepe to ask about her son there, she
saw her son's car parked in front of the police station. Nevertheless,
when she went inside, she was told, "There is no one detained here
under this name." Later, she could not find the records she saw earlier
either. Detained in the operation, Ahmet Öztürk, Ahmet Ok, Şaban
Arslan, Turgut Karataş and Fevzi Rakıcı witnessed the detention and
interrogation of Hayrettin Eren. Ahmet Öztürk said, "I am a witness,
I saw him both at the police station and the department of political
offenses."*[11]

—Saturday Mothers, Public Announcement, 786th Week

*In my dreams I switch on the dial and you appear in black and white.
I say: that's the boy who dreamed, that's the boy who dreamed.
When I awake there are only casualties on a large patio and scalps
Hanging from the antennas.*[12]

—Raúl Zurita, Song for His Disappeared Love

*After they took him, I first waited. Then I would go everywhere and
ask where he is. They told me that there is a graveyard, where they
bury people who died while in custody, so he is probably there. I went
to the graveyard, I saw that there was a grave, newly buried. It didn't
have a stone and a name; I thought it must be his. So I put some rocks
on top of each other, so that people wouldn't walk over it, and I put
some flowers. I started doing this, going there with flowers. But every
time I went there, the rocks would be scattered, so I would put them*

Interlude 87

*back up together. This happened so many times. Then I understood,
it is because his grave is not there.*[13]

—*Ölü ile Diri / Mîrî û jî sax*

*Fehmi Tosun, 35 years old and father of 5, and Huseyin Aydemir,
34 years old and father of 6, were from Lice. Because of the intense
pressure they were facing, they had to leave Lice and move to Istanbul. On the morning of October 19, 1995, Fehmi Tosun and Huseyin
Aydemir left the house of Tosun in Avcilar after having breakfast
together. Fehmi Tosun, in the evening, was brought to the curb in
front of his house by armed civilian police, in a white station wagon
Renault (Toros). His children and his wife saw him, and he shouted at
them, "I have been arrested, they will kill me!" When they ran towards
him, he was forced back into the car and taken away. The neighbors
around there witnessed this event as well. Hanim Tosun went immediately to the Avcilar Police Station, giving them the plate number of
the car. Checking the plate number, she was told that there were no
such cars registered. The Aydemir family learned that Huseyin had
been detained around the same time in Aksaray. They traced him as
he was moved between multiple cities; he was last seen in Ankara.*[14]

—*Saturday Mothers, 27th anniversary of
Fehmi Tosun's disappearance*

Others arrested/disappeared (who passed through La Escuelita):

*A 50-year-old woman who had a shop in Ingeniero White.
    She stayed for two days.*
*A 26-year-old man, a gardener. Guards tortured him, burning
    him with a blowtorch. They kept him outside of the building
    in a trailer. He was thin, approximately 6 ft. tall, with brown
    eyes and straight chestnut brown hair. He wore glasses. He was
    detained at the end of January 1977.*
*A young man with a deep chest wound, the result of torture. I heard
    him begging to have his wound dressed for several days, but,
    according to the guards, by the time they finally dressed the
    wound it had become severely infected.*
A couple who were kept outside in a trailer.
A soldier.
Another couple, captured on April 24, 1977.[15]

—*Alicia Partnoy, The Little School*

We know what happened, it is not in the dark. In the dark of course, but up to a certain point, we know, even in the dark. After that point, there is more than enough for us to know.[16]

—Ikbal Eren, the sister of Hayrettin Eren

Now that you got in here into our nightmares, through pure verse and guts: can you tell me where my son is?[17]

—Raúl Zurita, Song for His Disappeared Love

Part 2

✦

Nightmare Knowledges

Chapter 4

◆

The Epistemology of Loss

One of the longest curfews took place in Silopi, in Turkey. The residents could not leave their homes for a period of twenty-three days.[1] During the curfew, Taybet İnan was shot in front of her house. She was alive for about twenty hours afterwards, and her body remained on the street for seven days. During this period, her family was not able to leave the house to retrieve her body from the street.[2] At the end of seven days, İnan's body was taken first to the Şırnak Public Hospital, and then she was buried by local authorities at midnight.[3] According to the local authorities, there are no records of any calls made to remove the body, and they were only made aware of the incident after seven days. İnan's son, in a letter, wrote that no one in the house was able to sleep during those seven days, for everyone was worried that birds might land on the body.[4]

Many families moved to the vicinity of Newala Qesaba, the "River of Butchers," to be close to the river; in effect, they were living across from the city landfill that contains a currently unspecified number of dead bodies. While civilians are not allowed to enter the landfill because it is state-owned land, stray dogs and cats that entered have been periodically bringing bones back. In their years of interactions with various city and state officials, the families and those in the vicinity have been repeatedly told that there is nothing there, and that those bones are only animal bones. The families in Newala Qesaba, however, state that they know this cannot be the case, insofar as they have been going to the area right outside the landfill for quite a while now, in order to "talk to the river."[5] They know that their loved ones must be there, they say, for they have had so many nightmares, where their loved ones told them they cannot get out of trash, and so many other dreams, where their loved ones became a bird and flew out of the landfill.

This kind of insistence on sleep and sleeplessness, what someone knows because of what they learned in their sleep, and the associations of truth with sleep are not rare occurrences in the aftermath of improper burials. Indeed, many of the searchers for the disappeared discuss the disappearance precisely through their dreams and their nightmares. One of the Saturday Mothers in Turkey says of her son, "He is there before my eyes, and he will always remain.

91

For instance, when I am alone, the neighbors visit in the evening, we sit and chat, but when they leave, I am left alone here. Until twelve o'clock, or eleven o'clock. Then he suddenly comes and sits beside me. 'I see him now,' I say to myself, 'he is here.' "[6] Fabiola Lalinde, whose son disappeared after being put on a truck by the Colombian Army, describes similar dreams, saying, "More than dreams, they are real in that I see him return home with the smile that he always has, together with tranquility and ease, and when I ask him where he has been and he is about to answer, that's when I always wake up."[7]

This chapter works on discourses that are strange, discourses that do not "make sense," discourses that are enmeshed with nightmares, that emerge in the context of necrosovereign assemblages. The goal is to understand how and why they emerge, along with the ways in which they play into the power/knowledge assemblages of necrosovereignty. In particular, this chapter is about dreams and nightmares: how they are born, what they do, and what kinds of resistant capacities they may mark. To this end, the chapter consists of three main parts. The first part analyzes the relation between power and resistance, discussing under what conditions resistance can be possible and how resistance relates to power. Specifically, in this part, I analyze how resistance relates to necrosovereignty, to a kind of power that consists of allowing or disallowing individuals and populations to be dead. In the second part, I discuss epistemic resistance in the context of death and its knowledge: what is known and knowable about death and the organization thereof, we have seen, is an object of necrosovereignty. Just as the knowledge of death can be an object of power, however, so too can it be an object of resistance. Last, I will turn to an analysis of nightmares, discussing what is nightmarish about the kinds of knowledges that emerge out of necrosovereignty.

Power and Resistance

There is no mode of power, as Foucault says, that exists in a unilateral fashion and only operates as domination. The exercise of power is inextricably linked to the presence of resistance; each subject of power is at the same time a subject of resistance. Thus, in one of his most famous passages Foucault writes:

> Where there is power, there is resistance . . . a multiplicity of points of resistance. . . . These points of resistance are everywhere in the power network . . . Are there no great departures, massive binary divisions, then? Occasionally, yes. But more often one is dealing with mobile and transitory points of resistance, producing cleavages in a society that shifts about, fracturing unities and effecting regroupings, furrowing across individuals themselves, cutting them up and remolding them, marking off irreducible regions in them.[8]

The Epistemology of Loss

This correlation of power and resistance in Foucault's account opens up many questions. What does it mean to say that power and resistance are inseparable from each other? What kind of a relationship is operative between the two? One reason why this suggestion is controversial is that it seems to allude to two possibilities: either an automatic relationship between power and resistance, where resistance occurs as a side effect of power, or a quasi-ontological possibility, where the subject of power still appears to retain some sense of autonomy apart from the relations of power.

According to the former view, power and resistance have a mechanical, rather than organic relationship: where there is power there is resistance, insofar as power breeds resistance or in certain ways produces resistance. In this sense, there is no separating power from resistance; they are simply continuous with each other. Thus, if there are resistance movements in the context of necrosovereignty, such as those of the Saturday Mothers or the Mothers of the Plaza de Mayo, this is because the necessity of resistance emerges coextensively with the relations of power that mark necrosovereignty: insofar as the mode of power at hand works by disallowing mourning, then resistance automatically takes place precisely through mourning.

This view is appealing for the insistence that Foucault places on the ineliminable quality of resistance, for it accounts for the continuity of these movements. After all, movements such as those of the Plaza de Mayo are long durational movements, extending over decades; they feel as age-old as the techniques of improper burial. However, an insistence on automatism between power and resistance opens itself to the risk of assuming a certain parallel between the two and their work: such a parallel would suggest that modes of resistance can only emerge insofar as they are in line and in accordance with power. This, in turn, would call into question the actual possibility of the effectiveness of resistance; insofar as the possibility of resistance is conditioned by the existence of power relations, it would only go as far as the relations of power allow, thus not only finding its source but also its limitations in the parameters of power relations. The fatalism implicit in this automatism is thus about how far resistance can go and whether it is inevitably constrained by the limitations of power relations. Edward Said attributes the supposed parallel between power and resistance to Foucault's "singular lack of interest in the force of effective resistance."[9] According to this view, as espoused by Said, Foucault's account of the relation between power and resistance reduces all resistance to the same level and assumes that there is no mode of resistance that can be more effective than any other, since each and every resistance is coextensive with—and thus limited by—power relations.

According to the latter view, which Foucault terms "subjectification," the process of becoming a subject of power always includes a "remainder" that is left behind, so that power is never completely successful. Judith Butler, for example, argues that processes such as normalization can never fully encompass all the possibilities in subjects' capacity for resistance. The subject can and does always enact resistances that are beyond those that are produced in relations of power.[10] The resistance that is enacted by movements such as the Saturday Mothers is this kind of excess of subjectivity that remains beyond relations of power. The problem here, however, resides not simply at the level of the effectiveness of resistance but rather in the ontological possibility of resistance in the first place. According to this view, the problem in Foucault's account occurs precisely at the point of asserting resistance that has an ontological, or even ontic, capacity. This kind of dependence on an ontic categorization of subjectivity would not only belie the critique of political ontology that is prominent in Foucault's own theory, but it also risks taking away the possibilities of effective resistance that require, more than anything, particular actions. If any subject retains such a "capacity" to resist, this would attest to some sort of ontological description on the side of the subject, where the subject would persist beyond the relations of power; and yet the question of how and why particular subjects would side with particular acts of resistance remains obscure. In this vein, for example, Richard Bernstein notes that "what is never quite convincing in Foucault is why anyone should favor certain local forms of resistance over others,"[11] for the very relation between subject and resistance on an ontological level is precisely what is undertheorized from the Foucauldian perspective.

Granted that the question of resistance, of how and why it is possible, and what undergirds it, remains largely undertheorized, perhaps the most important aspect of Foucault's account of resistance is the idea that resistance need not take only a single form. Rather, resistance varies in its scope, object, and shape. This kind of emphasis on the variability of forms of resistance is very much in line with Foucault's emphasis on variations in the modes of power relations themselves. Inasmuch as power itself operates as a relational category, it works through a variety of relations: the lines of resistance that emerge from such varietal relations thus also take on different shapes. In this sense, rather than power working as a "conditioning" or "encompassing" category for resistance, it rather forms lines of interaction with forms of resistance. In the *Security, Territory, Population* lecture courses, Foucault clarifies this point: "Just as there have been forms of resistance to power as the exercise of political sovereignty, and just as there have been other, equally intentional forms of resistance or refusal that were directed at power in the form of economic exploitation, have there not been other forms of resistance to power?"[12] Indeed, even though certain modes of power, such as classical sovereignty, exist mostly in linear and adversarial terms, this is not the case for all forms of power, and different technologies deploy different relations.[13] Certain modes of power can exist, as Kevin Thompson says, in "purely instrumental, or even supportive relations."[14] This would mean that the resistance that takes place in such modes of power relations would be not

The Epistemology of Loss

95

only quantitatively, but also qualitatively different. In short, just as power does not exist in a single form, neither does resistance.

In this sense, if we are to talk about different formations of power that take different objects, we need to also consider different forms of resistance that take up different objects in relation to the objects and scope of power. The implications of this mode of analysis for our object are manifold. The first one would involve the direction of the analysis in terms of the methods of resistance in the context of necrosovereignty. We have said thus far that necrosovereignty is a mode of power that distributes the right to death by intervening in and regulating practices of mourning. Articulating resistance in the context of necrosovereignty thus requires analyzing different modes of resistance, understood both in oppositional terms and non-oppositional terms, as formulated in the context of the practices of mourning. What are the oppositional and non-oppositional ways in which mourning is mobilized resistantly? What are some specific examples of mobilizations of mourning that are not necessarily oppositional but nevertheless are resistant? Moreover, insofar as necrosovereignty is a mode of power that produces specific knowledges and memories of and around death, the question of resistance entails articulating the practices that are formulated around death. These practices would involve both those that take death itself as an object of resistance, and those that are formed in relation to the key scopes of necrosovereignty, working on epistemic and mnemonic levels. The question is, what are the kinds of resistances that are articulated around death? Moreover, how are such resistances articulated on the epistemic level, and how can knowledges of death be resistant? Adding to this, as we have seen, necrosovereignty is primarily an epistemic and mnemonic apparatus which works with the organization of memory, thus incorporating not only what is understood and known of death, but what is remembered of death, how it is remembered, and within what kinds of relations remembrance takes place. Bringing these to the scope of resistance would also thus mean incorporating the resistant use of memory, and specifically the collective use of the memory of death. Last but not least for us, there is the question of memories of death: how are memories of death mobilized, and what does it mean to talk about such mobilization?

Bargu refers to life and death not only as objects of power but also as objects of resistance.[15] Bargu provides an account of the corporeal mobilization of death as an object of resistance. Insofar as the biopolitical infusion of life is inseparable from the necropolitical work of death, resistances that work in the name of life are also coupled with those that weaponize life. While the former kind of resistances would be those that work in line with the biopolitical emphasis on life and well-being, such as demands for better living or working conditions, or other kinds of well-being, the kinds of resistances that weaponize life are those that utilize death against the biopolitical emphasis on life. Bargu refers to these forms of resistance as "necro-resistance," which "negates life and turns death against the power regime."[16] In this sense, insofar as biopolitics functions specifically as the valuation of life for the sake of the proliferation of a certain kind of life, one can articulate modes of resistances that negate such valuation in order to challenge the rationalities of biopolitical regimes. In Bargu's account, resistant practices of self-harm, self-destructive practices, or practices of self-inflicted death are examples of necro-resistance. As such, these practices take up death and utilize it: they are closely connected to the kinds of power they are produced in relation to, and yet they are neither parallel to, nor subsumable under, such models of power. While they emerge from specific conglomerations of power relations, and specifically asymmetrical power relations formulated around life and death, these practices formulate a relationship with life and death different than those delineated by the power relations from out of which they emerge. Moreover, necro-resistances emerge neither from the ontological capacities of the subjects nor from the sheer operation of power. Eschewing the questions around the origins of resistance in terms of subjective capacities or the primacy of power relations, necro-resistances formulate the resistant use of objects of power in counter-conduct. Instead, necro-resistances are based on the idea that the objects that are taken up and produced in relations of power can also be twisted and used against such power. In this sense, just as life and death are not solid categories that are separate from the field of power relations, so are they intimately linked to practices of resistance: if power can work on death, so too can death be politicized.

While Bargu's own analysis focuses on the corporeal mobilizations of necro-resistances, formulated in examples such as hunger strikes, death-fasts, and practices of self-immolation, thinking about mobilizations of death in the context of necrosovereignty means taking up this analysis on epistemic and mnemonic levels, and questioning what necro-resistance looks like when considered in the context of knowledges and memories of death. Indeed, inasmuch as life and death, and their deployment in power, work corporeally, such corporeal work does not exist on a different level than epistemic and mnemonic work. Becoming subjects in and through power relations entails not only the bodily production of subjectivity but also the epistemic and mnemonic categories that make up subjectivity. We have seen throughout that questions of what is known of death, how such knowledge is distributed, how it is told, and how it is remembered, are inseparable from the ways in which both life and death become infused with power. In shaping certain memories and erasing others, and targeting the temporal organization of memories and the logical coherence of testimonies, necrosovereignty deploys specific epistemic injustices around knowledges of death. Moreover, epistemic mechanisms are inseparable from mnemonic tactics: like knowledge, memory does not exist separately from power relations, and it is rather built and built over as necrosovereignty works not only on lives and deaths but also on spaces and territories. Locating resistances of death in the context

The Epistemology of Loss

of necrosovereignty thus means not only looking at the moments of direct opposition between power and resistance, but also investigating those cuts, molds, and cleavages in individuals and collectives, in memories and forgettings. An analysis of how death is produced as an object of politics and yet marks a contested category thus requires us to pay attention to the kinds of resistances that are played out around the knowledge of death.

Resistances and Impasses

How can the knowledge of death be taken up and politicized in order to challenge necrosovereignty? Such resistance depends on what I call "nightmare knowledges," knowledges that are born out of necrosovereignty and yet work to politicize the knowledge of death in response to its techniques. If necrosovereignty targets the coherence of testimony and the continuity of memory, nightmare knowledges demonstrate modes of epistemic resistance precisely because they work to mobilize perplexity by underlining the incoherence born out of these methods and making space for counter-memories that challenge necrosovereign discourses.

José Medina shows that, just as the epistemic effects of power are achieved by targeting the capacities of subjects as knowers, resistance can also take place specifically through the subjects' roles and interactions as knowers.[17] In this sense, just as there are modes of epistemic injustice that are taken up in the context of specific force relations, one needs to consider the variations of resistance within epistemic contexts as well. Thus, epistemologies of resistance are the kinds of epistemologies that are built on the premise that the subjects of epistemic injustice are not solely subjected to injustice but rather are endowed with the epistemic capacity to survive, build relations, and resist in the context of such injustice. "Resisting" in this context, however, does not only refer to an oppositional movement: it can take on different shapes. While resistance often has a reactive sense, resistances on the epistemic level can take many forms: they can be internal or external, positive or negative.[18] In a vein very similar to Foucault's account of resistance, Medina underlines that not only corporeal resistances but also epistemic resistances take many shapes, insofar as they are both multitudinous and relational. Thus, Medina argues that many cases of epistemic resistance actually take place not as a direct or oppositional refusal but rather as "perplexity." This perplexity, for Medina, is experienced as "being pulled in different directions from the inside," or "like feeling a rupture."[19] The knower is perplexed insofar as their experiential memory is disjointed from the dominant discourse, and yet the dominant discourse itself does not constitute a coherent whole. Indeed, this kind of perplexity, or the feeling of rupture, is a common element in the testimonies of the relatives of the disappeared, insofar as it is inseparable both from the hermeneutical injustices of necrosovereignty and the mnemonic methods through which the replacement of memory works. After all, targeting the coherence of testimony through methods such as gendered hysterization or invisibilization, or the targeting of memory through methods such as spatial reorganization, are key aspects of necrosovereignty. The inhabitants of death-worlds thus epistemically experience perplexity and are pulled in the directions of their experiential memory on the one hand, and the narrative silences of necrosovereignty on the other. In this sense, the perplexed testimonies of the families in Newala Qesaba, or the seemingly strange worry of Taybet İnan son about birds landing on her body, can be seen as instances of such perplexity, where the memory of mourning for a loved one lost does not match the discourses of necrosovereignty.

Insofar as power does not have a single locus, the fact that there are modes of resistance that go beyond oppositional movements is contextually understandable. The question to consider, however, is rather what it is about perplexity that can be resistant. Specifically, at the heart of this is the question of how a category that is often understood as an epistemic impasse can serve as a category of resistance: the risk at hand appears to be not only that of splitting the ties between rationality and resistance but also that of splitting off understanding from resistance. Does this mean to suggest, for example, that long-lasting movements such as the Mothers of the Plaza de Mayo or the Saturday Mothers are only the result of "unconscious" efforts that are based on the absence of understanding? Associating perplexity with resistance seems to risk disqualifying the agency and legitimacy of political movements. Second, it seems to jeopardize the possibility of the effectiveness of such movements, insofar as it predicates the possibility of resistance on the production of impasses. Last, there is of course the danger of romanticizing the effects of power. After all, is it not the case, as we have seen, that epistemic impasses are one of the very productions of power? Doesn't predicating resistance on an epistemic impasse do precisely the same thing that Said critiqued Foucault for: that of romanticizing the minute instances that are, in and of themselves, precisely the effects of power, and thus letting go of the very hope of effective resistances as a result?

One of the most fundamental aspects of the idea of epistemic resistance lies in the disjunction of the categories of resistance from categories that tie political agency to the characteristics of understanding. In this sense, cognitive success is not a requirement for political agency. Instead, the very elements of forgetting, of perplexity, silence, or "not understanding" form possibilities for interrupting power relations. Thus, Medina says, "when our cultural practices of remembering and forgetting are interrogated as loci where multiple power relations and power struggles converge, the first thing to notice is the heterogeneity of differently situated perspectives and the multiplicity of trajectories that converge in the epistemic negotiations in which memories are formed or de-formed, maintained alive or killed."[20] This kind of heterogeneity between epistemic standpoints and trajectories is a fundamental reason

The Epistemology of Loss 99

why tying political agency to cognitive success risks disqualifying the ways in which epistemic negotiations take place.

As Medina underlines, categories that are traditionally understood as epistemic impasses, such as silence or perplexity, nevertheless constitute forms of discursive practices. As such, these categories function in relation to discursive practices, and they nevertheless mark lines of interaction that consist in the interrogation and challenge of official narratives and discourses. These categories are never quite on the outside of the official discourse, but rather they are immanent to the official discourse, and this is precisely the reason why they have such a capacity to critique or challenge. Thus, Medina states: "There are constitutive silences, for the discursive practice proceeds in the way it does and acquires its distinctive normative structure by virtue of the exclusions that it produces, by virtue of those silenced voices and occluded meanings that let the official voices and meanings dominate the discursive space."[21] Building an epistemology of such silences necessitates conceptualizing a kind of politics that engages with categories that conventionally mark epistemic impasses, and disjointing these from political impasses. In the face of such omissions that are constitutive of silences, the possibilities are either to return to the origins of such omissions in order to produce new origins, or to develop practices that Medina calls "epistemic frictions." These frictions not only automatically arise in the context of force relations, but they also accumulate, and as such, can be cultivated as well. Thus, the emphasis of the relatives on their dreams and their nightmares, both in terms of how often they have these nightmares and what happens in them, can be seen as such a cultivated friction, a long-lasting effort to mobilize something that does not go through, or does not become fully subsumed by, the relations of power, a kind of experience that Glissant would call "opacity."

There is, however, something to be said about perplexity not only as an epistemic experience, but also as a political tactic. Glissant demonstrates that the mobilization of the categories that conventionally mark epistemic impasses is a particularly necessary political tactic that can be utilized to produce not only new categories of self-understanding but also ones of self-determination. In Glissant's account, the attempts to tie political projects to processes of cognitive success are part of a call for transparency, which is a characteristic of global and dominant modes of subjectivity. He describes these demands for transparency as inseparable from understanding political subjectivity as a "root" structure. In this model, subjectivity would resemble a root that takes up everything that it encounters to delineate colonial and dominant knowledge systems: "The root is unique, a stock taking all upon itself and killing all around it."[22] The expansion of root identity is legitimized through transparency; the root expands as much as it can assume clarity, as much as it can see. Transparent understanding is a mode of "grasping" the other. This "reductive transparency" is constituted by the assumption of a transparent subject, one capable of understanding and "grasping" the entirety of the earth. The "inner space" of this subject is "as indefinitely explorable as the spaces of the earth."[23] The transparent subject is capable of understanding their self, holding their memories, exploring their experiences, and more than anything, projecting their universality onto the rest of being. In necrosovereign contexts, as we have seen, this transparency is precisely what is inaccessible and impossible: the mnemonic methods of necrosovereignty target memory in a way that denies transparency to the inhabitants of death-worlds; necro-epistemic methods produce specific modes of knowledge around death, and the possibility of transparency in terms of (specifically political) subjectivity—and subjects' capacity to make sense of their experiences and memories—becomes not much more than a wistful dream, a privilege denied to those who inhabit necrosovereign spaces. Instead, many of the inhabitants of necrosovereign worlds describe their experience as a nightmare, one that does not end, that festers within: a nightmare, nevertheless, wherein they search for their loved ones, try to learn about their whereabouts, verify information, meet with others, and get together. A nightmare in and through which they learn and mobilize.

The idea of opacity as a political tactic is especially important in this context of nightmares that make up knowledges. In developing the term "opacity," Glissant points to what cannot be rendered completely visible or graspable. Inasmuch as the root imaginary denotes transparency, Glissant explains that the expansion of the root creates holes and cavities in the soil that cannot be completely enlightened. Opacity works through sediments and alluviums that build up in the motion of the root. Opacity is formed in challenges to the transparent identity by marking what is not totalizable or rendered transparent in the motion of the root. In this sense, Glissant explains that opacity has its basis in traumatic experience: experiences of forgetting, of not understanding, or of perplexity—those that constitute epistemic impasses—are inseparable elements of opacity. However, opacity is not reducible to, nor is it thwarted by, such experiences.

Opacity is formed in relation to such abyssal experience, and thus it is twofold: on the one hand, the experience out of which it arises is enmeshed in loss. The impossibilization of mourning that shapes all the spaces of necrosovereignty is such an abyssal beginning, as it involves the doing and redoing of memory, its erasure and its re-formation, its vicissitudes in the lives of individual and collective subjectivities. As John Drabinski explains, an abyssal beginning "asserts itself without reference to what precedes."[24] Opacity is formed precisely in relation to the abyssal beginning that is present inasmuch as it is absent and haunts the present. Berfo Kırbayır describes the disappearance of her son as when she started having the same nightmare: a nightmare in which he comes into the house in the middle of the night, sits across from her on the sofa and looks at her, without talking. As Glissant says, opacity is formed in loss, in the abyss, where it is not only impossible to grasp the loss but also impossible to resuscitate or explain

The Epistemology of Loss

the loss. Kırbayır's nightmare emerges, in this sense, from her loss; and yet, insofar as there is no loss to grieve, no space to mark the loss, the nightmare itself cannot be explained by the loss as such. It is not surprising that the accounts of the searchers shift between nightmares, dreams, and perplexities: the kinds of knowledges that are operative in necrosovereign contexts have their beginnings in the abyss, in the impossibility of transparent knowledge to be superimposed on the abyss.

Nevertheless, abyssal beginnings make transformations possible. Glissant writes: "The unconscious memory of the abyss served as the alluvium for metamorphoses."[25] The experience of the abyss does not incapacitate the subject, and the possibilities of resistance do not get lost in the abyss of forgetting. Instead, the abyss foregrounds the opacity that haunts the present. If the memory of the Basements of Atrocity in Cizre does not yield its place simply to memories of newly built condos, for example, and if the memory of Berfo Kırbayır's son does not yield its place to the memory of death, it is precisely due to the formation of an "opaque present" that is continuously haunted by its past. Even more important for this project, moreover, is that the opacity of such haunted presences is what the searchers mobilize in order to create metamorphoses, in order to become otherwise. Thus, Glissant writes: "For us, and without exception, and no matter how much distance we keep, the abyss is also a projection of and perspective into the unknown."[26] This is an "unknown that doesn't terrify," because it indicates that not all that is unknown is shaped by and incorporated into the depths of the abyss.[27] In other words, the so-called epistemic impasses of perplexity, dreams, and forgetting mark the possibilities of other modes of becoming, or mark a kind of unknown that is not produced by, and incorporated into, necrosovereignty. Most importantly, opacity is sedimented experience that constitutes a creative reservoir of resistance. Glissant writes: "Transparency no longer seems to be the bottom of the mirror in which Western humanity reflected the world in its own image. There is opacity now at the bottom of the mirror, a whole alluvium deposited by populations, silt that is fertile, but, in actual fact, indistinct and unexplored even today."[28] Opaque memories, forgettings, and perplexities do not undo the present of the inhabitants of necrosovereign spaces. Rather, opacity forms the alluvium on which relations are built. "Experience of the abyss lies inside and outside of the abyss," Glissant writes.[29] It is a "continuous/discontinuous thing": it involves the panic, the haunting, the alliance, and the renegotiation at once.[30] Such a possibility thus gives a different aspect to the question of the relation between power and resistance, this time not only on the corporeal and institutional levels but also on the epistemic and mnemonic levels. Power does not create resistance as such, nor is resistance limited by the constraints of power. Rather, resistance is formed in relation to opacity, in the silt of abyssal beginnings. Thus, resistance involves mobilizing these, working the silt, molding the sediments, opening up routes, and at times, filling in the routes opened by power.

It should be clear by now that the point here is not that the searchers are simply perplexed, forgetful, or dreaming. It is rather the case that there is a specific strategy of resistance that is found in performing perplexity and mobilizing nightmares, which proceeds through mobilizing epistemic impasses. The account of historical trauma in relation to personal experience that is put forth in Glissant's account is especially helpful, as it neither denotes the forgetfulness of singular subjects nor the impasses and blockages of trauma. Rather, opacity provides a reservoir for resistance, without assuming that either the trauma or the violence is something that can simply be done away with. It is important, in this sense, not to conflate opacity with "obscurity" and thereby overlook its specifically political capacity by identifying it as a pathology to be overcome. "The opaque is not the obscure, though it is possible for it to be so and be accepted as such."[31] The obscure denotes a stopping point, an incomprehensibility beyond experience. Opacity, however, is not obscure, because it is alive and because it haunts the subject: as such, it provides a reservoir of resistance, a strategy that can be and is continuously mobilized.

Opacity is not a pathology, and it is not a given either. It can be seen as an "achievement," as Ben Davis states, or even more so, as a tactical alignment, a strategy of resistance.[32] Glissant writes, "We clamor for the *right to opacity* for everyone."[33] This is a notoriously peculiar claim of Glissant's inasmuch as it treats opacity not as an ontological category that is shared by all subjects, but rather as a right to be claimed "for" everyone. Drabinski writes that the critical sense of the phrase "the right to opacity" "lies in its resistance to certain senses of knowing and understanding that would seek to absorb, reactivate, and possess; its resistance to the dialectic of legibility and intelligibility."[34] As such, the right to opacity denotes an epistemological concept, as it denotes a mode of resistance that takes place by mobilizing other ways of knowing, as well as other ways of unknowing. As such, if the searchers are insisting on the nightmares that they have in response to official narratives, or if they gather around every week for decades to tell stories that do not exist away from memories, this specifies a way of being not through the categories of knowing, but rather through unknowing, or through epistemic impasses. This opacity, however, is not a given capacity that the searchers have ownership of; rather, it is an activity that is realized precisely in telling stories, in organizing, in searching, and in remembering.

Thus, epistemic resistance can consist in mobilizing perplexity, a kind of epistemic resistance that involves insisting on things "not making sense," or on basing information on nightmares rather than records, dreams rather than spaces. Resistance, however, does not take place automatically; it does not just occur as a side effect of power: it is always "active," as in the case of perplexity, since such perplexity can be mobilized. The question is how it is mobilized, and what happens through such mobilizations.

The Epistemology of Loss

103

Mobilizing Perplexity: Nightmare Temporalities

We have said that epistemic resistance takes place in challenging claims of transparency: unlike the demands for transparency that are utilized by dominant discourses, resistance takes place through claiming opacity as a strategy of political resistance. Political agency is not limited to the possibilities either of transparency or cognitive success. Rather, agency becomes an achievement to be claimed precisely through mobilizing what is construed as an impasse. In this sense, epistemic resistance takes place precisely through mobilizing perplexities rather than categories of cognitive success. What does it mean, however, to mobilize perplexity? How can the perplexed knowledges of death be taken up and mobilized resistantly? Mobilizing perplexity as epistemic resistance entails two aspects: first, it challenges the dominant discourse by pointing to the incoherencies of the official discourse, and second, it claims experiential memory in order to reveal the ways in which what is recorded is no more credible than what has been experienced. In necrosovereignty, perplexity is produced precisely by necro-epistemic methods, which target the temporal and rational coherence of memory by discrediting the subjects and erasing their experiences. Nightmare knowledges, on the other hand, mobilize this perplexity by pointing to the incoherencies of the official discourse and challenging the boundaries of necropolitical rationalities, such as the boundaries between dream and reality, memory and imagination, or reason and unreason.

Many of the Saturday Mothers, when asked to explain their experiences of the last thirty years, describe them as a series of dreams. One of them describes a particularly repetitive dream: "I see him in my sleep. 'Ayşe,' he calls out to me. I look up, and I see my deceased son next to him, too. He asks me, 'Ayşe, do your eyes still see?' and 'Yes,' I reply. 'Do you see the white rock over there?' he asks me. 'Yes, I do,' I reply. 'Go there, you will find my clothes,' he says. There is a hill, a very high hill."[35] As much as this is a recurring dream for this mother, it does not belong uniquely to her. Many of the mothers have similar dreams, dreams where they find the person who has been lost, dreams where they go through cadavers trying to dig out the one that is theirs, or dreams where they come to the verge of finding a clue to the disappearance of the person. Some describe the last time they saw the person as a repetitive dream that they have, where the police put the person "in a white car and leave."[36] The white car that they see is a white Toros, a station wagon Renault, the type of car that was used by the Gendarmerie Intelligence organization and the pro-state militia in Turkey throughout the 1980s and 1990s. Many of them describe the same experience as Berfo Kırbayır, where the disappeared person comes and sits with them and looks at them long and hard. It should be remembered that Berfo Kırbayır herself did not lock her doors or close the windows of her house for thirty years, convinced that her son would return through those doors. All too often, the person in the dream who comes and sits with the mother is wearing pajamas, as they did when they were taken away.[37] Saturday Mothers' dreams are shared by others like Fabiola Lalinde, who in her dream constantly asks her son where he is, and he is always "just about to answer"; she is so close to getting an answer each time but is always only a bit too far from the answer.[38]

In the consistent repetition of Fabiola Lalinde's dreams, or in Berfo Kırbayır's practice of not locking her doors or windows, the perplexities involved in the experience of disappearance become clear. The first perplexity, of course, concerns the unknown fate of the disappeared person, and wondering where that person is who is now gone, who was last seen many years ago, a person who, according to official records, may or may not exist, or may or may not have been detained; a perplexity that has its answers all too often simply in death, in a ditch somewhere, or at the bottom of the ocean, or on top of a mountain, or in a trash-disposal area. Even more than that, however, is the perplexity that comes from wondering whether or not a person can actually "vanish" in the first place. As one of the Saturday Mothers says, a person is *not* a bird to fly away; after all, they cannot just disappear into oblivion. Amnesty International's way of saying this is that "disappearance is a misnomer. Many prisoners who have 'disappeared' may well, at worst, have ceased to be. None, however, is lost or vanished. Living or dead, each is in a very real place."[39] Perplexity acquires a mimetic quality: mobilizing this perplexity by referring to dreams reveals that a world in which people vanish into thin air is no less unbelievable or fantastic as it stands than the dreams that their relatives have. Indeed, Fabiola Lalinde, together with so many of the mothers of the disappeared, insists precisely on this kind of intermingling between dreams and reality, and says that the dreams they have in which they sit with their lost ones and the nightmares they have where they grope through bushes are "no less real" than the world that they wake up to. Indeed, the dreams of the pajamas or the white car all too often continue to haunt those who remain, and in this haunting there is even a collective quality: Lalinde says that her neighbors started having the same nightmares, in which the Saturday Mothers repeat similar patterns, with the pajamas, and the white car, and the piles of bodies.[40] Nightmares thus serve as a reminder that what is real and not a dream forms a thin thread that ties together nothing other than unbelievable facts. As Gordon says, "spiraling between unbelievable facts and potent fictions, the knowledge of disappearance cannot but be bound up with the bewitching and brutal breaks and armature of disappearance itself."[41] This perplexity about concrete reality and dreams, the constant repetition of perplexity over the fate of the person vanished and the person present, reveals a world in which what is official is no more realistic than dreams and what is recorded is no more reasonable than nightmares.

Most importantly, perplexity is not an impasse, just as the opaque is not the obscure. Rather, it is accompanied by a certain lucidity regarding not

The Epistemology of Loss

only the incredibility of the official discourse but also disappearance itself, and the cognitive attitudes that underlie necro-epistemic methods, as well as the cognitive limitations of these methods. Medina calls such lucidity "meta-lucidity," which "involves not just lucidity about the social world, but about the cognitive attitudes, cognitive structures, and cognitive repertoires of those who navigate the social world."[42] Meta-lucidity as connected to perplexity consists not only in understanding the incredulity of the official discourse, or the limitations of the epistemic subjects that are construed through necro-epistemic methods, but also the cognitive resources that are imaginable in relation to these methods. In this sense, the mothers of the disappeared know, for example, not only that the records of disappearance and those records' absence are misleading, but that the institutional agents that they interact with occupy specific epistemic positions with regard to the production of necro-epistemic methods. As one of the searchers states, "Sometimes, when I wake up from my dreams, I feel like I am going crazy. But then, I remember, it is not me, it is them that are crazy, the entire thing is crazy."[43] The cognitive repertoire of the field of rationality in necrosovereignty, in this sense, becomes apparent in the meta-lucidity of nightmare knowledges, where the subjects in their perplexity have access to the obscurities that are produced inseparably from necrosovereignty.

This meta-lucidity arises from a kind of "double consciousness," as Du Bois calls it, from looking inward and outward at the same time. It looks inward "insofar as it recognizes, through the internal friction of the perspectives available to itself, the limitations and obstacles of cognitive elements."[44] In this sense, nightmare knowledges emerge out of "looking inwards" as much as they refer to a certain knowledge that understands the limitations of the accounts offered in the official discourse, as well as the limitations of the cognitive repertoires operative in necro-epistemic methods. These "meta-insights" stem from having access to two different sets of cognitive attitudes and sources of information at once: on the one hand, those that emerge out of the discursive practices of necrosovereignty, which consist of erased archives, gendered hysterization, and the disruption of the coherence of memory; and on the other hand, the insights attained through dreams and nightmares, through the perplexity that arises from the incredulity of given accounts, and the insights that rest on the haunted memories of those who remain in spaces that are built anew. The elimination of records and the long-lasting forgetting that surround necrosovereignty thus provide the meta-insights that allow those who remain to become "critically aware of the body of ignorance surrounding the relations of oppression that goes along with the dominant perspective they have internalized."[45] The people in Newala Qesaba know, for example, that the bones that they see are not animal bones; and İnan's family knows that there were calls to report her body lying on the street, that what is nightmarish about what is real lies precisely in that blank space between the said and unsaid.

At the same time, these knowledges are the products of a certain "looking outwards," insofar as they come with the realization that what is taking place is not uniquely their own experience, and that necro-epistemic methods work not only on particular subjects but on groups, on entire parts of the population. The collective element of the dreams testifies to this kind of looking outwards: Fabiola Lalinde's friends, the whole family, and even the neighbors have the same dreams, for nightmares look outwards, they look into that gap between the said and the unsaid, the limbo of existence that consists of the undead and the unburied. If dreams take up so much space in their accounts, it is precisely because they know that these dreams are not products of individual psychic processes, but rather, of collective experiences. Nightmare knowledges mobilize this knowledge to remember that nightmarish gap between uncorroborated memories and unbelievable facts, a gap that consists precisely in the distribution and the redistribution of the right, not only to live, but also to die. Thus, when asked why, after these many years, they still keep searching for their loved ones, many of the survivors say they do it "because they are not alone," and because their loved one was "not the only one" and that their search, and their organization, their movement, their meetings, and the entirety of their activities stem particularly from the lucidity that comes from looking outwards, from realizing that they are not alone. The "looking outwards" in this sense consists in the elimination both of the singularity and the exceptionality of improper burial, where the solitariness of those who were taken in alone and never seen again constitutes an object of knowledge that is to be known, understood, shared, and circulated. Nightmare knowledges are the results of what Medina calls "guerrilla pluralisms," insofar as they work to multiply both the sources and methods of knowledge by shifting the space of credible knowledge from written words to memory. "Resistance is not simply something that happens to us, but rather is something we do (or fail to do)"; resistance is, indeed, a product of active remembering, mobilizing memory, and mobilizing the perplexity of the divide between the real and the surreal.[46]

Memory is something to be made, however, and is even trickier to make in spaces that have been built anew, archives that have been erased, and subjects who have either disappeared or been disqualified. Gordon states: "Disappearance is an exemplary instance in which the boundaries of rational and irrational, fact and fiction, subjectivity and objectivity, person and system, conscious and unconscious, knowing and unknowing, are constitutively unstable."[47] As much as these divides become unstable in themselves in nightmare knowledges, so does the distinction between complete and incomplete memories, between corroborated and uncorroborated remembrances: one of the ways in which resistant memories function is to remember and to remind the survivors that what took place is impossible to remember. The insistence of the Saturday Mothers and the relatives in Newala Qesaba on remembering the details, the color of the pajamas that the person was wearing, the exact

The Epistemology of Loss

words they said, and the white car that took them, is a work of making memory despite its absence from the official record. The act of remembering when there are no corroborated memories is a collective act of mobilizing memory as a resistant mechanism. Take the emphasis on the uniqueness of each individual: virtually every relative discusses the person lost as a "wonderful person," as a "person that everyone loved," as a person "who had never even hurt an ant in their lives."[48] In the absence of dead bodies or disappeared persons, such an emphasis functions to weave a person out of memory, in order to produce another frame than the one of the official discourses. As Acosta López states, "memory can make history precisely by erasing it."[49] The collective memory practices in Newala Qesaba and of the Saturday Mothers attest to this work of actively erasing the official history by producing frames that challenge that discourse by underlining the "unresolvable excess" that emerges in the death-worlds of necropolitics.[50]

Prolonged mourning and "waiting" for the disappeared, on the other hand, mobilize memory in order to disrupt necro-epistemic temporalities: they function as a method of claiming another a temporal regime other than the fractured time of necrosovereignty. One of the mothers in Newala Qesaba says she turned her home into a "funeral house" thirty years ago. As funeral houses are houses of grief, her house never leaves the state of mourning; she has been "crying for thirty years," and she will do so until she dies.[51] Many of the Saturday Mothers recall being told to "move on": some were told to find a new husband, others to devote themselves to their remaining children.[52] Instead, they all declare their commitment to not stop grieving, no matter how much time passes; and all of them state that they will "never forget," no matter how much time passes. Özgür Sevgi Göral says: "Although the waiting starts as an imposed and enforced process, it is transformed by the family members of the disappeared into a process that includes different forms of activity and political mobilization."[53] Active remembering reminds us that grief is not simply a personal process but a collective one, shared in funeral houses where there are no bodies, or in weekly meetings that are regularly disrupted. The insistence on collective and prolonged grief politicizes grief by way of disrupting the necrosovereign temporal order. As Göral states, it opens up a temporality where "the passing of time was declared irrelevant by the interviewed relatives; time stopped being a hindrance to waiting, searching and asking for the bones within this *longue durée*."[54] If the collective oblivion of necropolitics proposes a temporality that is composed of fractured moments and replaced memories, prolonged grief opens up counter-temporalities that extend over time, which work by adding together ruptured memories, by ceaselessly remembering and sharing what is meant to have been forgotten a long time ago.

Nightmare knowledges form a type of political-epistemic agency that produces modes of coherence out of the absence of temporal consistency; they produce memories in the impossibility of remembering as such, and work to

108   Chapter 4

create "counter-discourses" that are not only opposed to necro-epistemic discourses but also reveal the incoherence that is typical of those discourses. The world of necropolitics is "filled with ghosts," as Gordon says, and the work of nightmare knowledges is to "recognize the world that the ghost conjures up."[55] This conjuring requires a kind of resistance that Medina calls "guerrilla pluralism," which consists in developing counter-discourses, weaving words out of silences and memories out of forgettings. Nightmare knowledges attest precisely to such a work, a collective epistemic agency that is born out of dreams and reality, told and untold statements, uncorroborated memories: the work of nightmare knowledges is a work of conjuring up ghosts, insofar as these present the possibility of another kind of discourse, another kind of memory.

Conclusion: Nightmare Knowledges and Necro-Resistances of Knowledge

Methods of power do not exist in the absence of resistance. This does not mean that resistance is determined by power or that it is limited to the scope of power: rather, resistance emerges as a multiplicity of relations that accompany and extend beyond power relations. One of the greatest strengths of Foucault's account of resistance is that it is not limited to simply oppositional terms: this expansion of the notion of resistance, however, does not detract from concrete acts of resistance. Rather, it invites us to consider the ways in which resistance takes place by taking different objects, different forms, and different relations. Thus just as power can take on different objects, such as life, death, or bodies, so can resistance, as it can take up both life and death as its object, mobilize death against a power that is concerned with the optimization of life, and mobilize bodies against the disciplinary formulations of corporeality. In short, just as power does not have a single object or direction, neither does resistance, as it can take on objects and directions beyond oppositional relations and objects.

In the context of necrosovereignty, this insight is especially important. As we have seen, necrosovereignty is the mode of power that is concerned with distributing the right to die by regulating practices of mourning and by organizing the knowledges and memories of death and grief. However, just as death is an object not only of power but of resistance, so too is the knowledge of death, which is contested and politicized. Necro-epistemic methods do not work in a unilateral line without obstruction: instead, they open up cleavages of memory and forgetting, gaps between dreams and concrete reality, a world where living is not simply subsumed under death but rather is haunted by the dead. And yet, what emerges in and through necro-epistemic methods are nightmare knowledges, knowledges that do not fit within the proposed rationalities of death and dying.

The Epistemology of Loss

Nightmare knowledges are products of epistemic resistance, which challenge the proposed lucidity of the official discourse by mobilizing perplexities, and blurring the distinction between dream and reality in order to reveal what is not credible in the official account. Indeed, unlike the so-called transparency of necrosovereign knowledges, which work by totalizing the possibilities of knowledge production into archives, nightmare knowledges work by mobilizing opacities. These opacities function as challenges to the transparency of necrosovereign memories and knowledges: the transparencies of newly built condos over sites of destruction, of empty passages in archives that suggest only the nonexistence of people disappeared, and the official discourses that try to hystericize subjects and invisibilize their memories. Instead, nightmare knowledges mark what is not there, what is absent, what is opaque, in order to mobilize these. These knowledges assert, for example, that people are not birds that fly away, and bodies do not vanish into thin air, just as they assert that the unknown graves of bodies do not make the bodies themselves unknown. They show, more than anything, that opacity is a strategy of resistance: clamoring for the right to opacity, as Glissant does, is first and foremost a struggle for the right to be, the right to live, and in the context of necrosovereignty, the right to die. Nightmare knowledges demonstrate the ways in which opacity can be mobilized in order to challenge necrosovereign rationalities, in order to open up new ways of knowing, understanding, and remembering.

Insofar as necrosovereignty works through the production of an official knowledge that is shaped by oblivion, by rendering testimonies incredible and experiences incomprehensible, nightmare knowledges work to mobilize what does not "make sense" and yet typifies necro-epistemic methods. In Berfo Kırbayır's insistence on not locking her doors, the families of Newala Qesaba visiting the trash-disposal area in order to talk to the river, İnan's family worrying that birds may have landed on her body when it was on the street, in Fabiola Lalinde's dreams and nightmares that are shared by her family, friends, neighbors, and, as Michael Taussig says, "even us," what is at stake is the production of another discourse: a counter-discourse that looks inward and outward, that mobilizes both the knowledge of its own limitations and the knowledge of sharing these limitations with many others. Unlike the prima facie transparency of necrosovereignty, this discourse instigates a meta-lucidity as it multiplies the sources of knowledge, the sources of credibility, and the possibilities of communication. Countering the empty archives with nightmares and the absent graves with prolonged grief, nightmare knowledges attest to the reformulation of both political and epistemic agency in the necrosovereign regime. Weaving together unsaid statements, incomplete moments, and memories that reveal the arsenal of nightmare knowledges attests to the possibility of epistemic agency even in the death-worlds of necropolitics.

Knowledge production, however, is a question not only of knowledge formation but also of its distribution, transmission, and circulation. The question is, what does such an arsenal do, how is it utilized and mobilized, how and where is it activated, and what are its terms of circulation? How do nightmare knowledges circulate? What are their terms of discursive construction? What kind of information are produced in them, and how are these circulated? What stories do people tell, who tells them, and what happens through these tales? The next chapter is devoted to these questions.

Chapter 5

✦

Stories of Nothing

In 1979 in Chile, "Operation Television Withdrawal" entailed the excavation of Patio 29 and other official mass burial sites, where the bodies of the disappeared had been deposited in unmarked or anonymous graves.[1] As the excavations were under way, the military found a way to "disappear" the bodies once again: this time by exhuming nameless remains from Patio 29 in order to airdrop them over mountainous regions or over the ocean. In 1989, some families, around 300 of them, were each returned a set of bones, which the state claimed to be those of their loved ones. The bones often came in a bag, and exhibited signs of torture and physical violence done to the bodies. In 1996, the same families were informed that the DNA testing that had identified those sets of bones as the remains of their relatives was mostly faulty, and the bones probably belonged not to their loved ones but to other nameless persons who disappeared and encountered a fate similar to that of their loved ones. Doña Nena González, the caretaker of Patio 29, says that in the years that she was living in the cemetery as its caretaker, she witnessed many things, and if she could, she would tell the stories of these bodies to the rest of the world, but there were no longer any bodies there. So, since there are no bodies, what is there to tell the story of?

While Doña González speaks to the difficulty of telling stories in the absence of records, many of the relatives of the disappeared are insistent precisely on telling stories. For example, the Mothers of the Plaza de Mayo say that they will not stop meeting as long as they live, for they meet in order to tell the stories of their loved ones. In Turkey, the Saturday Mothers have been holding up the photographs of their disappeared ones and insisting on telling stories, both their own and those of others. In 2020, as the restrictions on public meetings due to COVID-19 reinforced the usual police disruptions of their weekly meetings, the Saturday Mothers moved their narrative activity primarily to the scope of social media, where each week a "Saturday Person" provides an account of their disappeared loved one in front of a camera, telling their story. The Saturday Mothers released a statement saying that they would not stop, and they would not be silenced. This kind of insistence on telling stories, finding venues and avenues of telling stories,

111

and the relentlessness in doing so is shared by many of the movements that arose in the aftermaths of improper burial. The Mothers of the Plaza de Mayo, the Saturday Mothers, the Mothers of Soacha, Ayatzinapa, and many other locales, in and through their nightmares, insist that they will "not be silenced," and not only will they continue speaking, but particularly, they will keep telling their stories. The question at hand is one that Saidiya Hartman asks: "How do you write a story of nothing?"[2]

The goal of this chapter is to turn to the relation between knowledge and narrative in order to take the demand to tell stories seriously. Instead of explaining "why" with respect to this insistence on telling stories that are long past, my goal is to analyze the "how" of it, in the sense of asking what this insistence *does*. In the searchers' insistence on finding the remains of the disappeared, and in their determination to keep telling their stories, I argue, what is at stake is the emergence of another kind of fable, which multiplies the possibilities of the present and the past precisely by telling stories of nothing. This chapter is divided into three main sections. The first section develops storytelling and fabulation from the perspective of an epistemology of resistance. In the second section, I turn to Foucault's discussion in "Lives of Infamous Men" of the modes of genealogical engagement built upon lives that are "about to disappear" into the archive. Enforced disappearances and the knowledge thereof, I argue, constitute examples of such fables, but they do not only mark obscure lives and deaths; they also play into the dramaturgy of the real. The last section of the chapter turns to the question of what such stories do by analyzing the actors, the events, and the time of such stories. Overall, this chapter demonstrates that stories work both to jeopardize the status of the event of necrosovereignty and to eventalize the agency and activities of the searchers' movements.

Necrosovereign Fabulation, Enchantments of Death

Necrosovereignty, we have said, amounts to the work of allowing and disallowing individuals and groups to be dead: the corporeal methods of improper burial are accompanied by epistemic and mnemonic methods, where the disappearance of the body is reinforced by the disappearance of the archive, and the erasure of memory is replicated by the building over of the sites of violence. However, in and through the work of mourning, nightmare knowledges emerge as products of epistemic resistance, marking what is not there, mobilizing perplexity, and producing modes of resistance that look both inward and outward, in order to mobilize that which does not "make sense" in the context of necrosovereignty. Resistance is a relational category: it exists not in the solitude of the dreams and nightmares of individuals but in the relations that are built, in the acts that are undertaken. Thus, understanding nightmare knowledges as products of epistemic resistance that emerge

Stories of Nothing

in the context of necrosovereignty means investigating not only how these knowledges emerge but how they are mobilized, how they are actualized, and in short, how the forgettings and perplexities that shape nightmare knowledges are narrativized.

One of the key elements of the insistence of the "remnants," as the Mothers of Soacha, the Mothers of the Plaza de Mayo, and the Saturday Mothers call themselves, on telling stories is the way in which these stories counter archival erasure. As we have seen, archival disappearance is a constitutive element of necrosovereignty as a power/knowledge assemblage. Necrosovereignty functions to produce a death that is not death, and disallows death by distributing the right to die: it is intimately tied to death, to the possibilities of seeing and understanding death. Taking, once again, the example of enforced disappearances, what one finds would be, if at all possible, the records of death: searching for remains means looking for the records of execution, for the prior detention, the correct set of bones, the correct site of burial, the correct tomb of existence. The absence of these is duplicated in the archival records. As Hartman says, "the archive is a death sentence, a tomb, a display of the violated body, an inventory of property."[3] Looking for records means looking for the death sentences, for the records of burial or dumping. The archive, at its best, can only provide testimony to death, where "to read the archive" would mean to "enter a mortuary," as Hartman says, and obtain "one final viewing and allowing for a last glimpse of the persons about to disappear."[4] And yet, when the best thing the archive can give is the mark or testimony of death, the very absence of any such records, any such marks of burial, of dumping, of arrest, entails the disappearance of not only the person but the very possibility of catching a last glimpse of that person. Neña González for example, the caretaker of Patio 29 for over forty years now, talks about the relatives of the disappeared coming to show her photographs in the hope that she can identify one of them, so that they can catch one last glimpse of their loved ones, even in the form of a mutilated body. The problem is that of all the dead bodies Gonzales has seen in Patio 29, she has never seen someone, only bodies that have been disfigured and often dismembered. So, no, she would always say, she has never seen them, neither the people in the photographs, nor their deaths.[5]

Telling stories becomes especially relevant to consider in the impossibility of bearing witness to the disappeared ones' lives and their deaths. If it is indeed the case that "catching one last glimpse" of the person who is about to disappear is impossible, what does it mean to insist on telling stories, or even attempting to approach the archive, or approach such voids in the archive? The archive is, at best, a death sentence, a mortuary, and at its worst, it is nothing, it is testimony to nothing, not life, not death, not even disappearance. So what does it mean to insist on telling such stories?

Perhaps the biggest point of caution involves the question of the relation between these stories and absence as such. In many ways, these stories

114   Chapter 5

do not so much fill up a void. The world of necrosovereignty is, as we have seen, not a world of emptiness, nor is it shaped by a void. The work of disallowing death is not a work of erasure: instead, it is the work of producing a haunted world, a world that is shaped by various utterances and incomplete sources of information, a world shaped by sites that are built anew, archives that are written over and redone, a world filled with nightmares, ghosts, perplexities, impasses. The absences of necrosovereignty are as meaningful as its presences, and its ghosts can be as vibrant as the living and dead bodies. The world of necrosovereignty is thus not so much a void inasmuch as it is its own fable. For example, in the case of Colombia, there are no records of the number of people who were buried in order to boost the body count of guerrillas killed. However, there are records of the number of weapons that were held by the Colombian military on a monthly basis, and gaps in these records indicate the number of weapons that the dead were given to be buried with.[6] For the "false positives," in the absence of the identity of the bodies, or a numerical count of them, what makes up the archive becomes not the sign of death but precisely the sign of enmity, the story of the enmity that remains there. In the absence of records or bodies, what remains is still a story: the story of the killing of an enemy. Indeed, to think that there is nothing would be to overlook the story of power itself, or as Mbembe says, the fact that "the work of power also involves a process of 'enchantment' in order to produce 'fables.'"[7] Many of the enforced disappearances were accompanied by various degrees of criminalization, which serves the purpose of providing legitimacy or intelligibility to what happened. If the "false positives" of Colombia were given identities through FARC uniforms, this was replicated in other cases of enforced disappearances, where the disappeared were represented as various kinds of enemies. In Argentina, as Diana Taylor explains, gendering the national "self" in Argentina worked to align moral categories with gender categories, where the disappeared fell into the tropes of "bad" men and women, fathers and mothers.[8] In Turkey, upon searching for the forcibly disappeared, if the "remnants" are not told that their relatives didn't even exist, they're told that they must have been anti-state militia, or else they were sympathizers with the militia. The gaps in the archive do not amount to nothing: they form fables, stories held by nightmares, and are nightmarish themselves.

Fables have their own rules of order, and they require neither rationality nor coherence in order to function. Mbembe says that "there can be no 'fable' without its own particular array of clichés and verbal conventions notable for their extravagance and self-regard, the purpose of which is to dress up silliness in the mantle of nobility and majesty."[9] The purpose of the fable is not to create a rational whole, or a complete "cover-up": what it covers up is nothing but the absence of records, or a gap in the level of intelligibility. The fable is "silliness": silences, pieces of information that do not fit, apart from the fact that they are present, said, and done. The world of necrosovereignty

Stories of Nothing

is shaped by fables: fables of enmity, fables of terror, fables with clichés and verbal conventions of various sorts. So the stories told by the "remnants" do not emerge in an absolute void, nor do they "fill up" what is empty. In this sense, many of the stories that the relatives of the disappeared insist on telling serve to counter the fabulations of necrosovereignty. These stories are counter-fabulations, or modes of "counter-conduct," ways of being and acting otherwise, ways of opening up other temporalities and other imaginaries.

Counter-conducts hold a different space than modes of resistance against sovereignty or modes of resistance against specific institutions. Unlike modes of critique against a given sovereign, as in revolts against authoritarian or exploitative sovereigns, counter-conducts are modes of resistance against the effects of power and against ways of being governed. The general point of a counter-conduct, in this sense, is not that "the sovereign X must be toppled because they are not a 'good' sovereign." The object of counter-conducts is neither the persona of the sovereign, in whom sovereignty as a mode of power is crystallized, nor is it the institutions that actuate sovereignty, such as courts and bodies of specific laws. Thus, just as counter-conducts are distinct from revolts against the sovereign, they are also distinct from the kinds of movements that demand change and reform in a given set of laws. Instead, counter-conducts are modes of resistance that "have as their objective and adversary a power that assumes the task of conducting men in their life and daily existence."[10] As such, they are modes of resistance that are against the governing of ways of being and living, of existing. The remnants telling stories of their loved ones as "good people," for example, as people who were valuable and important in their own right, are resistances against the fabulations that construe their loved ones as enemies, terrorists, bad mothers, or bad people. And thus, the remnants resist the ways in which the lives and deaths of their loved ones are conducted in necrosovereignty.

Moreover, the mode of resistance that is seen in the remnants' insistence on storytelling as a practice also fits what Foucault characterizes as "struggles against subjection." For one, storytelling, and especially public storytelling, as practiced by the remnants is a "transversal" act, insofar as they are not limited to the resistances to power that occur in one country only.[11] Indeed, from Argentina to Mexico, Chile to Turkey, one of the key characteristics of the remnants' movements is this shared emphasis on telling their stories and telling them regularly, meeting every week, releasing the stories either vocally or through the media, and building transnational alliances through their stories. Thus, while the Saturday Mothers have used their online presence to highlight the stories of the remnants by releasing one story every week, the Mothers of Soacha have issued regular press releases regarding the fates of their loved ones. Moreover, these are examples of "immediate struggles" insofar as, despite their prolonged temporality, they always look for a specific counterpoint, or an "immediate enemy," as Foucault says; that is, an immediate point of contact that is specific to a locale, such as the head of the gendarmerie in the town of Siirt in Turkey, or the military orders that were carried out during the execution of the "false positives." "Conflicts of conduct will occur on the borders and edge of the political institution," says Foucault.[12] Indeed, much of the activity of the remnants' movements occur at the edges of a variety of political institutions, yet they are not circumscribed by these institutions. The police, the military, the prison, the hospital, the state, all occur as regular counter-points of the stories: "I mean in the end it's the police, and it's the police who took him. I mean after all that's also the state. When I went there, when I went to the police, no one would go with me to the police,"[13] says Hasene; and similarly, Sevda says, "I was going between the jail and the police and the gendarmerie all the time."[14] Nevertheless, each of these interactions with institutions occurs at the liminal space of the institution, taking place either as informal conversations with the "officials" that are neither registered or recorded, or as habitual activities when confronting officials: "I used to go to the Gendarmerie every day. They would tell me come back six days later, then six months later. I would go, and I kept going for days, months, and years."[15] The institutions, and the interactions with them, become liminal elements in the remnants' stories, with the stories told occurring always at their edge, at a point of distance, and at a point of resistance.

The insistence of the remnants' movements on telling stories can thus be seen not as attempts to fill up the voids of necrosovereignty, but rather as counter-conducts, as struggles against subjection, as ways of demanding other ways of subjectivation. In the context of necrosovereignty, however, these are counter-conducts not against ways of living, but rather against ways of dying. Inasmuch as necrosovereignty shapes the ways in which the right to die is distributed, telling the stories of those who are gone is a way of claiming another kind of death, a revolt not against the way of living and being, but against the ways of dying and mourning that are conducted in necrosovereignty. Thus, unlike the fictions of enmity and absence that constitute necrosovereign fabulations, the stories of the remnants are filled with presences, random instances of solidarity, and more often than anything else, people who are returning in dreams, and others who are buried in nightmares. This insistence on telling the story of a person who is long gone, who according to the records neither lived, nor was detained, nor died, functions as a revolt against the way death is conducted: "They tell me my son is dead," says one of the mothers in Newala Qesaba. "How dare they tell me? Who are they to tell me my son is dead? I just saw him, he told me to wait for him!"[16] Similarly, telling stories, and specifically, telling stories about dreams of people returning or getting buried, functions as a rejection of the order of truth that is prescribed in necrosovereignty, or as a way of saying, according to Foucault, "We do not want this truth. We do not want to be held in this system of truth."[17]

Storytelling is a mode of counter-conduct that consists not in filling up emptinesses, but in actively producing counter-discourses. Necrosovereignty

Stories of Nothing

is not devoid of fabulations: power comes with its own enchantments, and the enchantments of necrosovereignty consist in producing undead deaths and erased narratives. There is, however, the question of what kind of counter-conduct is at stake: knowledge is inextricably enmeshed with the archive, and nightmare knowledges emerge out of specific relations and struggles with the archive. Understanding the practices of storytelling, specifically in relation to the work of necrosovereignty, requires excavating the relation between these stories and the archive. After all, as counter-conducts, they engage with the fables of necrosovereignty, and as struggles, they are struggles against the modes of truth that are recorded in archives. If they are not filling in absence, then, how do these stories counter the archives? What kind of a relation do they have with the archives of necrosovereignty, the gaps that are built into those archives, and the spaces that are built anew? In order to answer these questions, it is necessary to investigate what "archival counter-conduct" means, and what modes of counter-conduct are mobilized in the context of archives that have been erased or altered.

Infamously Disappeared

Inasmuch as necrosovereignty consists in making fables, its counter-conducts, or counter-fabulations, take place in dealing with the archive. This dealing, however, requires an engagement with stories as they are disappearing and deaths that disappear with those stories. In "Lives of Infamous Men," Foucault talks about genealogical engagement with the archive as a method of engaging with lives that are about to disappear into it. His treatment of the archive focuses on engagement with people who do not exist beyond the few lines within it. Those few lines, which record detention, arrest, confinement, being transported from one place to another, mental asylum records, or clinical records, don't center on the persons themselves at all; these are not lines "about" these people. Yet, the people exist in these lines, acquiring an "ashy existence" by virtue of these lines. Their existence acquired in and through these lines, in this sense, is on its way to disappearance even as those lines are being written; nevertheless, it is an existence that has a place in what is real, and not fictional. The people who make up genealogies, Foucault says, are very much real existences, not literary fictions or imaginary lives. In such genealogies, one should be able to "ascribe a place and date to them," so that they exist in one point and place in history.[18]

Nevertheless, the lives that Foucault engages with are "infamous" or "obscure" lives. There is not much that is special about them, that distinguishes them from others. Unlike the figures of history who are famous for their heroism, their beauty, or their nobility, when it comes to these "infamous" lives of Foucault, what matters is that "nothing prepared them for any notoriety" and "they would not have been endowed with any of the

118   Chapter 5

established and recognized nobilities."[19] There are no hidden facts or secrets that would place them in the key moments of history either; "the existence of these men and women comes down to exactly what was said about them: nothing subsists of what they were or what they did, other than what is found in a few sentences."[20] Like the infamous lives that Foucault talks about, who were working-class people, peasants, prostitutes, or people who lived and died in asylums, the bodies in Patio 29 or Newala Qesaba and the "false positives" can be seen in many ways to fit his description as well. These "infamous" existences were not marked by any element of notoriety or nobility, neither wealth, nor birth, nor any other form of celebrity. Inasmuch as they were very much real beings who "lived and died," in a certain way the distinctions between the real and the imaginary become blurred in their existences, precisely because their existence now comes down to what is said about them in a few lines in the archive.[21]

Nevertheless, these are "fable lives," lives that emerge in fables of power, inasmuch as engaging with the archive bears testimony to their interactions with power, to the work of power on these lives. The existence of these obscure lives comes down to a couple of lines, and those very lines record their interactions with power: in the case of Foucault's examples, the records of detention, asylum records, and police reports document how "obscure lives" were targeted by power. Foucault talks about these as "lives that are as though they hadn't been, that survive only from the clash with a power that wished only to annihilate them or at least to obliterate them."[22] The very work of power, in this sense, makes them emerge, as Huffer says, "out of the anonymous murmur of beings who pass without a trace."[23] What gives a story to these lives is precisely the work of power that struck them. Foucault says that in telling their stories, "the dream would have been to restore them their intensity in an analysis," or at least to "assemble a few rudiments for a legend of obscure men, out of the discourses that, in sorrow or in rage, they exchanged with power."[24] However, such a dream would not produce a story for such lives apart from their exchanges with power. Rather, doing so would primarily mean providing a witness for that flash of power that struck them, assembling a legend of the work of power on them, and thus witnessing their annihilation or obliteration not in their lives, as beings who lived and died unrelated to their interactions with power, but precisely in their exchanges with power.

And yet, when considering necrosovereign techniques, witnessing the power that flashes on them precisely becomes the problem. There are no records of the disappeared ones' "clash with power" since the very operation of necrosovereignty is the very obliteration of records. The eradication entailed by the enforced disappearances is not metaphorical but a physical and quite literal obliteration, and what disappears with them is specifically those victims' clash with power. The few lines that mark the existence of Foucault's infamous men, the detention records, the medical records, the records

Stories of Nothing

119

of confinement, the lines that testify to the work of power, simply do not exist. Necrosovereign fabulation works by erasing its own work. Whatever the work of necropolitics is, that work becomes precisely that which is not testified in necrosovereign assemblages.

Moreover, inasmuch as the impact of power on the lives of the forcibly disappeared is very difficult to bear testimony to, what makes them "infamous" is not their lives, nor even their death. It is rather the very absence of their deaths. There may be no records of detention, arrest, torture, or burial that mark the lives of the disappeared, and yet there are records of those who search for them: the meetings of the mothers, the records of detention of the searchers, the news articles that pertain to the mothers, and most importantly, the stories that are told by the mothers themselves. The Mothers of Soacha, of the Plaza de Mayo, and the Saturday Mothers all recount the day their loved ones disappeared: the color of the pajamas they were wearing, the exact time of their detention, the sound of the knock on the door, their daily activities at that moment, the last words that their mothers heard them say. What "remains" of them is not a written archive to provide a glimpse of them, but rather decades-long activism that transports their memory from location to location. Inasmuch as there are no single lines that provide a glimpse of such lives that are "about to disappear," there are nevertheless stories, stories of disappearance, that are carried over and retold in different geographies, over the span not of a moment about to disappear, but over decades and generations.

Interestingly, when Foucault talks about his choice of archival records, he notes that memoirs, or stories that resemble those of the mothers of the disappeared, are precisely the kinds of archives that he avoids. The reason he gives for this is "their relation to reality," or the way in which they take up a role in the battlefield of reality. Thus, he says:

> I ruled out all the texts that might be memoirs, recollections, tableaus, all those recounting a slice of reality but keeping a distance of observation, of memory, of curiosity, or of amusement. I was determined that these texts always be in relation, or, rather, in the greatest possible number of relations with reality. Not only that they refer to it, but they be operative within it, that they form a part of the dramaturgy of the real: that they constitute the instrument of a retaliation, the weapon of a hatred, an episode in the battle, the gesticulation of despair or jealousy, an entreaty or an order. I didn't try to bring together texts that would be more faithful to reality than others.[25]

Foucault's genealogies that are built on single lines in the archival records thus avoid stories that have tellers. It is worth noting that there are certain characteristics of such stories that have tellers or that fit within the category of testimonies. First, the stories that are told are just as "real" as archival records, and perhaps even more so. These stories have specific relations that they establish with reality, in the sense that they "do" things in reality; they are operative in that reality. In this sense, the reality that they refer to is not an objective substratum that can only be described. It is rather a dramaturgy that consists of relations that are played out and enacted. Second, these kinds of stories are weaponized in their relation to reality. Thus, the "dramaturgy of the real" functions as a battlefield, where what is played out are not only relations, but specifically power relations, within which stories not only do things but also switch the order of things.

Indeed, there are many ways in which telling a story, or recounting a memory, plays into the "dramaturgy of the real" for the remnants. In the context of necrosovereignty, this storytelling is particularly important to such dramaturgy and the ways in which the stories of the remnants play into it. In Patio 29, for example, when the first round of exhumation was completed and the first sets of bones were sent to the relatives, many of them tried to tell stories about the deceased by reading the traces on the bones. As Peter Read and Marivic Wyndham discuss, once the relatives acquired the bones, they carefully read and interpreted, in painstaking, excruciating detail, every sign of torture, every trace of injury that remained: "'This is the trajectory where the bullet entered and exited his brain,'[26] "This is how many pieces the hand was fractured.'"[27] The narrative of horror in its cruel and gruesome details becomes a way of attaching the body to its clash with power, a way of witnessing the work of power on the body, beyond the lines of the written archive. Moreover, this narrative recounting has legal and political implications in the dramaturgy of the real. For example, once a missing person is no longer "disappeared" but was "executed," their relatives become, as Read and Wyndham say, a part of the "'normal' community of mourners."[28] The wife of the disappeared becomes the widow of the executed and qualifies to receive a pension and a life insurance payout. The legal route of investigation becomes the investigation of a homicide; and the relatives can decide on a burial place where they can visit the bones, bring flowers on holidays, bring the youngest in the family to visit. In Turkey, the relatives can receive pensions once they can successfully claim that the disappeared is indeed dead, and they can file lawsuits, or they can request a support subsidy.[29] Stories, specifically in the form of memories, play into the "dramaturgy of the real" in this sense because they do things, they function in the general order of things, and become weapons to be used in the battlefield of necrosovereignty. In this sense, providing a story for the remains becomes a way of shifting the order of the real, a method of weaponizing stories in the battlefield of the real.

Nonetheless, this dramaturgy of the real does not follow any linear rules in necrosovereign assemblages, nor can the narratives of the remnants maintain the grip on reality that they claim. In the case of the first round of exhumations in Patio 29, many of the relatives who received a set of bones in bags learned later on that the bones most likely did not belong to their lost one.

Stories of Nothing

121

The traces that they had read in those remains, the fractured bones, the bullet holes, the pulled teeth, belonged to someone else who had been anonymously buried; the bones told the story of someone else, another deceased, another disappeared. Just as Neña González the caretaker of the cemetery lot, was unable to identify the deceased from the photographs, so was the state unable to derive names from the contorted bodies found there. Inasmuch as the relatives' stories themselves play into the battlefield of the real, that reality, they came to learn, was shaped in and through necrosovereign fables, with narratives of torture attached to the "wrong" sets of bones, or where the remains disappear once again. And so the relatives once again find themselves lost in fables of anonymous skeletons and the horrors of unknown corpses.

It is important to note that what the mothers' stories provide is not closure to the limbo of necrosovereignty, nor do their stories "reverse" the work of sovereignty or provide any sort of healing for the bereaved. Becoming part of the dramaturgy of the real implies that the stories do not fix the operation of power, nor do they mark a space beyond power. This becomes an especially important aspect of necrosovereign genealogies. Foucault, in *Speech Begins after Death*, talks about the genealogical work built upon the lines of the archive as "speaking over the corpses of others, to the extent that they are dead."[30] Catching a glimpse of infamous lives that are about to disappear in the archive is very much entangled with the death of these lives, a way of "postulating their death." In a similar vein to Hartman's image of the archive as a mortuary, Foucault's archive moves "from death to truth and from truth to death," where their plays into the dramaturgy of the real is countered by death.[31] And yet necrosovereign archives, when they do testify, testify to the impossibility of attaching an actual death to disappearance, the impossibility of "postulating their death," the impossibility of dealing with the death of others, "to the extent that they're already dead."[32] If the possibility of speech is conditioned upon the possibility of postulating such death, then in the cases of improper burial, that very impossibility puts the very status of speech and testimony in question. How can there be speech when there is no death? When the relatives insist on telling their stories, what is the status of their testimonies in the very absence of death?

There is something to be said about the narrative restraint that keeps the genealogist from both killing others in writing and dreaming of their resurrection in writing. Speech does not make the past alive, nor does it make the dead live again. "They think I am the silly one," says one of the Saturday Mothers, "they tell me I am the silly one; that I should know that he is dead now."[33] Many of the Saturday Mothers say they know that their loved ones will more than likely not reappear, just as they say that they will not stop grieving upon finding the bodies either. That the archive is shaped by necrosovereignty means that there is no miraculous closure that can be attained by telling their stories, that telling their stories will not bring about such recuperation. This is of particular interest when it comes to the decades-old demand of the

Mothers of the Plaza de Mayo, namely "*Aparición con vida*," that is, "Bring them back alive." In their demand, the inability of speech to bring someone back alive becomes clear: the mothers do not claim to be doing the work of resurrecting through telling the stories, and their demand stands as one that is merely posited.

Perhaps more important, however, when it comes to improper burial, is the possibility of putting the disappeared to rest. Inasmuch as speech cannot bring them back alive, that was never the point anyway. Perhaps their stories, or the emphasis the mothers use in telling those stories, the stories of the lives of their relatives, can be thought of in relation to the "realization that the past is dead."[34] Given that many of the cases of enforced disappearance have been unresolved for decades at this point, and given that what the relatives of the "false positives" have at hand are precisely bodies that are dead, the question may be less of bringing them back alive through telling their stories but rather of postulating their death.

And yet, it is no easy feat to "seize from the world and put to death what has previously been decreed to be nothing."[35] The archival temptation to provide closure where there is none, "to create a space for mourning where it is prohibited," or "to fabricate a witness to a death not much noticed," does not produce a dead body when there is none, or mourn deaths where there are too many to count.[36] Much too often, the task of "handing off their death," as the Saturday Mothers call it, is precisely what the relatives avoid. Telling the story of the death of a person alters things in the necrosovereign order of things: it makes one a widow, it allows state pensions to arrive, it creates "benefits" where there are none. And yet, in the absence of the stories or records of death, the remnants do not fabricate a witness to death or claim the death of the disappeared. Even when such deaths play into the necrosovereign dramaturgy of the real, many of the relatives speak of holding off on claiming the death, that is, on affirming that the person is legally dead in order to receive the state pension accruing to a widow. This restraint in decreeing the loved one dead is important in accounting for the impossibility of "undoing" the work of necrosovereignty through words or stories. Providing a story does not "bring back" the disappeared, nor does it put the disappeared to death. As much as necrosovereignty fabulates in order to create limbos, the relatives do not tell stories in order to provide closure to those limbos.[37]

The archive provides a glimpse of lives that are about to disappear, or it can provide testimony on the brief interactions between these obscure lives and the power that wishes to annihilate them. In the case of the stories of the remnants, the archive is an impossibility, and their interactions with the archive are an impossibility: as counter-conducts, their stories do not fill up the archive, nor do they "undo" the work of power or provide a glimpse of power and its impacts on the living and the dead. That very impossibility, however, is inseparable from the necrosovereign "dramaturgy of the real," which functions to weaponize their stories to play in the dramaturgy of the

Stories of Nothing

123

real. In necrosovereign fabulation, there is no life, but also no death. In the absence of either, there is no testimony to life, and no speech after death either. The question that remains is what do the stories do if they don't fill up gaps, bring the disappeared back, or provide testimony to life, death, and the work of power. The question here concerns fables: what the function of fables is, and in particular, what fables of disappearance do. In order to investigate this, however, we must pay attention to the stories.

What Is in a Story?

Many of the relatives express their determination to tell their story in different ways. They say, for example, that "they will not be silenced," and they announce they will "share their stories." María Ubilerme Salabria, one of the Mothers of Soacha, says that hers is a "tale [cuento]" that needs to be told, and the Saturday Mothers often simply say that they will continue "speaking."[38] In Spanish, the telling of historia can refer to either giving an account of "history" or recounting a "story," and many of the remnants still refer to this as telling a tale (cuento).[39] Similarly, in Turkey, the relatives refer almost exclusively to telling their story as telling a tale (hikâye), and in recounting what came upon them (başımıza gelenler). Foucault says that a "fable, in the proper sense of the term, refers to that which deserves to be told."[40] Inasmuch as necrosovereign fables consist of erasure and undoing, the demand of the remnants lies in this: that whatever happened deserves to be told, that there is an urgency in the story itself that requires such telling.

The stories at hand, however, are neither fairy tales nor literary fictions. They consist of information on the person who has disappeared, the events of the day of disappearance, the next few days after the disappearance, and any interactions with the remains, if there were any: when the bones were found, when they received the bones, when they were told of the existence of the remains at a certain location, what they were able to "read" from those remains (the signs of torture, the fracturing of bones, the lost limbs), and, if the remains are not theirs (as in the case of Patio 29), how they could tell that this was the case ("her hands are bigger," "his skull is rounder"). When describing fables, Hartman says: "'fabula' denotes the basic elements of story, the building blocks of the narrative," or as she cites Mieke Bal, a story is "a series of logically and chronologically related events that are caused and experienced by actors. An event is a transition from one state to another. Actors are agents that perform actions . . . To act is to cause or experience an event."[41] The events of a fable appear connected to each other through certain transformations of the actors. Similarly, many of the relatives of the disappeared refer to time in their stories in relation to their state or status: "I was still going to school then," "I was a pregnant woman then," or "I was a young bride then."[42] The event of disappearance prescribes a certain transformation in the states of the remnants, as when they went from being a pregnant woman to the wife of a disappeared, or from being a student to being a "remnant" or a "searcher." This transformation underlies the narrative of the story: as storytellers, they refer to themselves exclusively as "remnants" or as "searchers"; that is, specifically as identities that are established in relation to disappearance. If the traditional fable transcribes a transformation, fables of disappearance primarily transcribe the event which transforms someone from an "ordinary person" with an obscure life into someone who is a searcher and thus an agent who exists in relation to necrosovereign assemblages, who participates in the web of power relationships that constitute necrosovereignty.

According to Hartman, critical fabulation occurs not in the recounting of the event but rather in jeopardizing the status of the event. She says: "By playing with and rearranging the basic elements of the story, by re-presenting the sequence of events in divergent stories and from contested points of view, I have attempted to jeopardize the status of the event."[43] Insofar as the event refers to a transformation from one state to another, this "jeopardizing" involves shifting around the building blocks of the narrative, in order to displace the center of the narrative. For Hartman, this means "advancing a series of speculative arguments and exploiting the capacities of the subjunctive (a grammatical mood that expresses doubts, wishes, and possibilities) in fashioning a narrative, which is based upon archival research," in order to "tell an impossible story and to amplify the impossibility of its telling."[44] Hartman moves beyond the transgressive limits of the archive in order to fashion stories about those who disappear in the archive. This involves dealing with an archive that no longer has any witnesses beyond the gaps in it. In the stories that are told by the remnants, however, this method of jeopardizing the status of the event occurs through other means, through the transformations of the actors of the events, and by shifting the focus of the event. Many of the remnants, when telling the story of when their loved ones disappeared, discuss it precisely in relation not to the violence involved, but rather to everyday occurrences, situating it in the processes of everyday life. "I was making the bed," they say, or the "lentils weren't bleached yet," or "I was breast-feeding the kid."[45] Insofar as "to act is to cause or experience an event," the stories of the searchers consistently shift the focus of the event from the act of violence itself back to other kinds of acts that make up their everyday existence.[46] In this everyday existence, the "actors" are not the gendarmerie who detained the person in the middle of the night, but rather the searchers. In such stories, disappearance becomes flesh and bone; the disappeared is situated in another time than that of the disappearance, such as the time of the lentils bleaching, or the time of the kid being breast-fed, and unlike the time of disappearance, it is a time that exists somewhere.

As the time is that of lentils bleaching, the stories of the remnants attest to the "impossibility" of the event of the improper burial. The event of the lentils bleached, for example, is the time of the arrest or detention, and yet the

Stories of Nothing

story recalls a different event: "We were very poor, and they trampled on all our beds."[47] Sometimes the storyteller was not actually present at the time of the event: "I was breast-feeding the kid, and the neighbor told me they took him away."[48] The time of disappearance, moreover, is an absent time, a time that does not exist in the temporality of life or fit within the time of death. Halide Yurttaş, whose husband has been missing for over two decades, says, "Sometimes I think he might be alive, because I didn't see him dead."[49] While there is a transformation that occurs in the status of the remnants, the event that marks that transformation, that of disappearance, is precisely what is absent in their stories. There is no time of disappearance, and no event of disappearance either: the time is that of lentils bleaching, or that of breast-feeding, or the beds being turned down.

The task of jeopardizing the status of the event, however, is not just to shift the locus of the event from the work of necrosovereignty to another kind of agency by focusing on different activities or experiences.[50] Jeopardizing functions "to displace the received or authorized account," to open up another kind of account, in order to "imagine what might have happened or might have been said or might have been done."[51] Indeed, the question of other pasts and other presents is a question that haunts improper burial: what would have happened if they did not open that door? What would have happened if they did not know that person? What could have happened in the disappearance, if not death? The task of telling other stories or putting the "event" of the event into question becomes inseparable from the task of writing a history of the present, and yet that of another kind of present. Hartman says that writing "a history of the present strives to illuminate the intimacy of our experience with the lives of the dead."[52] In a sense, displacing the event from disappearance to that of beds turned down, and displacing the time from necrosovereignty to that of lentils bleaching, marks another kind of intimacy with the lives of the disappeared, where their absence is inseparable from the most mundane moments of existence, such as making beds, breast-feeding kids, harvesting plots, or bleaching the lentils. And yet, as Mbembe says, for the remnants "there opens a time after death,"[53] insofar as "death, as speech, does not imply silence, even less the end of possible representation of the dead."[54] The question of what could have happened if the disappeared were present is inseparable from what could have happened if they were absent. For the remnants, imagining a present in which the loved ones are alive is as hard as imagining a present where they are dead, and imagining one where the disappeared are walking around is as difficult as imagining one in which their disappeared loved one is in a grave. If the representation of the dead does not end with the moment of death, neither does that of their disappearance. Instead, it opens up other modes of the present, as well as other kinds of presences.

Critical fabulation is "a history of an unrecoverable past."[55] Many of the remnants, however, describe their stories as not being of the past, one that is

126   Chapter 5

recoverable or even approachable. Instead, they refer to the stories of their present, their stories of becoming searchers, or their stories of becoming remnants. For many of the searchers, the stories of the arrests, detentions, and the finding of the remains are inseparable from their stories of hearing about the meetings of the remnants, the stories of meeting each other for the first time, the stories of initially becoming searchers as political actors or activists. Encountering the stories of others is a life-changing event, and a shift to another status. "I was walking to the gendarmerie station for the second time," one of the Saturday Mothers says, "when I heard that there are these other women that meet up in Istanbul, so I decided to move to Istanbul to meet them."[56] The story of improper burial does not end with its impossibility, nor does it become the story of necrosovereignty only: just as the event is displaced, so is the subject, so disappearance becomes the search, the disappeared's relatives become the remnant, and the story of necrosovereignty becomes that of meeting, that of protesting, that of organizing.

At the same time, insofar as the actors of a fable are "agents that perform actions" and "to act is to cause or experience an event," jeopardizing the status of the event also entails a shift in the actors as well.[57] The process of becoming a searcher entails a shift not only of their status, but also of their activities, of the way they speak, the kinds of acts they perform, the way they spend their days. Nora Cortiñas, one of the Mothers of the Plaza de Mayo, explains that becoming a "Mother" meant getting used to "public life, new relationships, the loss of privacy, traveling a lot, using different forms of speech, preparing yourself to meet with people in power, speaking to the media, being recognized on the street."[58] Saturday Mothers discuss traveling all over the country, meeting others like them, organizing. When the event is a non-event, and the death is a non-death, there are no actors in those fables either, but rather other kinds of activities, other modes of organization and relations. Indeed, there opens a time after death, but the time after improper burial is another time, filled with other pasts, futures, and presents, not only in imagining what could have been, but also in multiplying the possibilities of the present. Fables of disappearance neither bring back to life nor put to death what is gone, but rather open other presents and other kinds of deaths, precisely by jeopardizing the status of the non-event and conjuring up the ghosts of the non-spaces.

Fables of disappearance, in this sense, are not merely stories to be told, nor do they function as stories told with the impossible hope of bringing back the dead or providing closure where there is none. They play into the dramaturgy of the real; they function in that blurry space between the real and the fictional; in short, as counter-conducts, they are stories that *do things*. They shift the time of the event, they disrupt the order of things, and, perhaps most importantly, they produce actors who contest necrosovereign fabulations by conjuring up the ghosts of such fabulations. In the demand of the relatives to tell stories, in their insistence on reading fables out of bodies, what is at stake

Stories of Nothing

is another kind of acting, doing, and telling, which jeopardizes the non-event that marks improper burial.

Necrosovereign Enchantments and Stories of Nothing

Necrosovereignty is a method of power that functions by allowing and disallowing individuals and groups to be dead. Through regulation of the practices of mourning, and impossibilizing the practices of mourning, necrosovereignty distributes the right to die, producing a kind of death that is not death, an absent death. What is at stake, in other words, is not the reduction of the deceased to nothing. Instead, it is the production of a kind of limbo for the disappeared, where the individuals or groups are neither dead nor alive. This necrosovereign work does not occur only through archival erasure, nor does it take place by making storytelling impossible; instead, necrosovereignty is invested in fabulation, fables of death and disappearance, fables of enmity, and fables of terror.

In this context, the insistence of the searchers on telling their stories is especially critical. Insofar as the very work of necrosovereignty is on the archive, in erasing it and rebuilding it, in both impossibilizing some knowledge and producing other modes of knowledge around death, storytelling in the mothers' movements functions as a mode of counter-conduct. First and foremost, it is a method of struggle that is widely deployed: it spans from Latin America to Turkey, and is not limited to specific countries. Moreover, it denotes struggles not against specific sovereigns or sovereignties, but against the effects of power: in the stories of the remnants, dreams and nightmares function to challenge the very effect of necrosovereignty on individuals, on their lives and deaths. Last, the stories denote struggles against the mode of conduct that is characteristic of necrosovereignty: as such, the stories work against the modes of truth produced in necrosovereign assemblages and function to reject that mode of truth.

It is important to consider these stories, however, not only as modes of counter-conduct that are mobilized, but also specifically as modes of archival counter-conduct, as methods of engaging with archives that are both erased and built anew. On the one hand, these are stories of obscure lives that attest neither to a life that is about to disappear, nor to a kind of death that can be brought back. Instead, they attest specifically to the workings of a kind of power that fabulates nothings out of persons, events, and things. Telling the stories of nothings, however, plays into the dramaturgy of the real: in this sense, they neither provide closure where there is none, as Hartman says, nor do they bring the past back alive, or bring the dead back. Instead, they conjure ghosts in order to play into the scene of the real, creating pasts, presents, and possibilities for the future. Fable is that which deserves to be told. The stories of the searchers jeopardize the account of what deserves to be told by putting the event in question. The time of the remnants' fables shifts from the time of arrest to the time of everyday events, to the lentils bleaching, to beds being made. The status of the event shifts from the event of violence to the event of a change in the actors, they become political actors, and actors in a different kind of event, that of meeting others, that of organizing. More than anything, the stories of the remnants reveal what is at stake in necrosovereignty: an event that is a non-event, a death that is not a death, a present that does not follow from the past. Necrosovereignty works through fables, through deliriums and fetishes, through disappearances and absences. The stories of the searchers, however, point to the production of another kind of past, another kind of present, and more than ever, another kind of life-death that jeopardizes the non-event and shifts the dramaturgy of the real. Death, indeed, does not imply silence, nor does disappearance: instead, they are filled with stories, ones that are built of nightmares.

Chapter 6

Fables That Stir the Mind

We have visited many places. There is Newala Qesaba, the trash-disposal area in eastern Turkey, which hosts an unknown number of bodies, and across from which the relatives of the inhabitants visited their loved ones; an area now turned into a lot for building condos. There is Patio 29 in the General Cemetery of Santiago, a mass gravesite that is emptied of remains, a graveyard without the dead. There is Cizre, which hosted the freezer in which the ten-year-old body of Cemile was kept, and there is also Suruç, with the street on which the body of Taybet Inan was left in front of her house. There is Soacha, a suburb of Bogotá, where young men have been disappearing for years now, only to be found a few hundred miles away, clothed in garments that are not their own. There are the Basements of Atrocity, where an unknown number of people died in a span of twenty days, a site now replaced by luxury condos; and there is the city center of Sur, a space of urban warfare, now being completely rebuilt with brand-new Ottoman and Seljuk-style architecture.

In each of these places there is death, and there is mourning: not only natural or experiential, but specifically political and politicized death and mourning. Death and mourning are entangled with power, and—in the contemporary sphere—with necrosovereignty. Nevertheless, they are also entangled with resistance, and are mobilized in order to resist power. Specifically, much of this mobilization takes place through methods of narrative and testimony, through formulating different modes of epistemic stances, accompanied by an insistence on storytelling: stories not only of grief and disappearance, but stories of other kinds of events, other kinds of deaths, other kinds of subjects. Together, each of these spaces is doubled by another space, a space that is "other," which testifies not only to the work of necrosovereignty, but also to that of its nightmares.

Take Galatasaray Square, on İstiklal Street in Istanbul: a city of close to 20 million that is by far the most populous and famous city of Turkey. İstiklal, the busiest street of the city, has a square that is defined by the gargantuan gates that were built for a sultan and are now no longer in use. The vigils of the Saturday Mothers take place in the square at noon, when the members lay down carnations there. Their meetings have faced two main periods of heavy pressure, when the members have been interrupted regularly by police presence. Like the meetings themselves, the periods of pressure have been long-lasting and point to the parallels between corporeal politics and spatial politics. The first period of heavy pressure, which lasted from 1995 to 1998, focused on corporeal methods: there were regular detentions, and several of the Saturday mothers forcibly disappeared. These detentions would take place early in the morning, and members would be taken from their houses. The second period of heavy pressure is the one we are still in now, since the 700th meeting on Saturday, August 25, 2018. This time the authorities have focused on spatial methods: each week, the square is blocked off by heavily armed police, armored vehicles, and barriers; the detentions are carried out "on site,"[1] and the pattern of the detentions points to those who read their stories or those who stand next to the reader. Those who are detained are released later in the day or the next day at sites far away from Galatasaray Square. The response given by the Saturday Mothers is similarly spatial: they say they will not stop going to the square no matter what the police do. Galatasaray Square, which itself is not a space of mass burial or enforced disappearance, is called a "place to meet with the disappeared,"[2] a place to conjure ghosts, a memory space, a space of resistance.

Understanding spaces of memory requires thinking about the tactics of reinvention and the spatial methods of reinventing spaces, and this is perhaps most clear in the case of the Plaza de Mayo. The oldest public square in Buenos Aires, the plaza has been the setting for various turning points in the history of Argentina, such as the second founding of the city and the Argentinian Revolution. Since 1977, however, the square has been the setting for the weekly meetings of the Mothers of the Plaza de Mayo on Thursdays at 3:30 p.m. While the meeting time and the main activities of the meetings (members wearing white cover-ups, holding up photographs, telling stories, and giving speeches) have not changed over the years, the mothers' tactic of occupying the space has taken various forms, by no means unified, and shaped by conflicts and contestations.[3] As Foucault says, resistance never takes place in a single fashion, and it does not have to be unified in order to be resistant. Over the years, the mothers have utilized conflicting strategies in approaching the space, by either commemorating the disappeared at the plaza by posting photographs of them there, or by marking the plaza as a site of human rights activism in general. In and through both these types of contestation, the Plaza de Mayo remains a space associated with *Las Madres* first and foremost: a memory space, a space of resistance. A resistance that takes space as its object means discussing the tactics that are deployed in resistance in reinventing spaces. One can also consider other much less public, but no less collective spaces that are reinvented, such as the houses of mourning in Newala Qesaba. Indeed, some of the relatives of those in Newala Qesaba call their homes "houses of mourning." While this phrase typically denotes

Fables That Stir the Mind

the house of the deceased's closest relatives for the forty-day period after the person's death, a time when others visit the home, these houses of mourning have been in operation for multiple decades now and are regularly used for community organizing.

There are no new places or people to visit in this chapter, or there are too many to visit in the confines of this book. Instead, the goal of this chapter is to think of other spaces that emerge in necrosovereignty, the spaces that exist in juxtaposition to, and which counter, spaces of death. Thus, this chapter focuses on the counter-spaces of nightmare knowledges, those that are both contested and invested through knowing and storytelling. The work of resistance in these spaces consists in reinvention against building anew: the reinvention not only of archives and memories but also of spaces and subjectivities. The chapter is organized around three main axes. The first section considers the "other spaces" that delineate distinct modes in relation to power, namely, "heterotopias," and questions the implications of the invention of heterotopias for nightmare knowledges. The second section will move on to the question of reinvention, or in Wynter's term, "autopoiesis," which works as a subjective and spatial reinvention, emphasizing the connections between the politics of subjects and spaces. The last section will discuss mobilizing practices of mourning in the heterotopias of necrosovereignty, which, I argue, is a tactic of inventing other modes of death and dying. Insofar as necrosovereignty consists in the production of an absent death, nightmare knowledges reinvent spaces in order to invent other vocabularies and other ways not only of living, but of dying as well. In this way, this final chapter concludes *Nightmare Remains* by demonstrating its principal thesis: that contemporary politics is invested in organizing and shaping practices of mourning, and that mourning is politicized to reinvent new modalities of knowing, remembering, and existing. Throughout, what we have is an account of nightmare knowledges as an autopoietic practice, a practice of redoing and rebuilding the spaces and subjects that exist in necrosovereign assemblages.

Memory Spaces, Spaces of Remembrance: Heterotopias of Mourning

One way to think about the "other spaces" that are formed in relation to power would be what Foucault calls "heterotopias," or "counter-spaces." Heterotopias, Foucault says, are distinct from utopias: utopias are spaces that do not have a real "place" but instead are inverted forms of the relations within a given society. In the context of necrosovereignty, a utopia would be a site where the work of improper burial is undone, where the deceased are fully mourned, where the bodies are found. It would be a utopian graveyard, like the one many of the searchers discuss having dreams about, a graveyard

132   Chapter 6

where each of those gone has a tombstone with a name, where each one has flowers on their grave.[4] As Foucault says, utopias "present society itself in a perfected form, or else society turned upside down, but in any case these utopias are fundamentally unreal spaces."[5] Utopias of necrosovereignty would be the spaces that open up in the dreams of the searchers. In these spaces the work of necrosovereignty is undone and is turned upside down, like the garden where one searcher says she meets with her son every night, where he is right there in front of her eyes, and nothing has ever happened to him; he has never disappeared, but just aged peacefully, and the light is beaming on his hair turned white just before he stops talking, as the dream turns into a nightmare.[6] Utopias are, indeed, fundamentally unreal places, as each of the searchers probably knows only too well.

Heterotopias are distinct from utopias, since they are rather "counter-sites." They are "very real places": these are spaces that exist very much within the dramaturgy of the real, that exist in relation to other kinds of spaces. Unlike the gardens of nightmares and the utopic cemeteries of wishful dreams, heterotopias are real spaces where the searchers can go, visit, and meet up regularly. Nevertheless, even though these spaces are distinct from utopias, they are similar to "effectively enacted utopias" in the sense that they are spaces where a mechanism of power is contested and inverted. The spaces of the regular public meetings such as Galatasaray Square become spaces to "meet up with the disappeared," as the searchers call it, or the Plaza de Mayo, a site of national history where the relatives of the disappeared come to be seen every Thursday.[7] As Foucault says, "places of this kind are outside of all spaces," and they are not determined by the conditions of possibility of the specific events taking place in them. Much like the non-spaces of necrosovereignty, such as the curfewed towns, heterotopias are not marked or determined by their locations, but rather are shaped by the inversion of relations in a given space.[8] Nevertheless, it may be possible to still mark such a location, give an address for such a space, and describe it in relation to other sites around it. Thus, Galatasaray Square as a place for "meeting with the disappeared," or a space for conjuring up their ghosts, is still inseparable from the public square that is located at the heart of İstanbul, since it is possible to describe its location, give its address, organize meetings there, and gather crowds. Moreover, even though heterotopias are not defined by their location, they are nevertheless capable of "juxtaposing in a single real place several spaces, several sites that are in themselves incompatible."[9] There are incompatibilities between a square that lies at the center of the city as defined by the old Sultanî Gates, and a square of regular activist meetings, a space that is defined by its relation to deaths that are absent. The sites in a heterotopia do not need to fit in to each other for them to function as they do: the imperial nostalgia of the gates, for example, does not annul the force of the meetings of the Saturday Mothers.

Every society produces heterotopias: from crisis heterotopias that emerge in relation to the breaking points of power relations, to deviation

Fables That Stir the Mind

heterotopias, which emerge in conjunction with relations of power. In the context of the mechanics of power that work specifically in relation to life and death, the function of heterotopias moves and shifts in relation to the work of power on death. For example, the cemetery is a heterotopia, Foucault argues, which has shifted its meanings along with the shifting relations to death in the conjunctions of sovereignty and biopolitics. Up until the end of the eighteenth century, the cemetery was placed at the heart of the city, in relation to other spaces of social gathering such as the church and the city center. One result of the biopolitical privatization of death, of the emergence of death as a singular and private affair, was a shift of the cemetery heterotopia into a private space that is situated on the outskirts of city life, with neatly organized private death-spaces: "It is from the beginning of the nineteenth century that everyone has a right to his or her own little box for her or his own little personal decay; but on the other hand, it is from the start of the nineteenth century that cemeteries began to be located at the outside border of cities."[10] In the case of the cemetery heterotopias, the biopolitical privatization of death made the cemetery into a space within which the private individual encounters their own limits.

Heterotopias thus emerge and shift in conjunction with changes in a society's relations to categories such as life and death: the emergence of new kinds of relations to life and death can bring about shifts in both the meaning and function of existing heterotopias, and the emergence of new kinds of heterotopias. Spaces such as Galatasaray Square or the Plaza de Mayo can, in this sense, form heterotopias that exist in specific relations to death and disappearance. Through the relatives' utilization of these spaces as sites where they "meet with the disappeared" or where "the disappeared become visible," the sites mark a space with a specific relation to death, to death that is absent, death that exists within the space of murmur between presence and absence. Ghosts always come with something to say and something to do; marking a space as one that conjures up ghosts testifies to the work of making that space a heterotopia for absent death: a heterotopia that is formed in the absence of the private cemetery that is the dream of biopolitics. The function of any space is inseparable from the meaning of that space, the memories and forgettings that are bound up with its sensory signs and its experience. After all, if the Saturday Mothers insist that Galatasaray Square is a memory space, it is because this space nevertheless exists in conjunction with memories and forgettings around death and disappearance, and similarly memories around gatherings, meetings, and struggles. One of the principles of heterotopias is that they are "linked to slices in time,"[11] they are linked to heterochronies that mark specific relations to time and memory. The cemetery heterotopia is inseparable from the heterochrony of both a society's and individuals' relations to death, marking both a passage and a space of mourning. Similarly, heterotopias can exist to accumulate time, just as a museum does, as if to produce the dream of an all-encompassing archive or to mark time in its most

134   Chapter 6

fleeting and precarious aspect, as in the space of a circus. Indeed, just as one can say that the cemetery of biopolitics, with its graves individually marked and privately reserved, marks a heterotopia for the biopolitical privatization of death, one can also think about spaces such as the Basements of Atrocity in Cizre or the city center of Sur as necrosovereign heterotopias. These are spaces that both exist and do not exist at the same time; they mark what was there, but they also testify to the necrosovereign aim of building anew, accumulating time and memory at once in the goal of building over and atop sites of violence. Spaces, indeed, exist in relation to memories: these memories involve remembering and forgettings. Heterotopias are the kinds of spaces that do things with memories and exist in relation to specific memories around life and death.

Insofar as the Plaza de Mayo or Galatasaray Square are heterotopias, however, other relations to time and memory are revealed: not too unlike the temporality of museums, time is accumulated in and through the weekly meetings of the mothers. However, unlike the museum's frozen time that preserves something that was lost, these meetings prolong time in order to preserve the loss and disappearance itself. Many of the mothers say that time stops at Galatasaray Square: their talk about how it has been decades since their loved one vanished, and how they have shown up at the square every week for hundreds of weeks, is both unbelievable and yet all too real. Nevertheless, as one of the mothers says, "Galatasaray is here, and it will always be here, for as long as our disappeared are here."[12] The time of the square moves in accordance with the temporality of disappearance; it stretches out beyond the limits of events and even the time spans of the searchers, it stretches on, and perhaps, as Foucault says, it "never stops building up and topping its own summit."[13] Nonetheless, this time, even though it stretches forward into the future, is also a fractured time: as the mothers meet and march every week, the square's space continues on all other days as a space of commerce: a space for the hustle and the bustle of the living, a space of exchange, a space for the everyday activities of life in ordinary neoliberal economies. The seeming eternity of prolonged mourning in necrosovereignty becomes fractured from meeting to meeting, rather than forming a linear totality that extends continuously, forming a kind of prolongation that is, at the same time, "absolutely temporal."[14]

Even though heterotopias emerge in both power and resistance, they are nevertheless not automatic, nor do they simply arise naturally. Rather, they are spaces that are done and made, that take the deployment of specific tactics. This is best exemplified by the Plaza de Mayo, where the contestation between different groups of mothers takes place in spatial terms, along with the meaning that the space upholds in relation to the lives and deaths of individuals. Indeed, the most prominent conflicts among the mothers involve different strategies of using the space. Of the two key groups that currently fall under the general umbrella of the *madres*, members of the Madres-Linea

Fables That Stir the Mind 135

Fundadora focus on remembering and honoring the disappeared, while those of the Asociación de Plaza de Mayo prefer to do so by constructing sites such as memorials, thus marking the Plaza de Mayo as a dynamic space, as a space of meeting, rather than focusing on the identities of the disappeared.[15] The immediate result of this conflict is marked by the weekly reinventions of the space: each week, identifying the space of the Plaza de Mayo as a space where the disappeared come to be seen, the *madres* of Linea Fundadora march around the plaza with the pictures of the disappeared pinned to their clothes and to their handkerchiefs, thus recalling the disappeared as specific persons, as they march around the Plaza with ashy faces and their fading photographs. The mothers of the Asociación de Plaza de Mayo, however, use the plaza as a platform: a space where violence is addressed in the various shapes it takes, a space haunted not by the people of the disappeared but by disappearance itself, by the fact that it takes place, by the fact that it exists.[16] In and through the contestations of the *madres*, the Plaza de Mayo emerges as a space of invention, one that is reinvented each week as a heterotopia where the nightmares of necrosovereignty come to be seen: nightmares of people who have disappeared never to be seen again, mothers who march with old photographs pinned to their bodies, and everyday spaces being inescapably marked by the very absence of death. It is important, however, to analyze what invention and reinvention mean on the spatial level: how do "knowledges" invent or reinvent spaces?

"Fables That Stir the Mind"

We said in the previous chapter that a fable is what deserves to be told: it is a story that shifts the eventness of the event, that opens up a new temporal order of things in the haunted spaces of necrosovereignty. Fables, however, are connected not only to orders of temporality, but to spatial organization as well: spaces are molded or shifted in practices of resistance, and are taken up in relation not only to power, but to resistance. Necrosovereign fabulation works through the production of both spaces of mourning (such as haunted spaces, spaces of forgetting) and spaces of destruction and building anew: it marks spaces such as the Basements of Atrocity with memories of violence and forgetting. Nightmare knowledges, however, shift not only the temporality of necrosovereignty but also its spatial organization. In short, nightmare knowledges are the kinds of knowledge that do things, not only at the level of memory and subjectivity but also at the level of spatiality. To understand this spatial reorganization, however, we must interrogate what fables have to do with space in the first place.

Both the work of and resistance to necrosovereignty take place in relation to the production of power/knowledge assemblages and are inseparable from the work of memory, archiving, storytelling, and fabulation in such assemblages. Sylvia Wynter discusses these assemblages as "founding fables" that give not only legitimacy but also intelligibility to a certain order of things, making the systems and structures of that order understandable, valid, and necessary. In this sense, founding fables are those that make up a general order of things, shaped not only by how and where things are situated at a given moment, but also how and where they could be situated, and how or where they could move as well. Thus, Wynter writes, "each 'general notion of the world' contains within it . . . a specific idea of order."[17] This idea of order legitimates not only the presences but also the potentialities involved in that general notion of the world. In this sense, there are three key aspects of founding fables. First, they are shaped by their delineations of both subjectivity and otherness. Second, they refer to a spatial politics that is shaped by subjective formation. Third, they are shaped by invention, and as such, they have the possibility to be reinvented.

Each founding fable is simultaneously shaped by spaces of otherness. We have seen that in necrosovereignty, the orders of discourse are shaped by delineating not only what is known but also what is knowable, memorable, or in the case of storytelling, tellable. Archival disappearances function to delineate the limits of discourse of necrosovereignty; what is recorded of the person disappeared, or the event of their disappearance, and whether their remains are found and how they are found, delineates what is known and knowable regarding the death of that person. Moreover, the general terms of discourse, specifically involving the categories of otherness, are shaped along the lines of such founding fables. Wynter writes: "Each absolutized 'notion of order' then functions as the 'space of otherness'; anchoring the foundational principles of each society in a realm beyond the reach of human desire and temptation as the condition of its stability across time."[18] The space of otherness thus stabilizes the general notion of order of a founding fable. For the "false positives," for example, whose bodies are found with weapons that don't belong to them, their place in the space of otherness of terror keeps the general order of death in place, creating a semblance of intelligibility for narratives that would otherwise not appear coherent. In this sense, founding fables have a dual relationship to their space of otherness, where otherness marks both the general coherence of the order of discourse within the founding fable, and what does not belong within that order of discourse. Just as necrosovereign archives are shaped by the erasures in them, founding fables are shaped by what is inconceivable from within the terms of the fable.

Archives, however, do not just exist at the level of discourse. Rather, spaces themselves are archives of sorts: the demolished town center of Sur functions as an archive of the work of death, and the tactics of archives in such spaces can involve reconstruction as much as erasure. Wynter suggests that founding fables are "cosmogenic" categories: they mark not only how space is dealt with but also how space is "invented." Wynter makes this point by taking a historical standpoint to discuss the voyages of Columbus as the emergence of

Fables That Stir the Mind 137

a new founding fable. According to Wynter, these voyages marked the emergence not only of a new political era but that of a new cosmogony, where the relationship between political subjects and the earth shifted, together with the space of otherness, and its order in this founding fable.[19] The shift occurred in this sense: the very possibility of the colonial reorganization of the globe was founded on the possibility of reconceiving a kind of poetics that would allow for such reorganization in the first place. The orders of discourse that are operative in founding fables thus shape the ways in which space is organized and treated. In this sense, the production of death-worlds, such as the curfewed town or sites of mass burial, in necrosovereignty are shaped by the founding fables that define necrosovereignty, wherein the space is conceived as a space of death, a space that is made for and shaped by death.

Moreover, spatial politics are inseparable from subjective politics, wherein the very meaning of the "subject of politics" shifts together with the reinvention of space. Thus, the fact that the earth is made for humans to be explored means not only that the earth is explorable, but that the subject of such spatial politics would be one who is capable of such exploration and understanding. The hegemonic conception of the political subject is "overrepresented," and so what it means to be human, and what it means to be a subject, both get defined through spatial politics. This conception of the overrepresentation of Western subjectivity in turn defines not only the existential or epistemic capacities of subjectivity but also its political commitments, such as the modern state, or the biopolitical state apparatus. In this sense, founding fables produce a kind of spatial politics that is inseparable from both the production of political subjects and from the schema for political subjectivity in general: what kinds of acts are intelligible as "political acts," or what kinds of commitments are legible as political commitments become inseparable from the spatial politics of founding fables. Indeed, as we have seen in chapter 3, necrosovereignty operates through a specific spatial politics, wherein the very organization of the right to die is shaped by its spatial politics, of the organization of spaces of mourning. Second, the spatial politics of necrosovereignty governs not only death and mourning, but also the scope of political action, as well as which acts count as political acts. Third, both the spatial politics of necrosovereignty and its mnemonic and epistemic assemblages are constituted by "founding fables," fables that provide an order of discourse for life and death, together with the possibilities and practices of grief. In this sense, certain processes of fabulation produce not only what is done "within" a given space, but also the very shape and orientation of the space of politics, together with the acts that constitute the rule-governing behaviors of that space.

What is crucial in Wynter's account of resistance, considering specifically resistances that are marked in relation to death, is the emphasis placed on the role of invention, and in particular, the role of invention as a subjective and spatial configuration. Nightmare knowledges work with stories of nothing,

138   Chapter 6

we have said: they mark modes of knowledge that do things, that transform archives, that mobilize perplexities in challenging necro-epistemologies. As Wynter suggests, however, knowledges are inseparable from invention: each founding fable is a mode of invention. In this sense, nightmare knowledges not only attest, they also invent. One of the mothers of the disappeared who has been seeking the traces of her lost brother for thirty-eight years states: "We will follow this case for as long as this earth exists." This is at once a very common and a very odd formulation. On the one hand, it attests to the ongoing struggle, and the temporal continuation of struggle, that is asserted by so many of the searchers. It is another way of saying what Berfo Kırbayır died doing, a way of saying that they will continue searching, and will continue demanding, until the end of their lives; their search and their struggle will outlive them, which is sadly neither surprising nor unusual, considering both the amount of state violence that is routinely directed at searchers, and the temporal longevity of their searches. However, it is also an odd formulation, because the mothers state that they will follow the case not only as long as they live, but as long as the earth, and particularly this earth, exists. This is a way of connecting resistance in the context of necrosovereignty not only to the deaths of the disappeared and to their own lives, but to the earth itself.

Wynter notes that each founding fable is marked by invention, and as such, each founding fable carries with it the possibility of reinvention. The possibility of reinvention is an inalienable aspect of each founding fable, albeit one that can go in various directions, not only in accordance with resistance, but also in accordance with power as well. As David Marriott says, "invention is more or less an event of epistemic breakthrough, at any rate, a kind of rupture."[20] Whereas the possibilities of rupture are always immanent in founding fables, each rupture in turn appears "outside" of these fables; just as each founding fable is shaped by its own space of otherness, each fable both produces and negates its own ruptures. The constant possibility of reinvention is what shapes the possibility of opening the spaces of otherness. This possibility is not only of fabulating otherwise, but of reinventing spaces, subjects, lives, and deaths: in the tripartite production of fables (which are simultaneously spatial, subjective, and narratival), reinventing would mean reinventing a new subject, space, and fable for politics. Wynter's account, in this sense, provides a possibility for understanding practices, such as telling stories of nothing and mobilizing perplexity, or meetings beyond the hope of finding remains, at the levels of spatial and subjective formation. These practices around deaths that do not exist, spaces that are built anew, and archives that have disappeared mark the ongoing work of reinventing a new order of things, which constitutes not only a new political organization but a new kind of space, subject, and the relationship between them. The question lies in the conjunction of these two possibilities: "How can we make these 'fables that stir the mind' subject to a new order of knowledge"[21] while considering the possibilities of reinventing a "new world order"? In other

Fables That Stir the Mind

words, under what conditions does the reinvention of a new order go hand in hand with its actualization, so that reinvention in the order of knowledge takes place on the level of spatial reorganization? When it comes to necrosovereign assemblages, the work of power/knowledge functions specifically on the order of death, around the meaning of death and dying, alongside its organization, regulation, and management. What are the orders of death that are invented and reinvented, and what is the role of the spaces, stories, and subjects around death and mourning in the necrosovereign order of death? Specifically, what are the ways in which reinvention works as a spatial tactic through which other spaces of necrosovereignty emerge as spaces of resistance that can shift the order and vocabulary of death?

Inventing Worlds, Inventing Spaces:
Autopoiesis and Spatial Reorganization

"Autopoiesis" is the term Wynter gives to the processes of reinvention that produce both new spaces and new subjects interrelatedly. This term, which she borrowed from the Chilean biologists H. R. Maturana and F. J. Varela, in Varela's words, "focuses on the interpretive capacity of the human as an agent which doesn't discover the world but rather constitutes it."[22] The juxtaposition between being and inventing, in which the subject not only occupies the role of one who is situated within a given context but who is capable of articulating new contexts and relations, lies at the heart of the conceptions of invention and reinvention. A given subject does not merely relate to a space and a political context in the way that these "give themselves" to the subject, but rather produces methods of interaction, and through that, produces the very contexts and spaces within which the subject exists. In this sense, neither the searchers nor the inhabitants of Newala Qesaba exist only as those subjected to the functioning of necrosovereignty. Their resistance, moreover, takes place not just in the sense of simple opposition or in the form of individualistic negation. Their interactions with necrosovereignty also take place as methods of invention. As noted by Max Hantel, "autopoiesis repositions the observer, the object of observation, and the experience of truth, imagining a circular and self-perpetuating relationship in which 'seeing for oneself' is not simply to adjudicate reality but to experience it and make sense of it through the same domain of the seeable that defines 'oneself' and is, in turn, partially created by 'oneself.'"[23] It is no wonder, then, that "making sense" of death-worlds in the context of necrosovereignty follows different rules than official discourse and the dominant discourses that determine lives and deaths, credible and discardable knowledges, memories and forgettings. Autopoiesis is the process of taking up another position within the context of a power relation in order to invent the terms of reality within which one is positioned, as a searcher, a victim, a remnant.

140   Chapter 6

Importantly, autopoiesis involves not only the subjective reinvention of a perspective or a viewpoint, but the reinvention of the founding fables that mark the relation between subjects and spaces. The repositioning that marks autopoiesis relates not only to the questions of who the subject is and how their subjectivity (or subjectivation) takes place, but also of where and which kinds of spaces the subject inhabits. Insofar as power works primarily on the spatial level, autopoiesis is the practice of reinventing spaces and subjects simultaneously in and through acts of resistance. As Riley Snorton says, "throughout her writings, Wynter often refers to 'autopoiesis' as a formal praxis of the sociogenic principle."[24] The Fanonian principle of sociogeny, which stands "beside phylogeny and ontogeny,"[25] denotes the invention of new power relations that take place on the level of the production of new subjects. If, for example, the subjects of necrosovereignty shift between mourners and searchers, or the dead and the disappeared, this takes place as the invention of new subjects, or the invention of other relations to living and dying that differ from and invert the contexts prescribed by necrosovereignty. Sociogeny requires negotiations of spatial relations at each turn, and so does autopoiesis.[26] As Elisabeth Paquette notes, "sociogeny is the method through which one can address power differentials within social and political spaces."[27] This addressing of power differentials prescribes the new spaces of subjective production. This subjective production is necessarily a spatial one, which means producing other kinds of spaces within which political subjectivity can exist.

This invention of new power relations and the possibilities for resistance takes place in Wynter's account as the articulation of, as Riley Snorton calls it, "a new vocabulary of living and dying."[28] In this sense, autopoiesis is not the action of identifying death where it exists, or that of making live what is dead, or of allowing the dead to die. In the context of nightmare knowledges, this point is of particular importance. Indeed, what is at stake in the searchers' organizations is not forensic investigation, which aims to establish where, how, and why their loved ones died. Hantel calls autopoiesis a "move away from autopsy," since it does not aim to identify death where it exists. Instead, "far from confirming the truth of that regime, these 'liminal subjects' conjugate alternative imaginaries that open a relationship to a world-otherwise."[29] These alternative imaginaries mark a new vocabulary for the seemingly neutral and natural categories of living and dying that are continuously infused with and through necrosovereignty.

However, there is something particular, and perhaps peculiar, about saying that such a vocabulary is filled with ghosts and the mobilization of nightmares. As Maturana and Varela assert, "All doing is knowing, and all knowing is doing."[30] In the context of nightmare knowledges, both knowing and doing pertain to the production of vocabularies of living and dying by mobilizing opacity, the epistemic resistance of perplexities and impasses, and stories of nothing. As Foucault said, there are many ways of dying, and death does not

Fables That Stir the Mind

exist merely on the individual level, but takes place inextricably on social and political levels. In Wynter's terms, humans "never live merely animate lives. Rather, we live our lives according to the regulatory representations of that which constitutes symbolic *life* and of that which constitutes its Lack, its mode of symbolic *death*."[31] These regulatory representations or founding fables around life and death are precisely what nightmare knowledges counter by shifting their terms and producing other modes of archives. Working in and through historicization and temporal displacement, nightmare knowledges mobilize the kind of opacity that is at stake in not accepting the terms of death that are produced in necrosovereignty: rather than politicizing death as opposed to life, what is at stake is the production of new terms of dying, new modes of knowing, understanding, and remembering dying. The prolonged grief and active memory of the searchers, and the decades-long organizations that take the time of grief beyond disappearances or death, attest to the kind of resistance that is operative in changing the terms of death, or as Foucault called it, changing its "currency."[32] When the searchers state that they will tell their stories even though there are no records, even when those who would be in the stories are lost in time, and even when they do not *know* if the person is indeed dead, what is at stake is the kind of resistance that consists in rejecting the terms of such deaths; in Wynter's terms, this forms an autopoietic practice that reinvents such deaths, and most importantly, the subjects of such death.

A fundamental point to take from Wynter's analysis is the importance of spatial practices not only in the discursive categories of living and dying, but also in the practices of reinvention and autopoiesis. Power works spatially: it takes up space, bulldozes it, it deploys infrastructural warfare, and so thinking about spatial methods of power requires thinking about the "how" of power. In understanding the spaces of autopoiesis, the spaces that are reinvented in nightmare knowledges, it is also necessary to think about the "how" of resistance: not in terms of how resistance should or could take place, but how it takes up space, how it takes up ordinary spaces and works on them, and deploys specific tactics on and through them. The memory spaces of the mothers' movements, such as Galatasaray Square or the Plaza de Mayo, demonstrate this kind of reinvention, one that shifts the necrosovereign order of death on the spatial level and opens up other modalities of death and dying: these form counter-spaces that alter the vocabulary of death and dying, they reinvent spaces as well as the meaning of the right to die.

This kind of reinvention works as a counter-spatial movement to the necrosovereign work of building anew: building anew on the sites of death is a way of prolonging the work of death by replacing and reconstituting the sensuous signs of space. The spatial methods of necrosovereignty forge memories around death. This kind of memory formation takes place not only through the destruction of sites, but also by building new sites that convey completely new sensations. The impact of such building anew furthers the work of death, so that the necrosovereign work of disallowing death extends in space beyond the temporality of the physical lives and deaths of the inhabitants. The reinvention of spaces as heterotopias, however, works as a counter-movement against this tendency of prolonging the work of death, precisely by prolonging the work of mourning: in spaces such as Galatasaray Square or the Plaza de Mayo, rather than a site that is built anew, tactics are deployed to invest these spaces of life with mourning. An image of the Plaza de Mayo, for example, has been printed on white handkerchiefs in order to recall the *madres* and their losses, for that symbol has come to mark not only the mothers but also, as one of the members of the Asociación said, to mark their losses, to mark the fact that disappearances occur and are a thing to be reckoned with.[33] Through the mothers' weekly meetings, the temporality of spaces of regular activity becomes both fractured and prolonged: spaces become reinvented as heterotopias, as "other spaces," with other rules of entry and exit, other temporalities, and other subjects.

It is not surprising, then, that we have visited many places, and each space is doubled by another space: spaces of mourning to counter spaces of death, sites of nightmares to counter nightmarish sites. Autopoiesis, as Wynter suggests, consists in the reinvention of spaces: this reinvention is not the necrosovereign building anew over sites of death, but rather the invention of heterotopias, spaces that counter the death-zones of necropolitics. Between the Plaza de Mayo, Newala Qaseba, Soacha, Ayatzinapa, and İstiklal Street, what is at stake is the making of new places and spaces of resistance. Through tactics of mourning, each space of death becomes a site of resistance: not only implicitly, taking place in the psyches of the subjects, but also through collective gatherings, subject formations, and prolonged resistances. Through the stories that the searchers keep on telling, the nightmares that they keep on sharing, each of these spaces is reinvented as a heterotopia. Through the work of the mourners of Newala Qaseba, a landfill becomes not just a gravesite, but a space for collective action; the Mothers of Soacha make a suburb into a place of resistance, and the Mothers of the Plaza de Mayo turn a plaza into the site of one of the longest-living social movements of recent history. Turning spaces of violence into spaces of resistance is a tactic for mobilizing nightmare knowledges. Doing so means reinventing such spaces, not into ones that are unconditionally resistant because they are new, but into ones that are resistant because they challenge what is seemingly clear, transparent, or rational. Just as a temporary house of mourning becomes a decades-long house of organizing, a public square becomes a memory space, and the mourners become searchers. Nightmare knowledges indeed attest to an entire arsenal, one that is continuously mobilized, claiming and clamoring in opacity not only for the dead and the living, but also for the ghosts that conjure entire temporalities. Insofar as "all knowing is doing" and "all doing is knowing," nightmare knowledges attest to a kind of doing that consists in producing not only new vocabularies for death and dying, but also new spaces of mourning, remembering, and resisting.

"Of Other Spaces"

Wynter asks, "How can we make these 'fables that stir the mind' subject to a new order of knowledge?"[34] This possibility of another order of knowledge, another mode of knowing, a new kind of founding fable, is particularly challenging when it comes to the necrosovereign order of things. After all, death is not just a physical or natural category: it belongs to a symbolic order of things that is enacted in necropolitics, and to an entire vocabulary of living and dying. Throughout, we have called this order of things "necrosovereignty"; this order consists not only of taking life of various sorts, but of letting die, of letting individuals, groups, and populations be dead. Necrosovereignty takes shape not only through the categorization and recategorization of objects of knowledge, but through erasures, gaps in knowledge, memories that are built anew: it is the kind of symbolic order that is filled with ghosts, voids, absences, epistemic impasses. Wynter's question thus asks not only how to change the way we make sense of things, but how we can make sense when sense-making is precisely what is targeted.

There is no power without resistance, and each symbolic order carries the possibilities of reinvention within itself. Reinvention means not only the shifting the terms, but also overhauling the entire vocabulary: it is the production of another arsenal of knowledges that can reinvent both subjects and spaces. In the case of nightmare knowledges, this reinvention takes place spatially: through the reinvention of everyday spaces as heterotopias of mourning, through meetings and storytelling, and through conjuring the ghosts of those spaces in order to change not only the sensuous signs, but the very vocabulary of spaces. This reinvention is both real and material: it takes shape in the ghosts of the disappeared who are recalled by the mothers as they march, as much as it does in the mothers' contestations of the impossibility of death in necrosovereignty. Autopoiesis takes place as a counter-movement within the work of power on subjects and spaces: resistance produces counter-sites to spaces of death as counter-sites of mourning, where the archive of the space shifts from the work of necrosovereignty to reinvent what it means to live and what it means to die. Necrosovereignty consists in the production of a kind of death that is absent, we have said: it consists in the work of producing limbos of disallowed death, where the spaces of death are disallowed and disqualified as much as the subjects thereof. Nightmare knowledges reinvent spaces, not to create a grave where there is none, but rather, in order to conjure the ghosts of spaces, in order to reinvent what it means to live, and what it means to die.

Nightmare knowledges consist in the invention of other spaces in necrosovereignty: mobilizing dreams, nightmares, impasses, and erasures, they invent spaces of prolonged mourning, spaces that shift what it means to live and what it means to die. Such spaces emerge by challenging what is seemingly clear, by making opaque what is seemingly transparent. Through memories that are not complete, records that are missing, and stories that are not corroborated, nightmare knowledges challenge not only what is sayable, but also what is possible, what is doable. The knowledges born in nightmares attest not only to the possibility, but to the constant making and remaking of new vocabularies for living and dying, new spaces for grieving, new subjects for resistance. Resistance does not occur in a void, nor does it only take place individually, or as a possibility to come. Nightmare knowledges attest to a constant arsenal, mobilized in weekly meetings, decades-long resistances, and grief, so that death is prolonged beyond what is allowed. As such, nightmare knowledges are indeed "fables that stir the mind," attesting to the constancy of new orders of knowledge that emerge in living, dying, and mourning.

CODA

> Honestly, I left out a part, I forgot . . . it is incomplete, hold on,
> let me tell it again.
> —Interview with Sevda, *Holding Up the Photograph.*

The work of a conclusion: to provide an ending, to wrap everything into a nice whole, to draw out deductions and the implications of the work, and to point to where one goes next, now that the work here is done. There is no conclusion in this case. The temporality of improper burial does not move in the direction of linear time: it wraps around and extends, it spirals and circles back. Testimony repeats itself; stories remain incomplete. Most importantly, the content that makes up *Nightmare Remains* is shaped by incompleteness: from people who have never returned to long-durational movements, there are no endings to be drawn out, final words to be spoken, or summaries that can be provided. Many of the people who make up the subjects of this book, from the Mothers of the Plaza de Mayo to the Saturday Mothers, continue to meet regularly, to tell their stories, to search for their loved ones.

As such, I do not attempt to provide any last words, summaries, or final conclusions: where the stories of the searchers and the remnants are ever continuing, those are not my words to seal, nor are they my narratives to finalize. *Nightmare Remains* ends instead with the words of Sevda, once again circling back to some other time and to some other space: "it is incomplete, hold on, let me tell it again."

NOTES

Introduction

1. Michel Foucault, *The History of Sexuality: The Will to Knowledge*, trans. Robert Hurley (London: Penguin, 1976), 138.

2. Achille Mbembe, "Necropolitics," trans. Libby Meintjes, *Public Culture* 15, no. 1 (2003): 40, original emphasis.

3. Mbembe, "Necropolitics," 12.

4. It is worth noting that Mbembe's account of necropolitics, deployed throughout this book, is different from Hans Ruin's use of the term. Ruin uses the term to "encircle the sense and implications of how the political space is constituted and upheld by both the living and the dead." See Hans Ruin, *Being with the Dead: Burial, Ancestral Politics, and the Roots of Historical Consciousness* (Stanford, CA: Stanford University Press, 2018), 7.

5. Jacques Derrida, *Specters of Marx*, trans. Peggy Kamuf (New York: Routledge, 1993), 9.

6. Verena Erlenbusch-Anderson, *Genealogies of Terrorism: Revolution, State Violence, Empire* (New York: Columbia University Press, 2018), 2.

7. Charles Mills, *The Racial Contract* (Ithaca, NY: Cornell University Press, 1999), 5.

8. "NN" letters used in various locations in Latin America (most notably in Chile and Argentina) signify nameless burials and stand as an acronym for various phrases that designate the same thing and that are used interchangeably: no name, *no nombre, non nombre, ningún nombre, nomen nescios*.

9. Valérie Loichot, *Water Graves: The Art of the Unritual in the Greater Caribbean* (Charlottesville: University of Virginia Press, 2020), 7.

10. Thomas Lacquer, *The Work of the Dead: A Cultural History of Mortal Remains* (Princeton, NJ: Princeton University Press, 2015), 18, 81. Lacquer brilliantly traces a history of Western modernity in terms of the different treatments of the dead body.

11. Ruin, *Being with the Dead*, 7.

12. Michel Foucault, "The Subject and Power," in *Power*, vol. 3 of *Essential Works of Foucault, 1954–1984*, ed. James D. Faubion, trans. Robert Hurley (New York: New Press, 2001), 341.

13. For Foucault's well-known formulation of this notion, see *History of Sexuality: The Will to Knowledge*.

14. José Medina, *The Epistemology of Resistance: Gender and Racial Oppression, Epistemic Injustice, and Resistant Imaginations* (Oxford: Oxford University Press, 2013).

15. Indeed, the first specialized body to search for disappeared people under the auspices of the United Nations was formed in a 1981 agreement between the

Greek and Turkish Cypriot communities. See Grazyna Baranowka, "*Shedding Light on the Fate of the Disappeared? Committee on Missing Persons in Cyprus,*" 3 *INT'L J. RULE L., TRANSITIONAL JUST. & HUM. RTS.* 101, 103 (2012); Ariel E. Dulitzky "The Latin-American Flavor of Enforced Disappearances," *Chicago Journal of International Law* 19, no. 2 (2019): Article 3.

16. Banu Bargu, *Starve and Immolate: The Politics of Human Weapons* (New York: Columbia University Press, 2014), 101. For a detailed analysis of Turkish politics prior to the coup, see *Starve and Immolate*, chapter 2; and Ali Yenen, "Legitimate Means of Dying: Contentious Politics of Martyrdom in the Turkish Civil War," *Behemoth: A Journal on Civilization* 12, no. 1 (2019): 14–34.

17. Murat Ergin, *Is the Turk a White Man? Race and Modernity in the Making of Turkish Identity* (Chicago: Haymarket Books, 2018).

18. Ergin, *Is the Turk a White Man?*

19. Gökçen Alpkaya, "Kayiplar Sorunu ve Turkiye," *Ankara Universitesi Siyasal Bilgiler Fakultesi Dergisi* 50, no. 3 (1995): 31–61.

20. Regional states of exception, as opposed to total and national states of exception, are constituted through increased state presence and control in particular regions, with the deployment of extra-state and paramilitary organizations, along with provisional immunities provided to these groups. The regional states of exception were in effect in most eastern regions of Turkey off and on between 1987 and 2002, and then starting again in 2015 and ongoing since then.

21. María Lugones, "Playfulness, 'World'-Traveling, and Loving Perception," in Lugones, *Pilgrimages/Peregrinajes* (Lanham, MD: Rowman and Littlefield, 2003).

22. The work of Hakikat, Adalet, Hafiza Merkezi (Truth, Memory, and Justice Center) constitutes one of the only systemic studies. For some of the few resources on this topic in Turkey, see Göral's *Unspoken Truth: Enforced Disappearances*, Bozkurt and Kaya's *Holding Up the Photograph*, and Alpkaya's "Kayiplar Sorunu ve Turkiye."

23. For two of the very few resources in the international field, see Banu Bargu, "Sovereignty as Erasure: Rethinking Enforced Disappearances," *Qui Parle* 23, no. 1 (2014): 35–75; and Meltem Ahiska, "Counter-Movement, Space, and Politics: How the Saturday Mothers of Turkey Make Enforced Disappearances Visible," in *Space and Memories of Violence*, ed. Estela Schindel and Pamela Colombi (New York: Palgrave Macmillan, 2018), 162–75.

24. Notable among the few studies are Alpkaya's "Kayiplar Sorunu ve Turkiye," Göral's *Unspoken Truth: Enforced Disappearances*, Bozkurt and Kaya's *Holding Up the Photograph*, and the work done by Insanliga Hizmet Vakfi (Association for Service to Humanity, Turkey) and and Insan Haklari Dernegi (Human Rights Association, Turkey).

25. Fabrice Lehoucq and Aníbal Pérez Liñán, "Regimes, Competition, and Military Coups in Latin America," paper presented at the American Political Science Association's 2009 annual meeting in Toronto, available at SSRN: https://ssrn.com/abstract=1449035.

26. Dulitzky, "The Latin-American Favor of Enforced Disappearances."

27. Dulitzky, "Latin-American Flavor."

28. Dulitzky, "Latin-American Flavor."

29. Dulitzky, "Latin-American Flavor."

Notes to Pages 15–19

30. See *Timurtas V. Turkey,* App. No. 23531/94, Eur. H.R. Rep. ¶¶ 82–86 (1998); and *Varnava and Others v. Turkey,* 2009-V Eur. Ct. H.R. 13, ¶ 147 (2009).

31. Gülsüm Baydar and Berfin İvegen, "Territories, Identities, and Thresholds: The Saturday Mothers Phenomenon in İstanbul," *Signs* 31, no. 3 (Spring 2006): 689, 691, explain that the Turkish case of the Saturday Mothers was inspired at its founding by the *madres* in Argentina.

32. G. W. F. Hegel, *The Phenomenology of Spirit,* trans. A. V. Miller (Oxford: Oxford University Press, 1977), §446, 266.

33. Ruin, *Being with the Dead,* 4.

34. Katherine Verdery, *The Political Lives of Dead Bodies.*

35. Sylvia Wynter, "1492: A New World View," in *Race, Discourse, and the Origin of the Americas: A New World View,* ed. Vera Lawrence Hyatt and Rex Nettleford (Washington, DC: Smithsonian Institution, 1995).

36. Édouard Glissant, *Poetics of Relation,* trans. Betsy Wing (Ann Arbor: University of Michigan Press, 2010), 8.

37. Saidiya Hartman, *Lose Your Mother: A Journey along the Atlantic Slave Route* (New York: Farrar, Straus and Giroux, 2008), 32.

38. Christina Sharpe, *In the Wake: On Blackness and Being* (Durham, NC: Duke University Press, 2016), 14.

39. Hartman, *Lose Your Mother,* 32.

40. Hartman, *Lose Your Mother,* 32.

41. It is important to highlight that I do not speak for or on behalf of Blackness or theorize Blackness as such. Invaluable work by Black thinkers exists that inhabits "the wake," speaking of, for, and on behalf of Blackness. Doing so is not my task here, as the unreflective appropriation of Blackness marks one of the key epistemic stances in histories of colonialism. In turn, the epistemic position of speaking for others is rarely, if ever, afforded to Black thought.

42. Glissant, *Poetics of Relation,* 1.

43. Anibal Quijano, "Coloniality of Power, Eurocentrism, and Latin America," *Nepantla: Views from South* 1, no. 3 (2000): 533–80.

44. María Lugones, "Heterosexualism and the Colonial/Modern Gender System," *Hypatia* 22, no. 1 (2007): 186–209.

45. Quijano gives France and Spain as examples of internal colonization. For an analysis of Russia with respect to this, see Alexander Etkind, *Internal Colonization: Russia's Imperial Experience* (Cambridge: Polity, 2011).

46. Quijano, "Coloniality of Power," 556.

47. Quijano, "Coloniality of Power," 556.

48. Quijano, "Coloniality of Power," 556.

49. Welat Zeydanlıoğlu, "The White Turkish Man's Burden: Orientalism, Kemalism and the Kurds in Turkey," *Neo-Colonial Mentalities in Contemporary Europe* 4, no. 2 (2008): 1. For further discussion of the formation of Kurdish identity as "uncivilized," see Zeynep Türkyılmaz, "Maternal Colonialism and Turkish Woman's Burden in Dersim: Educating the 'Mountain Flowers' of Dersim," *Journal of Women's History* 28, no. 3 (2016): 162–86; Zeynep Gambetti, "Decolonizing Diyarbakir: Culture, Identity and the Struggle to Appropriate Urban Space," in *Comparing Cities: The Middle East and South Asia,* ed. Kamran Asdar Ali and Martina Rieker (New York: Oxford University Press, 2010), 97–129.

50. Nelson Maldonado Torres, "On the Coloniality of Being: Contributions to the Development of a Concept," *Cultural Studies* 21, nos. 2–3 (2007): 249.

51. Diana Taylor, *Disappearing Acts* (Durham, NC: Duke University Press, 1997), 258.

52. Bilge Demirtaş, Alper Elitok, Can Gündüz, Murat Kocaman, and Osman Şişman, dirs., *Ölü ile Diri / Mirî û jî sax [The Dead and the Living]* (Siirt, Turkey, 2015).

53. "Newala Qesaba: Villas Being Built on Buried Pain," Bianet, January 5, 2023, https://m.bianet.org/english/politics/272410-newala-qesaba-villas-being -built-on-buried-pain.

54. For a map of the identified mass graves in Turkey, see http://www .ihddiyarbakir.org/Map.aspx. Unfortunately, this map is no longer available online. For references to the map, see "Mass Graves Interactive Map to Be Presented by IHD," https://anfenglishmobile.com/news/mass-graves-interactive-map -to-be-presented-by-ihd-4085.

55. Özgür Sevgi Göral, Ayhan Işık, and Özlem Kaya, *Unspoken Truth: Enforced Disappearances* (Istanbul: Truth, Justice, and Memory Center, 2013). Further reports on enforced disappearances can be found in *Turkey: Torture, Extrajudicial Executions,* "Disappearances," Report, No: eur 44/039/1992, April 30, 1992; Amnesty International, *Turkey: A Time for Action,* Report, No: eur 44/013/1994.

56. Antonius C. G. M. Robben, "Exhumations, Territoriality, and Necropolitics in Chile and Argentina," in *Necropolitics: Mass Graves and Exhumations in the Age of Human Rights,* ed. Francisco Ferrándiz and Antonius C. G. M. Robben (Philadelphia: University of Pennsylvania Press, 2015), 53–75.

57. Regional states of exception were regularly used throughout the 1990s until 2002, and were employed mostly in eastern and southeastern Turkey, in regions that are inhabited by the Kurdish population. They were then re-implemented through curfews beginning in May 2015; see http://hakikatadalethafiza.org/en /curfews-and-civillian-deaths-in-turkey/.

58. For the news on Cemile's death, see http://www.diken.com.tr/cizrede-10 -yasinda-bir-cocuk-yasamini-yitirdi-cenazesi-buzdolabinda-bekletiliyor/.

59. Foucault, *The History of Sexuality: The Will to Knowledge,* 138.

60. Michel Foucault, *Society Must Be Defended: Lectures at the Collège de France, 1975–1976,* trans. David Macey, ed. Mauro Bentani and Alessandro Fontana (New York: Picador, 1997), 240.

61. Foucault, *The History of Sexuality: The Will to Knowledge,* 136.

62. Foucault, *The History of Sexuality: The Will to Knowledge,* 138.

63. Foucault, *The History of Sexuality: The Will to Knowledge,* 139.

64. Foucault, *The History of Sexuality: The Will to Knowledge,* 138.

65. Foucault, *Society Must Be Defended,* 240.

66. For further treatment of Foucault's account of biopolitics in relation to the optimization of life, see Penelope Deutscher, *Foucault's Futures: A Critique of Reproductive Reason* (New York: Columbia University Press, 2019).

67. Jacques Derrida, *The Death Penalty, Volume 1,* trans. Peggy Kamuf (Chicago: University of Chicago Press, 2017).

68. Derrida, *The Death Penalty.*

Notes to Pages 28–34

69. Judith Butler, "Sexual Inversions," in *Feminist Interpretations of Michel Foucault*, ed. Susan J. Hekman (University Park: Penn State University Press, 1996), 63. Butler asks this question in order to refer specifically to the San Francisco AIDS epidemic and states that the slowness of the government's response to the epidemic testifies to the way in which gay men were made into a population that is cathected to death, a population akin to death.

70. Michel Foucault, *Security, Territory, Population*, trans. Graham Burchell (New York: Picador, 1997), 108.

71. Mbembe, "Necropolitics," 12.

72. Mbembe, "Necropolitics," 39.

73. Foucault, *Society Must Be Defended*, 254.

74. Foucault, *Society Must Be Defended*, 255.

75. Verena Erlenbusch-Anderson, *Genealogies of Terrorism* (New York: Columbia University Press, 2018), 10.

76. United Nations Human Rights Office, "International Convention for the Protection of All Persons from Enforced Disappearance (ICCPED)," *United Nations Human Rights Office of the High Commissioner,* 1980, http://www.ohchr.org/EN/HRBodies/CED/Pages/ConventionCED.aspx.

77. Bargu, "Sovereignty as Erasure," 41.

78. Avery F. Gordon, *Ghostly Matters: Haunting and the Sociological Imagination* (Minneapolis: University of Minnesota Press, 2008), 80.

79. Foucault, *Society Must Be Defended*, 240.

80. Gordon, *Ghostly Matters*, 80.

81. Gordon, *Ghostly Matters*, 74.

82. Banu Bargu, *Starve and Immolate*, 51.

83. Bargu, *Starve and Immolate*, 52.

84. Banu Bargu, "Another Necropolitics," *Theory and Event* 19, no. 1 (2016): 39, muse.jhu.edu/article/610222.

85. Bargu, "Another Necropolitics," 39.

86. Jean Bodin, *On Sovereignty: Four Chapters from "The Six Books on the Commonwealth,"* trans. Julian H. Franklin (Cambridge: Cambridge University Press, 1992).

87. Carl Schmitt, *Political Theology: Four Chapters on the Concept of Sovereignty*, trans. George Schwab (Chicago: University of Chicago Press, 2005).

88. Giorgio Agamben, *State of Exception,* trans. Kevin Attell (Chicago: University of Chicago Press, 2005).

89. WGEID, "Report of the Working Group on Enforced or Involuntary Disappearances," UN General Assembly, A/hrc/22/45, January 28, 2013, http://www.ohchr.org/Documents/HRBodies/HRCouncil/RegularSession/Session22/A.hrc.22.45_English.pdf.

90. WGEID, "Report of the Working Group."

91. Bargu, "Sovereignty as Erasure," 41.

92. Valérie Loichot, *Water Graves: The Art of the Unritual in the Greater Caribbean* (Charlottesville: University of Virginia Press, 2020).

93. Loichot, *Water Graves*.

94. Bilge Demirtaş, Alper Elitok, Can Gündüz, Murat Kocaman, and Osman Şişman, dirs., *Ölü ile Diri / Mirî û jî sax* [*The Dead and the Living*] (Siirt, Turkey, 2015).

152   Notes to Pages 34–40

95. Lynne Huffer, *Foucault's Strange Eros* (New York: Columbia University Press, 2020), 3.

96. Hatice Bozkurt and Özlem Kaya, *Holding Up the Photograph: Experiences of the Women Whose Husbands Were Forcibly Disappeared* (Istanbul: Hakikat Adalet Hafıza Merkezi, 2014).

97. Robben, "Exhumations, Territoriality," 68.

98. Rudolf Mrázek makes a similar point in relation to camp life: modernity did not ebb away in the camps: rather, they were painfully modern, and in many ways, constitutive of modernity. See Rudolf Mrázek, *The Complete Lives of Camp People* (Durham, NC: Duke University Press, 2020).

99. Ruin, *Being with the Dead*, 3.

100. See Seyla Benhabib, "Multiculturalism and Gendered Citizenship," in *The Claims of Culture: Equality and Diversity in the Global Era* (Princeton, NJ: Princeton University Press, 2002), 82–104; and Mary C. Rawlinson, "Beyond Antigone: Ismene, Gender and the Right to Life," in *The Returns of Antigone*, ed. Tina Chanter and Sean D. Kirkland (Albany: State University of New York Press, 2014), 101–24.

101. Bonnie Honig, "Antigone's Laments, Creon's Grief," in *The Returns of Antigone*, ed. Tina Chanter and Sean D. Kirkland (Albany: State University of New York Press, 2014), 29.

102. Ruin, *Being with the Dead*, 7.

103. G. W. F. Hegel, *Phenomenology of Spirit*, trans. A. V. Miller (Oxford: Oxford University Press, 1977).

104. Cecilia Sjöhölm, "Bodies in Exile," in *The Returns of Antigone,* ed. Tina Chanter and Sean D. Kirkland (Albany: State University of New York Press, 2014), 288.

105. Judith Butler, *Frames of War: When Is Life Grievable?* (New York: Verso, 2010), 38.

106. Butler, *Frames of War*, 38.

107. Sharpe, *In the Wake*, 17.

108. For further information on social death, see Orlando Patterson, *Slavery and Social Death* (Cambridge, MA: Harvard University Press, 1982).

109. Calvin Warren, *Ontological Terror: Blackness, Being, and Emancipation* (Durham, NC: Duke University Press, 2018).

110. Sharpe, *In the Wake*.

111. Foucault, *Society Must Be Defended*, 240.

112. Foucault, *Society Must Be Defended*, 240.

113. See Michel Foucault, *The Punitive Society: Lectures at the Collège de France, 1972–1973*, trans. Graham Burchell, ed. Arnold Davidson (Basingstoke, UK: Palgrave Macmillan, 2015). Here the basic distinction Foucault is drawing concerns the mechanisms of punishment involved in these situations: he underlines that the methods involved in systems that see death as the repayment of debt are drastically different from death in societies of confinement that understand death as "absolute closure" and "absolute security."

114. Foucault, *The Punitive Society*.

115. Foucault, *The History of Sexuality: The Will to Knowledge*, 138.

116. Foucault, *Society Must Be Defended*, 248.

117. Foucault, *Society Must Be Defended*, 248.

Notes to Pages 40–46

118. One might think here about the practices that make death into an abstract, private, and individual phenomenon as well as a phenomenon of consumption, such as overly expensive casket prices and funerals and the debate between cremation and inhumation; these practices aim to claim that even in death we will have control over the bodies of the dead. See Derrida, *The Death Penalty*.

119. As Banu Bargu notes, one of the overarching themes of the hunger strikes in Turkey between 2000 and 2007 was articulated in light of the right to die. See *Starve and Immolate*.

120. Gordon, *Ghostly Matters*, 78.

121. Demirtaş et al., *Ölü ile Diri / Mîrî û jî sax*.

122. Gordon, *Ghostly Matters*, 113.

Chapter 2

1. Rachelle Krygier, "Colombia Is Exhuming Graves of Civilians Allegedly Killed by Soldiers," *Washington Post*, December 18, 2019, https://www.washingtonpost.com/world/the_americas/colombia-exhuming-graves-of-civilians-allegedly-killed-by-soldiers/2019/12/17/0d99e428-20e5-11ea-b034-de7dc2b5199b_story.html.

2. Colombia Reports, "Extrajudicial Executions," 2019, https://colombiareports.com/false-positives/.

3. Mike Gatehouse, "Colombia: False Positives, Failed Justice," Latin America Bureau, 2018, https://lab.org.uk/colombia-false-positives-failed-justice/.

4. Human Rights Watch, "Colombia: Top Brass Linked to Extrajudicial Executions," 2015, https://www.hrw.org/news/2015/06/24/colombia-top-brass-linked-extrajudicial-executions#.

5. Joe Parkin Daniels, "Colombian Army Killed Thousands More Civilians Than Reported, Study Claims," *The Guardian*, 2018, https://www.theguardian.com/world/2018/may/08/colombia-false-positives-scandal-casualties-higher-thought-study.

6. Achille Mbembe, *On the Postcolony*, trans. A. M. Berrett, Janet Roitman, Murray Last, Achille Mbembe, and Steven Rendall (Berkeley: University of California Press, 2001).

7. Michel Foucault, "Prison Talk," in *Power/Knowledge: Selected Interviews and Other Writings*, trans. Colin Gordon, Leo Marshal, John Mepham, and Kate Sopher, ed. Colin Gordon (New York: Pantheon, 1980), 51–52.

8. Foucault, "Prison Talk," 51–52.

9. Hubert L. Dreyfus and Paul Rabinow, *Michel Foucault: Beyond Structuralism and Hermeneutics* (Chicago: University of Chicago Press, 2014), 117.

10. For more information, see Foucault's *History of Sexuality: The Will to Knowledge*, his *Abnormal* lectures, and *Discipline and Punish*.

11. Foucault, *History of Sexuality: The Will to Knowledge*, *Abnormal* lectures, and *Discipline and Punish*.

12. Mary Beth Mader, "Knowledge," in *The Cambridge Foucault Lexicon*, ed. Leonard Lawlor and John Nale (Cambridge: Cambridge University Press, 2014), 233, original emphasis.

13. Colin Koopman, *Genealogy as Critique: Foucault and the Problems of Modernity* (Bloomington: Indiana University Press, 2013), 35.

14. Koopman, *Genealogy as Critique*, 37.

15. Foucault, *The History of Sexuality: The Will to Knowledge*, 42.

16. Jasbir K. Puar, *Terrorist Assemblages: Homonationalism in Queer Times* (Durham, NC: Duke University Press, 2007), 35.

17. Butler, *Frames of War*, 34.

18. The question of whether this is what Foucault is doing is one that I will not delve into here, as there are invaluable accounts in Foucault scholarship to complicate his relationship to his theory. For further discussion, see Amy Allen, *The Politics of Ourselves* (New York: Columbia University Press, 2013); Koopman, *Genealogy as Critique*; Ladelle McWhorter, *Bodies and Pleasures* (Bloomington: Indiana University Press, 1999); and Lynne Huffer, *Mad for Foucault: Rethinking the Foundations of Queer Theory* (New York: Columbia University Press, 2009).

19. Michel Foucault, *The Archaeology of Knowledge*, trans. Rupert Swyer (New York: Penguin Random House, 2012), 127.

20. Samir Haddad, "Examining Genealogy as Engaged Critique," *Foucault Studies* 1, no. 28 (2020): 4–9.

21. Allen, *The Politics of Ourselves*, 42.

22. Foucault, *Society Must Be Defended*, 11.

23. Foucault, *Society Must Be Defended*, 6.

24. Foucault, *Society Must Be Defended*, 6.

25. Gordon, *Ghostly Matters*, 225.

26. Robben, "Exhumations, Territoriality."

27. Gordon, *Ghostly Matters*. 80.

28. Alpkaya, "Kayiplar sorunu ve Turkiye," 48.

29. Bargu, "Sovereignty as Erasure," 61.

30. Bargu, "Sovereignty as Erasure," 61.

31. Human Rights Watch, "Colombia: Top Brass Linked to Extrajudicial Executions."

32. Taylor, *Disappearing Acts*, 148.

33. Taylor, *Disappearing Acts*, 150.

34. Taylor, *Disappearing Acts*.

35. Quoted in Taylor, *Disappearing Acts*, 148.

36. Foucault, *Society Must Be Defended*, 6.

37. Foucault, *Society Must Be Defended*, 6.

38. Foucault, *Society Must Be Defended*, 6.

39. Foucault, *Society Must Be Defended*, 9.

40. Foucault, *Society Must Be Defended*, 9.

41. Miranda Fricker, *Epistemic Injustice: Power and the Ethics of Knowing* (Oxford: Oxford University Press, 2007), 19.

42. Mária Fernanda Perez Solla, *Enforced Disappearances in International Human Rights* (Jefferson, NC: McFarland, 2006), 8.

43. Göral, Işık, and Kaya, *Unspoken Truth: Enforced Disappearances*, 38.

44. Göral, Işık, and Kaya, *Unspoken Truth: Enforced Disappearances*, 42.

45. Fricker, *Epistemic Injustice*, 4.

46. Kristie Dotson, "A Cautionary Tale: On Limiting Epistemic Oppression," *Social Epistemology* 28, no. 2 (2014): 26.

47. Alpkaya, "Kayiplar sorunu ve Turkiye," 48.

48. Alpkaya, "Kayiplar soruni ve Turkiye," 48.

49. Fricker, *Epistemic Injustice*, 1.

Notes to Pages 57–66

50. Bozkurt and Kaya, *Holding Up the Photograph*.
51. Bozkurt and Kaya, *Holding Up the Photograph*.
52. Taylor, *Disappearing Acts*, 187–88.
53. Taylor, *Disappearing Acts*, 187–88.
54. Taylor, *Disappearing Acts*, 187–88.
55. Diana Taylor explains the performative dimensions of the mothers' movements as being a trap as much as a strategy.
56. Fricker, *Epistemic Injustice*, 37.
57. Gordon, *Ghostly Matters*, 72.
58. BBC, "Davutoğlu: Cizre'de tek bir sivil kayıp yok," 2015, https://www.bbc.com/turkce/haberler/2015/09/150910_davutoglu_cizre.
59. María del Rosario Acosta López, "One Hundred Years of Forgottenness," special issue on "Philosophy in Colombia," *Philosophical Readings* 11, no. 3 (2019): 165.

Chapter 3

1. A version of this chapter first appeared in *Theory and Event* 25, no. 1 (January 2022): 25–46.
2. For further information on the specific context of Turkey's "war on terror" between 2015 and 2017, see Bargu, "Another Necropolitics."
3. Serra Hakyemez, "Sur: A City of Imagination, a City under Occupation," *Middle Eastern Report* 287 (Summer 2018): 47.
4. Hakyemez, "Sur: A City of Imagination," 47.
5. See TOKI, "Sur Yeniden Insa Ediliyor," October 2017, https://www.toki.gov.tr/haber/sur-yeniden-insa-ediliyor.
6. See Mehmet Efe Altay, "Cizre'de Bodrum Kat Karanligi: Ilk gunden bugune neler yasandi?" [The Darkness of Basements in Cizre: What Happened since Day One?]. T24, September 8, 2016, https://t24.com.tr/haber/cizrede-bodrum-kat-karanligi-ilk-gunden-bugune-neler-yasandi,327392.
7. See the project plans at TOKI, "İllere Göre Projeler," https://www.toki.gov.tr/illere-gore-projeler/749.
8. Mbembe, *On the Postcolony*, 26.
9. Mbembe, *On the Postcolony*, 40.
10. Mbembe, *On the Postcolony*, 27–28.
11. Taybet İnan, for example, lost her life in Cizre when she was returning from her neighbor's house. Her body remained on the street for seven days while her family, inside the house, was not allowed to bring her body inside. See İlgili Haberler, "Taybet İnan 23 gün sonra defnedildi: Eşi ve çocukları cenazeye katılamadı," T24, October 11, 2016, http://t24.com.tr/haber/taybet-inan-23-gun-sonra-defnedildi-esi-ve-cocuklari-izin-verilmedigi-icin-cenazeye-katilamadi,323748; and Ali Bozan, dir., *7 Roj 7 Şev*. (Silopi, Turkey, 2017).
12. Mbembe, "Necropolitics," 27–28.
13. Mbembe, "Necropolitics," 29.
14. Mbembe, "Necropolitics," 29.
15. Mbembe, "Necropolitics," 29. It is worth noting that Mbembe's examples specifically refer to Palestine under siege, though the spatial methods of necropolitics are not necessarily geographically specific.
16. See Hakyemez, "Sur: A City of Imagination," 49.

17. Michel Foucault, *Security, Territory, Population: Lectures at the Collège de France, 1977–1978,* trans. Graham Burchell, ed. Michel Senellart (London: Picador, 2004), 30.

18. Michel Foucault, "Of Other Spaces," trans. Jay Miskowiec, *Diacritics* 16, no. 1 (Spring 1986): 23.

19. Foucault, "Of Other Spaces," 23.

20. Marcel Proust, *In Search of Lost Time, Volume 1: Swann's Way,* trans. C. K. Scott Moncrieff and Terrence Kilmartin (New York: Random House, 1992), 60–63.

21. Hakyemez, "Sur: A City of Imagination," 48.

22. Alia Al-Saji, "Memory of Another Past: Bergson, Deleuze, and a New Theory of Time," *Continental Philosophy Review* 37 (2004): 212.

23. Keith Ansell-Pearson, "Deleuze and the Overcoming of Memory," in *Memory: Histories, Theories, Debates,* ed. Susannah Radstone and Bill Schwarz (New York: Fordham University Press, 2010), 166.

24. Gilles Deleuze, *Proust and Signs,* trans. Richard Howard (Minneapolis: University of Minnesota Press, 2000), 57.

25. See Ayça Söylemez, "Cizre Bodrumları AİHM'de Görüşülecek," Bianet, November 12, 2018, http://bianet.org/bianet/insan-haklari/202537-cizre-bodrum lari-aihm-de-gorusulecek; and Vecdi Erbay, "79 Gün Sonra Cizre," Bianet, March 3, 2016, https://bianet.org/bianet/insan-haklari/172647-79-gun-sonra-cizre.

26. Ansell-Pearson, "Deleuze and the Overcoming of Memory," 163.

27. Al-Saji, "Memory of Another Past," 210.

28. Gilles Deleuze, *Difference and Repetition,* trans. Paul Patton (New York: Columbia University Press, 1968), 102.

29. Diken, "TİHV raporu: Diyarbakır'ın Sur ilçesindeki sokağa çıkma yasakları dünya rekoru," Diken.com, August 8, 2017, http://www.diken.com.tr/tihv-raporu-diyarbakirin-sur-ilcesindeki-sokaga-cikma-yasaklari-dunya-rekoru/.

30. Cathy Caruth, *Unclaimed Experience: Trauma, Narrative, History* (Baltimore: Johns Hopkins University Press, 1996), 4.

31. Caruth, *Unclaimed Experience,* 17.

32. Maria del Rosario Acosta López, "Gramáticas de lo inaudito as Decolonial Grammars: Notes for a Decolonization of Listening," *Research in Phenomenology* 52, no. 2 (2022): 203–22. Acosta López explains this as a "colonizing aspect" of trauma, wherein erasure works to sustain violence.

33. Gordon, *Ghostly Matters,* 164.

34. Gordon, *Ghostly Matters,* xvi.

35. Gordon, *Ghostly Matters,* xvi.

36. Gordon, *Ghostly Matters,* 98.

37. Derrida in "Archive Fever" discusses the work of the archive as fundamentally connected to the death drive, where the aim of remembering and archiving is inseparable from the danger of forgetting. See Jacques Derrida, "Archive Fever: A Freudian Impression," trans. Eric Prenowitz, *Diacritics* 25, no. 2 (Summer 1995): 9–63.

38. Walter Benjamin, "Excavation and Memory," in *Selected Writings, Vol. 2, Part 2 (1931–1934),* ed. Marcus Paul Bullock, Michael William Jennings, Howard Eiland, and Gary Smith (Cambridge, MA: Belknap Press of Harvard University Press, 2005), 576.

Notes to Pages 74–83

39. Benjamin, "Excavation and Memory," 576.

40. Achille Mbembe, "Power of the Archive and Its Limits," in *Refiguring the Archive*, ed. Caroline Hamilton, Verne Harris, Jane Taylor, Michele Pickover, Graeme Reid, and Razia Saleh (Dordrecht: Springer, 2002), 21.

41. Mbembe, "Power of the Archive," 22.

42. Mbembe, "Power of the Archive," 22.

43. Derrida, "Archive Fever," 9.

44. See Yusuf Nazim, "Sur'un Gözyaşları—II," T24, March 21, 2016, https://t24.com.tr/yazarlar/yusuf-nazim/surun-gozyaslari-ii,14154.

45. See Hatice Kamer, "Cizre Koca Bir Mezarliga Donmus," BBC, March 3, 2016, https://www.bbc.com/turkce/haberler/2016/03/160303_cizre_hatice_kamer_izlenim.

46. Kamer, "Cizre Koca Bir Mezarliga Donmus."

47. Michel Foucault, "Nietzsche, Genealogy, History," in *Aesthetics, Methods, and Epistemology*, vol. 2 of *Essential Works of Foucault, 1954–1984*, ed. James D. Faubion (New York: New Press, 1994), 377.

48. Foucault, "Nietzsche, Genealogy, History," 377.

49. Michel Foucault, "Lives of Infamous Men," in *Power*, vol. 3 of *Essential Works of Foucault, 1954–1984*, ed. James D. Faubion (New York: New Press, 2001), 163.

50. See Antoinette Burton, "Introduction: Archive Fever, Archive Stories," in *Archive Stories: Facts, Fictions, and the Writing of History*, ed. Antoinette Burton (Durham, NC: Duke University Press, 2005), 9.

51. See Altay, "Cizre'de Bodrum Kat Karanligi."

52. Kathy Ferguson, "Theorizing Shiny Things," *Theory and Event* 11, no. 4 (2008), muse.jhu.edu/article/257578.

53. Ferguson, "Theorizing Shiny Things." Ferguson discusses this possibility in the relation between "specific archives" and "general archives," with the latter referring to the orders of intelligibility that tie archival sets together.

54. Hartman, *Lose Your Mother*, 17.

55. Gordon, *Ghostly Matters,*152.

56. Foucault, "Nietzsche, Genealogy, History," 385.

57. Söylemez, "Cizre Bodrumları AİHM'de Görüşülecek," Bianet, http://bianet.org/bianet/insan-haklari/202537-cizre-bodrumlari-aihm-de-gorusulecek.

58. Mbembe, "Necropolitics," 36.

Interlude

1. "A Letter from Emine Ocak. The Mother of Hasan Ocak," *Cumhuriyet*, August 29, 2019, https://www.cumhuriyet.com.tr/haber/hasan-ocakin-annesi-emine-ocaktan-mektup-1556175.

2. Özgür Sevgi Göral, Ayhan Işık, and Özlem Kaya, *Unspoken Truth: Enforced Disappearances*, trans. Nazim Hikmet Richard Dikbas (Istanbul: Truth, Justice, and Memory Center, 2013), 69; interview, Şırnak-Cizre, 04.12.2012.

3. "Campos Barra Eduardo Alejandro," Memoria Viva, https://memoriaviva.com/nuevaweb/detenidos-desaparecidos/desaparecidos-c/campos-barra-eduardo-alejandro/.

4. *Unspoken Truth*, 54: interview, İstanbul, 10. 8. 2012.

158 Notes to Pages 83–92

5. "Saturday Mother Zeycan Yedigol Has Passed Away," *Bianet*, November 23, 2020, https://m.bianet.org/english/life/234850-saturday-mother-zeycan-yedigol-has-passed-away.

6. "Carlos Gustavo Contiñas," Comisión de Trabajo por la Reconstrucción de Nuestra Identidad, https://www.argentina.gob.ar/obraspublicas/comision-ddhh/corti%C3%B1as-carlos-gustavo.

7. *Unspoken Truth*, 79, interview, Şırnak-Cizre, February 9, 2012.

8. "860 Week Call for Gathering," *Cumartesi Anneleri (Saturday Mothers)*, https://www.youtube.com/watch?v=EBLAl5XYivk.

9. "Children Born in Captivity: Jeger-Gonzalez, Olga Gonzales, Maurice Jeger," Abuelas.org, https://abuelas.org.ar/idiomas/english/cases/cautiverio/14-jeger-gonzalez.htm.

10. "Cemil Kirbayir Dosyasi, Zaman Asimi Sebebiyle Kapatilmak Uzere" [The Case of Cemil Kirbayir is About to Be Closed due to the Statute of Limitations], *Cumartesi Anneleri (Saturday Mothers)*, https://www.youtube.com/watch?v=jW9oWsedfAA.

11. "Cumartesi Annesi Elmas Eren Hayatini Kaybetti" [Saturday Mother Elmas Eren Loses Her Life], Bianet, https://m.bianet.org/bianet/human-rights/211898-saturday-mother-elmas-eren-loses-her-life.

12. Raul Zúrita, *Song for His Disappeared Love*, trans. Daniel Borzutsky (Notre Dame, IN: Action Books, 2010), 11.

13. Demirtaş et al., *Ölü ile Diri / Mirî û jî sax*.

14. "Gozaltinda Kaybedilislerinin 27. Yilinda Fehmi Tosun ve Huseyin Aydemir' I Unutmadik" [On the 27th Anniversary of Their Disappearance under Custody, We Have Not Forgotten Fehmi Tosun and Huseyin Aydemir], *Cumartesi Anneleri (Saturday Mothers)*, https://www.youtube.com/watch?v=GcFX7dIvBLA.

15. Alicia Partnoy, *The Little School: Tales of Disappearance and Survival*, trans. Alicia Partnoy, Lois Athey, and Sandra Braunstein (San Francisco: Cleis, 1986), 127.

16. "Hayrettin Eren," *Cumartesi Anneleri (Saturday Mothers)*, https://www.youtube.com/watch?v=UFtrWLTFyMg.

17. Zurita, *Song for His Disappeared Love*, 9.

Chapter 4

1. Human Rights Foundation of Turkey, "16 Ağustos 2015–16 Ağustos 2017 Bilgi Notu," http://tihv.org.tr/16-agustos-2015-16-agustos-2016-tarihleri-arasinda-sokaga-cikma-yasaklari-ve-yasamini-yitiren-siviller-bilgi-notu/.

2. Seyhmus Cakan, "Turkish 'Cleansing' Operation Rocks Southeastern Cities," Reuters, October 25, 2015, https://www.reuters.com/article/us-turkey-kurds-idUSKBN0U80FQ20151226.

3. "Taybet İnan 23 gün sonra defnedildi: Eşi ve çocukları cenazeye katılamadı," T24, January 11, 2016, http://t24.com.tr/haber/taybet-inan-23-gun-sonra-defnedildi-esi-ve-cocuklari-izin-verilmedigi-icin-cenazeye-katilamadi.323748.

4. Bozan, *7 Roj 7 Şev*.

5. Demirtaş et al., *Ölü ile Diri / Mirî û jî sax*.

6. Göral, Işık, and Kaya, *Unspoken Truth: Enforced Disappearances*.

7. Michael Taussig, *The Nervous System* (New York: Routledge, 1992), 20.

8. Foucault, *History of Sexuality: The Will to Knowledge*, 95–96.

Notes to Pages 93–103

9. Edward Said, "Foucault and the Imagination of Power," in *Foucault: A Critical Reader*, ed. David Couzens Hoy (Cambridge, MA: Blackwell, 1986), 151.

10. For more on the discussion of Foucault and resistance, see John Mucklebauer, "On Reading Differently: Through Foucault on Resistance," *College English* 63, no. 1 (2000): 71–94; Jana Sawicki, *Disciplining Foucault: Feminism, Power, and the Body* (New York: Routledge, 1991); Brent Pickett, *On the Use and Abuse of Foucault for Politics* (Lanham, MD: Lexington Books, 2005); and Judith Butler, *Bodies That Matter* (New York: Routledge, 1993).

11. Richard Bernstein, "Foucault: Critique as a Philosophic Ethos," in *Critique and Power: Recasting the Foucault/Habermas Debate*, ed. Michael Kelly (Cambridge, MA: MIT Press, 1994), 76.

12. Foucault, *Security, Territory, Population*, 195.

13. Kevin Thompson, "Forms of Resistance: Foucault on Tactical Reversal and Self-Formation," *Continental Philosophy Review* 36, no. 2 (2003): 118.

14. Thompson, "Forms of Resistance," 118.

15. Bargu, *Starve and Immolate*, 54.

16. Bargu, *Starve and Immolate*, 85.

17. José Medina, *The Epistemology of Resistance: Gender and Racial Oppression, Epistemic Injustice, and Resistant Imaginations* (Oxford: Oxford University Press, 2013).

18. Medina distinguishes between "positive" and "negative" in the sense of "beneficial" or "harmful": thus, the internal opposing force one experiences in the face of epistemic injustice, for Medina, can be positive in the sense that it may be beneficial to a subject because it unmasks bodies of ignorance, and yet it can also be harmful because it can display a reluctance to learn or a refusal to believe. See Medina, *The Epistemology of Resistance*, 50.

19. Medina, *The Epistemology of Resistance*, 6.

20. José Medina, "Toward a Foucauldian Epistemology of Resistance: Counter-Memory, Epistemic Friction, and *Guerilla Pluralism*," *Foucault Studies* 12 (2011): 10.

21. Medina, "Toward a Foucauldian Epistemology," 16.

22. Glissant, *Poetics of Relation*, 11.

23. Glissant, *Poetics of Relation*, 62.

24. John E. Drabinski, *Glissant and the Middle Passage: Philosophy, Beginning, Abyss* (Minneapolis: University of Minnesota Press, 2019), 16.

25. Glissant, *Poetics of Relation*, 9.

26. Glissant, *Poetics of Relation*, 8.

27. Glissant, *Poetics of Relation*, 8.

28. Glissant, *Poetics of Relation*, 187.

29. Glissant, *Poetics of Relation*, 7.

30. Glissant, *Poetics of Relation*, 7.

31. Glissant, *Poetics of Relation*, 191.

32. Benjamin Davis, "The Politics of Édouard Glissant's Right to Opacity," *CLR James Journal* 25, no. 1–2 (2019): 59–70.

33. Glissant, *Poetics of Relation*, 194.

34. Drabinski, *Glissant and the Middle Passage*, 13

35. Göral, Işık, and Kaya, *Unspoken Truth: Enforced Disappearances*, 78.

36. Bozkurt and Kaya, *Holding Up the Photograph*.

160   Notes to Pages 104–116

37. Göral, Işık, and Kaya, *Unspoken Truth: Enforced Disappearances*, 87.

38. Taussig, *The Nervous System*, 21

39. Gordon, *Ghostly Matters*, 87.

40. Taussig, *The Nervous System*, 29.

41. Taussig, *The Nervous System*, 76.

42. Medina, *The Epistemology of Resistance*, 196.

43. Göral, Işık, and Kaya, *Unspoken Truth: Enforced Disappearances*, 88.

44. Göral, Işık, and Kaya, *Unspoken Truth: Enforced Disappearances*, 88.

45. Medina, *The Epistemology of Resistance*, 197.

46. Medina, *The Epistemology of Resistance*, 196.

47. Gordon, *Ghostly Matters*, 102.

48. Göral, Işık, and Kaya, *Unspoken Truth: Enforced Disappearances*, 75.

49. Acosta López, "One Hundred Years of Forgottenness," 169.

50. Acosta López, "One Hundred Years of Forgottenness," 169.

51. Demirtaş et al., *Ölü ile Diri / Mirî û jî sax*.

52. Bozkurt and Kaya, *Holding Up the Photograph*.

53. Özgür Sevgi Göral, "Waiting for the Disappeared: Waiting as a Form of Resilience and the Limits of Legal Space in Turkey," *Social Anthropology/Anthropologie Sociale* 29, no. 3 (2021): 805.

54. Göral, "Waiting for the Disappeared," 807.

55. Gordon, *Ghostly Matters*, 66.

Chapter 5

1. Peter Read and Marivic Wyndham, *Narrow but Endlessly Deep: The Struggle for Memorialisation in Chile since the Transition to Democracy* (Sydney: Australian National University Press, 2016).

2. Hartman, *Lose Your Mother*, 17.

3. Saidiya Hartman, "Venus in Two Acts," *Small Axe* 12, no. 2 (2008): 2.

4. Hartman, *Lose Your Mother*, 19.

5. Read and Wyndham, *Narrow but Endlessly Deep*, 45.

6. Paul Angelo, "Colombia: False Positives, Failed Justice," Latin American Bureau, May 24, 2018, https://lab.org.uk/colombia-false-positives-failed-justice/.

7. Achille Mbembe, "Provisional Notes on the Postcolony," *Africa: Journal of the International African Institute* 62, no. 1 (1992): 15.

8. Diana Taylor, "Military Males, 'Bad' Women, Dirty War," in *Disappearing Acts: Spectacles of Gender and Nationalism in Argentina's "Dirty War"* (Durham, NC: Duke University Press, 1997), 84–85.

9. Mbembe, "Provisional Notes," 15–16.

10. Foucault, *Security, Territory, Population*, 267.

11. Foucault, "The Subject and Power," 330.

12. Foucault, *Security, Territory, Population*, 265.

13. Interview with Hasene, in Hatice Bozkurt and Özlem Kaya, *Holding Up the Photograph: Experiences of the Women Whose Husbands Were Forcibly Disappeared* (Istanbul: Hakikat Adalet Hafıza Merkezi, 2014), 32–33.

14. Bozkurt and Kaya, *Holding Up the Photograph*, 33.

15. Bozkurt and Kaya, *Holding Up the Photograph*, 33–34.

16. Interview in Demirtaş et al., *Ölü ile Diri / Mirî û jî sax*.

17. Foucault, *Security, Territory, Population*, 265.

Notes to Pages 117–126

18. Foucault, "Lives of Infamous Men," 160.
19. Foucault, "Lives of Infamous Men," 160.
20. Foucault, "Lives of Infamous Men," 162.
21. Foucault, "Lives of Infamous Men," 162.
22. Foucault, "Lives of Infamous Men," 165.
23. Lynne Huffer, "Foucault's Fossils: Life Itself and the Return to Nature in Feminist Philosophy," *Foucault Studies* 20 (2015): 139.
24. Foucault, "Lives of Infamous Men," 158, 162.
25. Foucault, "Lives of Infamous Men," 160.
26. Read and Wyndham, *Narrow but Endlessly Deep*, 54.
27. Read and Wyndham, *Narrow but Endlessly Deep*, 54.
28. Read and Wyndham, *Narrow but Endlessly Deep*, 54.
29. Göral, Işık, and Kaya, *Unspoken Truth: Enforced Disappearances*, 48–49.
30. Michel Foucault, *Speech Begins after Death*, ed. Philippe Artières, trans. Robert Bononno (Minneapolis: University of Minnesota Press, 1968), 40.
31. Foucault, *Speech Begins after Death*, 45.
32. Foucault, *Speech Begins after Death*, 40.
33. Göral, Işık, and Kaya, *Unspoken Truth: Enforced Disappearances*, 40.
34. Foucault, *Speech Begins after Death*, 44.
35. Mbembe, *On the Postcolony*, 172.
36. Hartman, "Venus in Two Acts," 8.
37. Nowhere is this as clear as in the demand of the Mothers of the Plaza de Mayo: "*Aparición con Vida*." The task of demanding is not to "put to death" what is in limbo. The goal is a demand to bring back alive.
38. Natalia Sabogal Escobar and Ivonne Mondragón Alonso, "Capítulo 1, 'Nada más que la verdad': Relato de un 'falso positivo,'" in *El Camino hacia la paz: Investigaciones sobre la violencia y la paz en colombia* (Bogotá: Ediciones USTA, 2017), 31; Human Rights Watch, "Colombia: Top Brass Linked to Extrajudicial Executions."
39. Human Rights Watch, "Colombia: Top Brass Linked to Extrajudicial Executions."
40. Foucault, "Lives of Infamous Men," 168.
41. Hartman, "Venus in Two Acts," 11
42. Bozkurt and Kaya, *Holding Up the Photograph*, 58.
43. Hartman, "Venus in Two Acts," 11.
44. Hartman, "Venus in Two Acts," 11.
45. Göral, Işık, and Kaya, *Unspoken Truth: Enforced Disappearances*, 31.
46. Hartman, "Venus in Two Acts," 12.
47. Göral, Işık, and Kaya, *Unspoken Truth: Enforced Disappearances*, 33.
48. Göral, Işık, and Kaya, *Unspoken Truth: Enforced Disappearances*, 33.
49. Göral, Işık, and Kaya, *Unspoken Truth: Enforced Disappearances*, 33.
50. Mbembe, *On the Postcolony*, 206.
51. Hartman, "Venus in Two Acts," 11.
52. Hartman, "Venus in Two Acts," 11.
53. Mbembe, *On the Postcolony*, 206.
54. Mbembe, *On the Postcolony*, 206.
55. Hartman, "Venus in Two Acts," 12.
56. Bozkurt and Kaya, *Holding Up the Photograph*, 52.

57. Hartman, "Venus in Two Acts."

58. Mabel Bellucci, "Childless Motherhood: Interview with Nora Cortiñas, a Mother of the Plaza de Mayo, Argentina," *Reproductive Health Matters* 7, no. 13 (May 1999): 83–88.

Chapter 6

1. For more, see "Galatasaray Square: A Recognized Memory Space," Hafiza Merkezi, August 13, 2020, https://hakikatadalethafiza.org/en/galatasaray-square -a-recognized-memory-space/.

2. "Galatasaray Square: A Recognized Memory Space," Hafiza Merkezi.

3. Fernando J. Bosco, "Human Rights Politics and Performances of Memory: Conflicts among *Madres de Plaza de Mayo* in Argentina," *Social and Cultural Geography* 5, no. 3 (2004): 381–402.

4. Bozkurt and Kaya, *Holding Up the Photograph*.

5. Michel Foucault, "Of Other Spaces," trans. Jay Miskowiec, *Diacritics* 16, no. 1 (Spring 1986): 24.

6. Unspoken Truth, 79, interview, Sirnak-Cizre, 02.09.2012.

7. Foucault, "Of Other Spaces," 24.

8. Foucault, "Of Other Spaces," 24.

9. Foucault, "Of Other Spaces," 25.

10. Foucault, "Of Other Spaces," 25.

11. Foucault, "Of Other Spaces," 25.

12. Göral, Işık, and Kaya, *Unspoken Truth: Enforced Disappearances*, 38.

13. Foucault, "Of Other Spaces," 26.

14. Foucault, "Of Other Spaces," 26.

15. Fernando J. Bosco, "The Madres de Plaza de Mayo and Three Decades of Human Rights Activism: Embeddedness, Emotions, and Social Movements," *Annals of the Association of American Geographers* 96, no. 2 (2006): 342–68.

16. Bosco, "The Madres de Plaza Mayo."

17. Sylvia Wynter, "Columbus, the Ocean Blue, and Fables That Stir the Mind," in *Poetics of the Americas: Race, Founding, Textuality*, ed. Bainard Cowan and Jefferson Humphries (Baton Rouge: Louisiana State University Press, 1997), 154.

18. Wynter, "Columbus, the Ocean Blue," 154.

19. In Wynter's account, this shift occurred from a worldview shaped by Scholasticism, which understood the earth as bounded by the limits of the grace of God to the poetics of "propter nos." The shift was from a world shaped by the distinction between "inhabitable and uninhabitable lands" to a world made for humankind to be explored; from a political subject that is fallen to one that is rational; and from a space of otherness shaped by nonhuman monstrosity to one of racialized hierarchization. For further treatment, see Selin Islekel, "Totalizing the Open: Roots and Boundary Markers in Wynter and Glissant," *CLR James Journal* 24, no. 1–2 (2018): 107–23.

20. David Marriott, "Inventions of Existence: Sylvia Wynter, Frantz Fanon, Sociogeny, and 'the Damned,'" *CR: The New Centennial Review* 11, no. 3 (2011): 49.

21. Wynter, "Columbus, the Ocean Blue," 162.

22. Francisco J. Varela, "The Early Days of Autopoiesis," in *Emergence and Embodiment: New Essays on Second-Order Systems Theory*, ed. Bruce Clarke

Notes to Pages 139–143

and Mark B. N. Hansen (Durham, NC: Duke University Press, 2009), 63. Cited in Elisabeth Paquette, "Autopoietic Systems: Organizing Cellular and Political Spaces," *Radical Philosophy Review* (2020): 2, https://doi.org/10.5840/radphilrev2020325109.

23. Max Hantel, "What Is It Like to Be Human? Sylvia Wynter on Autopoeisis," *philoSOPHIA* 8, no. 1 (2018): 62.

24. C. Riley Snorton, *Black on Both Sides: A Racial History of Trans Identity* (Minneapolis: University of Minnesota Press, 2017), 238n 23.

25. Frantz Fanon, *Black Skin, White Masks*, trans. Richard Philcox (New York: Grove, 2008), 11.

26. This can best be seen with respect to Fanon's work on the impacts of colonization on the psyche: decolonization in terms of the reorganization of space is a fundamental part of each psychic therapeutic process, Fanon demonstrates. For more, see Fanon, *Black Skin, White Masks*.

27. Paquette, "Autopoietic Systems," 6.

28. Snorton, *Black on Both Sides*, 238, fn 23.

29. Hantel, "What Is It Like to Be Human?" 62.

30. Humberto R. Maturana and Francisco J. Varela, *The Tree of Knowledge: The Biological Roots of Human Understanding* (Boston: Shambhala, 1992), 27.

31. Sylvia Wynter, "Beyond the Word of Man: Glissant and the New Discourse of the Antilles," *World Literature Today* 63, no. 4 (1989): 641.

32. Michel Foucault, *The Courage of Truth: The Government of the Self and Others II, Lectures at the Collège de France, 1983–1984*, trans. Graham Burchell (New York: Palgrave Macmillan, 2011), 227.

33. Bosco, "Human Rights Politics and Performances of Memory," 396.

34. Wynter, "Columbus, the Ocean Blue."

BIBLIOGRAPHY

Acosta López, María del Rosario. "Gramáticas de lo inaudito as Decolonial Grammars: Notes for a Decolonization of Listening." *Research in Phenomenology* 52, no. 2 (2022): 203–22.

———. "One Hundred Years of Forgottenness." *Philosophical Readings* 11, no. 3, special issue on "Philosophy in Colombia" (2019): 163–71.

Agamben, Giorgio. *Homo Sacer: Sovereign Power and Bare Life.* Translated by Daniel Heller-Roazen. Stanford, CA: Stanford University Press, 1998.

———. *State of Exception.* Translated by Kevin Attell. Chicago: University of Chicago Press, 2005.

Al-Saji, Alia. "Memory of Another Past: Bergson, Deleuze, and a New Theory of Time." *Continental Philosophy Review* 37 (2004): 203–39.

Allen, Amy. *The Politics of Ourselves: Power, Autonomy, and Gender in Contemporary Critical Theory.* New York: Columbia University Press, 2013.

Alpkaya, Gökçen. "Kayiplar sorunu ve Turkiye." *Ankara Universitesi Siyasal Bilgiler Fakultesi Dergisi* 50, no. 3 (1995): 48.

Altay, Mehmet Efe. "Cizre'de Bodrum Kat Karanligi: Ilk Günden bugüne neleryasandi?" [The Darkness of Basements in Cizre: What Happened since Day One?]. T24, February 8, 2016. https://t24.com.tr/haber/cizrede-bodrum-kat-karanligi-ilk-gunden-bugune-neler-yasandi.327392.

Angelo, Paul. "Colombia: False Positives, Failed Justice." Latin American Bureau, May 24, 2018. https://lab.org.uk/colombia-false-positives-failed-justice/.

Ansell-Pearson, Keith. "Deleuze and the Overcoming of Memory." In *Memory: Histories, Theories, Debates,* edited by Susannah Radstone and Bill Schwarz, 161–64. New York: Fordham University Press, 2010.

Bargu, Banu. "Another Necropolitics." *Theory and Event* 19, no. 1 (2016). muse .jhu.edu/article/610222.

———. "Sovereignty as Erasure: Rethinking Enforced Disappearances." *Qui Parle: Critical Humanities and Social Sciences,* no. 23 (2014): 35–75.

———. *Starve and Immolate: The Politics of Human Weapons.* New York: Columbia University Press, 2014.

BBC. "Davutoğlu: Cizre'de tek bir sivil kayıp yok." 2015. https://www.bbc.com /turkce/haberler/2015/09/150910_davutoglu_cizre.

Bellucci, Mabel. "Childless Motherhood: Interview with Nora Cortiñas, a Mother of the Plaza de Mayo, Argentina." *Reproductive Health Matters* 7, no. 13 (May 1999): 83–88.

Benhabib, Seyla. "Multiculturalism and Gendered Citizenship." In *The Claims of Culture: Equality and Diversity in the Global Era,* 82–104. Princeton, NJ: Princeton University Press, 2002.

Benjamin, Walter. "Excavation and Memory." In *Selected Writings, Vol. 2, Part 2 (1931–1934)*. Edited by Marcus Paul Bullock, Michael William Jennings, Howard Eiland, and Gary Smith, 576–94. Cambridge, MA: Belknap Press of Harvard University Press, 2005.

Bernstein, Richard. "Foucault: Critique as a Philosophic Ethos." In *Critique and Power: Recasting the Foucault/Habermas Debate*, edited by Michael Kelly, 211–42. Cambridge, MA: MIT Press, 1994.

Bodin, Jean. *On Sovereignty: Four Chapters from "The Six Books on the Commonwealth."* Translated by Julian H. Franklin. Cambridge: Cambridge University Press, 1992.

Bosco, Fernando J. "Human Rights Politics and Performances of Memory: Conflicts among the *Madres de Plaza de Mayo* in Argentina." *Social and Cultural Geography* 5, no. 3 (2004): 381–402.

———. "The Madres de Plaza de Mayo and Three Decades of Human Rights' Activism: Embeddedness, Emotions, and Social Movements." *Annals of the Association of American Geographers* 96, no. 2 (2006): 342–68.

Bozan, Ali, dir. *7 Roj 7 Şev*. Silopi, Turkey, 2017.

Bozkurt, Hatice, and Özlem Kaya. *Holding Up the Photograph: Experiences of the Women Whose Husbands Were Forcibly Disappeared*. Istanbul: Hakikat Adalet Hafıza Merkezi, 2014.

Burton, Antoinette. "Introduction: Archive Fever, Archive Stories." In *Archive Stories: Facts, Fictions, and the Writing of History*, edited by Antoinette Burton, 1–24. Durham, NC: Duke University Press, 2005.

Butler, Judith. *Bodies That Matter*. New York: Routledge, 1993.

———. *Frames of War: When Is Life Grievable?* New York: Verso, 2010.

———. "Sexual Inversions." In *Feminist Interpretations of Michel Foucault*, edited by Susan J. Hekman, 59–73. University Park: Penn State University Press, 1996.

Çakan, Şeyhmus. "Turkish 'Cleansing' Operation Rocks Southeastern Cities." Reuters, October 25, 2015. https://www.reuters.com/article/us-turkey-kurds -idUSKBN0U80FQ20151226.

Caruth, Cathy. *Unclaimed Experience: Trauma, Narrative, History*. Baltimore, MD: Johns Hopkins University Press, 1996.

Chanter, Tina. *Whose Antigone? The Tragic Marginalization of Slavery*. Albany: State University of New York Press, 2011.

Colombia Reports. "Extrajudicial Executions." 2019. https://colombiareports .com/false-positives/.

Crimp, Douglas. *Melancholia and Moralism: Essays on AIDS and Queer Politics*. Cambridge, MA: MIT Press, 2004.

Daniels, Joe Parkin. "Colombian Army Killed Thousands More Civilians Than Reported, Study Claims." *The Guardian*, May 8, 2018. https://www .theguardian.com/world/2018/may/08/colombia-false-positives-scandal -casualties-higher-thought-study.

Davis, Ben. "The Politics of Édouard Glissant's Right to Opacity." *CLR James Journal* 25, no. 1–2 (2019): 59–70.

Deleuze, Gilles. *Difference and Repetition*. Translated by Paul Patton. New York: Columbia University Press, 1968.

Bibliography 167

———. *Proust and Signs*. Translated by Richard Howard. Minneapolis: University of Minnesota Press, 2000.

Demirtaş, Bilge, Alper Elitok, Can Gündüz, Murat Kocaman, and Osman Şişman, dirs. *Ölü ile Diri / Mirî û jî sax [The Dead and the Living]*. Siirt, Turkey, 2015.

Derrida, Jacques. "Archive Fever: A Freudian Impression." Translated by Eric Prenowitz. *Diacritics* 25, no. 2 (Summer 1995): 9–63.

———. *The Death Penalty, Volume 1*. Translated by Peggy Kamuf. Chicago: University of Chicago Press, 2019.

———. *Specters of Marx*. Translated by Peggy Kamuf. New York: Routledge, 1993.

Deutscher, Penelope. *Foucault's Futures: A Critique of Reproductive Reason*. New York: Columbia University Press, 2019.

Diken. "TİHV raporu: Diyarbakır'ın Sur ilçesindeki sokağa çıkma yasakları dünya rekoru." Diken.com, August 8, 2017. http://www.diken.com.tr/tihv-raporu-diyarbakirin-sur-ilcesindeki-sokaga-cikma-yasaklari-dunya-rekoru/.

Dotson, Kristie. "A Cautionary Tale: On Limiting Epistemic Oppression." *Social Epistemology* 28, no. 2 (2014).

Drabinski, John E. *Glissant and the Middle Passage: Philosophy, Beginning, Abyss*. Minneapolis: University of Minnesota Press, 2019.

Dreyfus, Hubert L., and Paul Rabinow. *Michel Foucault: Beyond Structuralism and Hermeneutics*. Chicago: University of Chicago Press, 2014.

Erbay, Vecdi. "79 Gün Sonra Cizre." Bianet, March 3, 2016. https://bianet.org/bianet/insan-haklari/172647-79-gun-sonra-cizre.

Erlenbusch-Anderson, Verena. *Genealogies of Terrorism: Revolution, State Violence, Empire*. New York: Columbia University Press, 2018.

Escobar, Natalia Sabogal, and Ivonne Alonso-Mondragón. "Capítulo 1: 'Nada más que la verdad': Relato de un 'falso positivo.'" In *El Camino hacia la paz: Investigaciones sobre la violencia y la paz en Colombia*, 14–45. Bogotá: Ediciones USTA, 2017.

Fanon, Frantz. *Black Skin, White Masks*. Translated by Richard Philcox. New York: Grove, 2008.

Ferguson, Kathy. "Theorizing Shiny Things." *Theory and Event* 11, no. 4 (2008). muse.jhu.edu/article/257578.

Foucault, Michel. *Abnormal: Lectures at the Collège de France, 1974–1975*. Translated by Graham Burchell. London: Picador, 2004.

———. *Archaeology of Knowledge*. Translated by Rupert Swyer. New York: Penguin Random House, 2012.

———. *The Courage of Truth: The Government of the Self and Others II: Lectures at the Collège de France, 1983–1984*. Translated by Graham Burchell. New York: Palgrave Macmillan, 2011.

———. *Discipline and Punish: The Birth of the Prison*. Translated by Alan Sheridan. New York: Vintage Books, 1995.

———. *The History of Sexuality: The Will to Knowledge*. Translated by Robert Hurley. London: Penguin, 1976.

———. "Lives of Infamous Men." In *Power*, vol. 3 of *Essential Works of Foucault, 1954–1984*, edited by James D. Faubion, translated by Robert Hurley. New York: New Press, 2001.

———. "Nietzsche, Genealogy, History." In *Aesthetics, Method, and Epistemology*, vol. 2 of *Essential Works of Foucault, 1954–1984*. edited by James D. Faubion. New York: New Press, 1999.

———. "Of Other Spaces." Translated by Jay Miskowiec. *Diacritics* 16, no. 1 (Spring 1986): 22–27.

———. "Prison Talk." In *Power/Knowledge: Selected Interviews and Other Writings*. Translated by Colin Gordon, Leo Marshal, John Mepham, and Kate Sopher. Edited by Colin Gordon, 51–52. New York: Pantheon, 1980.

———. *The Punitive Society: Lectures at the Collège de France, 1972–1973*. Translated by Graham Burchell. Edited by Arnold Davidson. Basingstoke, UK: Palgrave Macmillan, 2015.

———. *Security, Territory, Population: Lectures at the Collège de France, 1977–1978*. Translated by Graham Burchell. Edited by Michel Senellart. London: Picador, 2004.

———. *Society Must Be Defended: Lectures at the Collège de France, 1975–1976*. Edited by Mauro Bentani and Alessandro Fontana. Translated by David Macey. New York: Picador, 1997.

———. *Speech Begins after Death*. Edited by Philippe Artières. Translated by Robert Bononno. Minneapolis: University of Minnesota Press, 1968.

———. "Structuralism and Post-Structuralism." In *Aesthetics, Method, and Epistemology*, vol. 2 of *Essential Works of Foucault, 1954–1984*. Edited by James D. Faubion. New York: New Press, 1999.

———. "The Subject and Power." In *Power*, vol. 3 of *Essential Works of Foucault, 1954–1984*. Edited by James D. Faubion. Translated by Robert Hurley. New York: New Press, 2001.

Fricker, Miranda. *Epistemic Injustice: Power and the Ethics of Knowing*. Oxford: Oxford University Press, 2007.

"Galatasaray Square: A Recognized Memory Space." Hafiza Merkezi, August 13, 2020. https://hakikatadalethafiza.org/en/galatasaray-square-a-recognized-memory-space/.

Gambetti, Zeynep. "Decolonizing Diyarbakir: Culture, Identity and the Struggle to Appropriate Urban Space." In *Comparing Cities: The Middle East and South Asia*, edited by Kamran Asdar Ali and Martina Rieker, 97–129. New York: Oxford University Press, 2010.

Gatehouse, Mike. "Colombia: False Positives, Failed Justice." Latin America Bureau. https://lab.org.uk/colombia-false-positives-failed-justice/.

Glissant, Édouard. *Caribbean Discourse: Selected Essays*. Translated by J. Michael Dash. Charlottesville: University of Virginia Press, 1999.

———. *Poetics of Relation*. Translated by Betsy Wing. Ann Arbor: University of Michigan Press, 1997.

Göral, Özgür Sevgi. "Waiting for the Disappeared: Waiting as a Form of Resilience and the Limits of the Legal Space in Turkey." *Social Anthropology/Anthropologie Sociale* 29, no. 3 (2021): 800–815.

Göral, Özgür Sevgi, Ayhan Işık, and Özlem Kaya. *Unspoken Truth: Enforced Disappearances*. Translated by Nazim Hikmet Richard Dikbas. Istanbul: Truth, Justice, and Memory Center, 2013.

Gordon, Avery F. *Ghostly Matters: Haunting and the Sociological Imagination*. Minneapolis: University of Minnesota Press, 2008.

Bibliography

Haberler, İlgili. "Taybet İnan 23 gün sonra defnedildi: Eşi ve çocukları cenazeye katılamadı." T24, October 11, 2016. http://t24.com.tr/haber/taybet-inan-23-gun-sonra-defnedildi-esi-ve-cocuklari-izin-verilmedigi-icin-cenazeye-katilamadi,323748.

Haddad, Samir. "Examining Genealogy as Engaged Critique." *Foucault Studies* 1, no. 28 (2020): 4–9.

Hakyemez, Serra. "Sur: A City of Imagination, a City Under Occupation." *Middle Eastern Report* 287 (Summer 2018): 44–48.

Hantel, Max. "What Is It Like to Be Human? Sylvia Wynter on Autopoiesis." *philoSOPHIA* 8, no. 1 (2018): 61–79.

Harootunian, Harry. *The Unspoken as Heritage: The Armenian Genocide and Its Unaccounted Lives.* Durham, NC: Duke University Press, 2019.

Hartman, Saidiya. *Lose Your Mother: A Journey along the Atlantic Slave Route.* New York: Farrar, Straus and Giroux, 2007.

———. "Venus in Two Acts." *Small Axe* 12, no. 2 (2008): 1–14.

———. *Wayward Lives, Beautiful Experiments: Intimate Histories of Riotous Black Girls, Troublesome Women, and Queer Radicals.* New York: W.W. Norton, 2020.

Hegel, G. W. F. *Phenomenology of Spirit.* Translated by A. V. Miller. Oxford: Oxford University Press, 1977.

Honig, Bonnie. "Antigone's Laments, Creon's Grief." In *The Returns of Antigone*, edited by Tina Chanter and Sean D. Kirkland. Albany: State University of New York Press, 2014.

Huffer, Lynne. "Foucault's Fossils: Life Itself and the Return to Nature in Feminist Philosophy." *Foucault Studies* 20 (2015): 122–41.

———. *Foucault's Strange Eros.* New York: Columbia University Press, 2020.

———. *Mad for Foucault: Rethinking the Foundations of Queer Theory.* New York: Columbia University Press, 2009.

Human Rights Foundation of Turkey. "16 Ağustos 2015—16 Ağustos 2017 Bilgi Notu." http://tihv.org.tr/16-agustos-2015-16-agustos-2016-tarihleri-arasinda-sokaga-cikma-yasaklari-ve-yasamini-yitiren-siviller-bilgi-notu/.

Human Rights Watch. "Colombia: Top Brass Linked to Extrajudicial Executions." 2015. https://www.hrw.org/news/2015/06/24/colombia-top-brass-linked-extrajudicial-executions#.

Islekel, Selin. "Totalizing the Open: Roots and Boundary Markers in Wynter and Glissant." *CLR James Journal* 24, no. 1–2 (2018): 107–23.

Kamer, Hatice. "Cizre koca bir mezarliga donmus." BBC, March 3, 2016. https://www.bbc.com/turkce/haberler/2016/03/160303_cizre_hatice_kamer_izlenim.

Koopman, Colin. *Genealogy as Critique: Foucault and the Problems of Modernity.* Bloomington: Indiana University Press, 2013.

Kryger, Rachelle. "Colombia Is Exhuming Graves of Civilians Allegedly Killed by Soldiers." *Washington Post*, December 17, 2019. https://www.washingtonpost.com/world/the_americas/colombia-exhuming-graves-of-civilians-allegedly-killed-by-soldiers/2019/12/17/0d99e428-20e5-11ea-b034-de7dc2b5199b_story.html.

Lacquer, Thomas. *The Work of the Dead: A Cultural History of Mortal Remains.* Princeton, NJ: Princeton University Press, 2015.

Loichot, Valérie. *Water Graves: The Art of the Unritual in the Greater Caribbean.* Charlottesville: University of Virginia Press, 2020.

Lugones, María. "Heterosexualism and the Colonial/Modern Gender System." *Hypatia* 22, no. 1 (2007): 186–209.

Mader, Mary Beth. "Knowledge." In *The Cambridge Foucault Lexicon*, edited by Leonard Lawlor and John Nale. Cambridge: Cambridge University Press, 2014.

Maldonado Torres, Nelson. "On the Coloniality of Being: Contributions to the Development of a Concept." *Cultural Studies* 21, nos. 2–3 (2007): 240–70.

Marriott, David. "Inventions of Existence: Sylvia Wynter, Frantz Fanon, Sociogeny, and 'the Damned.'" *CR: The New Centennial Review* 11, no. 3 (2011): 45–89.

———. *Whither Fanon: Studies in the Blackness of Being.* Stanford, CA: Stanford University Press, 2018.

Maturana, Humberto R., and Francisco J. Varela. *The Tree of Knowledge: The Biological Roots of Human Understanding.* Boston: Shambhala, 1992.

Mbembe, Achille. "Necropolitics." Translated by Libby Meintjes. *Public Culture* 15, no. 1 (2003): 11–40.

———. *On the Postcolony.* Translated by A. M. Berrett, Janet Roitman, Murray Last, Achille Mbembe, and Steven Rendall. Berkeley: University of California Press, 2001.

———. "Power of the Archive and Its Limits." In *Refiguring the Archive*, edited by Caroline Hamilton, Verne Harris, Jane Taylor, Michele Pickover, Graeme Reid, and Razia Saleh, 19–27. Dordrecht: Springer, 2002.

———. "Provisional Notes on the Postcolony." *Africa: Journal of the International African Institute* 62, no. 1 (1992): 3–37.

McWhorter, Ladelle. *Bodies and Pleasures: Foucault and the Politics of Sexual Normalization.* Bloomington: Indiana University Press, 1999.

Medina, José. *The Epistemology of Resistance: Gender and Racial Oppression, Epistemic Injustice, and Resistant Imaginations.* Oxford: Oxford University Press, 2013.

Mills, Charles. *The Racial Contract.* Ithaca, NY: Cornell University Press, 1999.

Mrázek, Rudolf. *The Complete Lives of Camp People: Colonialism, Fascism, Concentrated Modernity.* Durham, NC: Duke University Press, 2020.

Mucklebauer, John. "On Reading Differently: Through Foucault on Resistance." *College English* 63, no. 1 (2000): 71–94.

Nazim, Yusuf. "Sur'un gözyaşları—II." T24, March 21, 2016. https://t24.com.tr/yazarlar/yusuf-nazim/surun-gozyaslari-ii,14154.

Nelson, Diane. *Reckoning: The Ends of War in Guatemala.* Durham, NC: Duke University Press, 2009.

———. *Who Counts: The Mathematics of Death and Life after Genocide.* Durham, NC: Duke University Press, 2015.

Paquette, Elisabeth. "Autopoietic Systems: Organizing Cellular and Political Spaces." *Radical Philosophy Review* (2020). https://doi.org/10.5840/radphilrev2020325109.

Patterson, Orlando. *Slavery and Social Death.* Cambridge, MA: Harvard University Press, 1982.

Bibliography

Pickett, Brent. *On the Use and Abuse of Foucault for Politics*. Lanham, MD: Lexington Books, 2005.

Proust, Marcel. *In Search of Lost Time, Volume 1: Swann's Way*. Translated by C. K. Scott Moncrieff and Terrence Kilmartin. New York: Random House, 1992.

Puar, Jasbir K. *Terrorist Assemblages: Homonationalism in Queer Times*. Durham, NC: Duke University Press, 2007.

Quijano, Anibal, and Michael Ennis. "Coloniality of Power, Eurocentrism, and Latin America." *Nepantla: Views from South* 1, no. 3 (2000): 533–80.

Rawlinson, Mary C. "Beyond Antigone: Ismene, Gender and the Right to Life." In *The Returns of Antigone*, edited by Tina Chanter and Sean D. Kirkland, 101–24. Albany: State University of New York Press, 2014.

Read, Peter, and Marivic Wyndham. *Narrow but Endlessly Deep: The Struggle for Memorialisation in Chile since the Transition to Democracy*. Sydney: Australian National University Press, 2016.

Robben, Antonius C. G. M. "Exhumations, Territoriality, and Necropolitics in Chile and Argentina." In *Necropolitics: Mass Graves and Exhumations in the Age of Human Rights*, edited by Francisco Ferrándiz and Antonius C. G. M. Robben, 53–75. Philadelphia: University of Pennsylvania Press, 2015.

Ruin, Hans. *Being with the Dead: Burial, Ancestral Politics, and the Roots of Historical Consciousness*. Stanford, CA: Stanford University Press, 2018.

Said, Edward. "Foucault and the Imagination of Power." In *Foucault: A Critical Reader*, edited by David Couzens Hoy, 149–56. Cambridge, MA: Blackwell, 1986.

Sawicki, Jana. *Disciplining Foucault: Feminism, Power, and the Body*. New York: Routledge, 1991.

Schmitt, Carl. *Political Theology: Four Chapters on the Concept of Sovereignty*. Translated by George Schwab. Chicago: University of Chicago Press, 2005.

Sjöhölm, Cecilia. "Bodies in Exile." In *The Returns of Antigone*, edited by Tina Chanter and Sean D. Kirkland, 281–96. Albany: State University of New York Press, 2014.

Snorton, C. Riley. *Black on Both Sides: A Racial History of Trans Identity*. Minneapolis: University of Minnesota Press, 2017.

Solla, Mária Fernanda Perez. *Enforced Disappearances in International Human Rights*. Jefferson, NC: McFarland, 2006.

Söylemez, Ayça. "Cizre Bodrumları AİHM'de Görüşülecek." Bianet, November, 12, 2018. http://bianet.org/bianet/insan-haklari/202537-cizre-bodrumlari-aihm-de-gorusulecek.

Taussig, Michael. *The Nervous System*. New York: Routledge, 1992.

"Taybet İnan 23 gün sonra defnedildi: Eşi ve çocukları cenazeye katılamadı." T24, January 11, 2016. http://t24.com.tr/haber/taybet-inan-23-gun-sonra-defnedildi-esi-ve-cocuklari-izin-verilmedigi-icin-cenazeye-katilamadi.323748.

Taylor, Diana. *Disappearing Acts: Spectacles of Gender and Nationalism in Argentina's "Dirty War."* Durham, NC: Duke University Press, 1997.

———. *!Presente! The Politics of Presence*. Durham, NC: Duke University Press, 2020.

Thompson, Kevin. "Forms of Resistance: Foucault on Tactical Reversal and Self-Formation." *Continental Philosophy Review* 36, no. 2 (2003): 113–38.

TOKI. "İllere Göre Projeler." https://www.toki.gov.tr/illere-gore-projeler/749.
———. "Sur Yeniden İnsa Ediliyor." October 2017. https://www.toki.gov.tr/haber/sur-yeniden-insa-ediliyor.
Türkyılmaz, Zeynep. "Maternal Colonialism and Turkish Woman's Burden in Dersim: Educating the 'Mountain Flowers' of Dersim." *Journal of Women's History* 28, no. 3 (2016).
United Nations Human Rights Office. "International Convention for the Protection of All Persons from Enforced Disappearance (ICCPED)." United Nations Human Rights Office of the High Commissioner, 1980. http://www.ohchr.org/EN/HRBodies/CED/Pages/ConventionCED.aspx.
Varela, Francisco J. "The Early Days of Autopoiesis." In *Emergence and Embodiment: New Essays on Second-Order Systems Theory*, edited by Bruce Clarke and Mark B. N. Hansen, 62–76. Durham, NC: Duke University Press, 2009.
Verdery, Katherine. *The Political Lives of Dead Bodies: Reburial and Postsocialist Change*. New York: Columbia University Press, 2000.
Warren, Calvin. *Ontological Terror: Blackness, Being, and Emancipation*. Durham, NC: Duke University Press, 2018.
Working Group on Enforced or Involuntary Disappearances. "Report of the Working Group on Enforced or Involuntary Disappearances." UN General Assembly, A/hrc/22/45, January 28, 2013. http://www.ohchr.org/Documents/HRBodies/HRCouncil/RegularSession/Session22/A.hrc.22.45_English.pdf.
Wynter, Sylvia. "Beyond the Word of Man: Glissant and the New Discourse of the Antilles." *World Literature Today* 63, no. 4 (1989): 637–48.
———. "Columbus, the Ocean Blue, and Fables That Stir the Mind." In *Poetics of the Americas: Race, Founding, Textuality*, edited by Bainard Cowan and Jefferson Humphries, 141–64. Baton Rouge: Louisiana State University Press, 1997.
Zeydanlıoğlu, Welat. "The White Turkish Man's Burden: Orientalism, Kemalism and the Kurds in Turkey." *Neo-Colonial Mentalities in Contemporary Europe* 4, no. 2 (2008): 1.
Zurita, Raúl. *Song for His Disappeared Love / Canto a su amor desaparecido*. Translated by Daniel Borzutzky. Notre Dame, IN: Action Books, 2010.

INDEX

Abu Ghraib prison, 48
Acosta Lopez, Maria del Rosario, 59,
72, 107
activism, 119, 132; human rights, 130.
See also resistances
Agamben, Giorgio, 33–34
agency: collective epistemic, 22, 108;
disqualifying the agency of political
movements, 98; necrosovereign
reformulation of political and
epistemic, 109; political-epistemic, 60,
107, 109
Allen, Amy, 48
Allende, Salvador, 14
Al-Saji, Alia, 69–70
Amnesty International, 14, 104
Ansell-Pearson, Keith, 69
Antigone (Sophocles), 16, 26, 36–38
archive: erasure of, 6, 8, 10, 19–21,
34, 50–53, 58–61, 113, 127, 136;
genealogical engagement with, 117,
119; necropolitics of, 74–76, 78, 80;
necrosovereign work on, 7, 53, 76,
109, 121, 127; reconstruction of space
as, 79–80; statistical, 31; struggles
against the modes of truth that are
recorded in, 117; as testimony to
death, 113; transgressive limits of,
124. *See also* knowledges; memories
Arendt, Hannah, 18
Argentina, 9, 14–15, 19, 25, 31, 33, 50,
114–15; Dirty War in, 52, 57. *See also*
Buenos Aires; Madres de Plaza de
Mayo
Argentine National Commission on the
Disappeared, 31
Arslan, Günay, 25, 34
Atlantic slave trade, 17
autopoiesis, 139–43. *See also*
reinvention; Wynter, Sylvia
Ayotzinapa, 112. *See also* Mexico

Bal, Mieke, 123
Bargu, Banu, 30, 32, 34, 51, 95–96
Benjamin, Walter, 74, 76
Bergson, Henri, 69, 79
Bernstein, Richard, 94
Bilir, Ramazan, 56
biopolitics, 7–8, 26–33, 40; and the
absence of the private cemetery, 133;
cemeteries of, 134; death function
of, 29; epistemic dimensions of, 48;
rationalities of, 96; sovereignty and,
133; state apparatus of, 137; as
technology of sovereign power, 39.
See also politics; sovereignty
Birlik, Kemal, 50
Blackness, 38, 149n41
bodies: absence of records and, 114; air-
dropped, 31, 38, 50; counts of, 51–52,
114; invisible, 42, 51–52; unknown
graves of, 109; witnessing the work of
power on, 120. *See also* death
Bodin, Jean, 7, 33
Buenos Aires: Plaza de Mayo, 16, 130,
132–35, 141–42. *See also* Argentina
bulldozing, 66, 71–74; and demolition,
67; and fragmentation, 68;
infrastructural warfare and, 76, 141;
and reconstruction, 73, 78. *See also*
rebuilding
burial: aftermath of improper, 91,
112, 125–26; "impossibility" of
the event of improper, 124, 126;
nameless (NN), 147n8; possibility
of putting the disappeared to rest
in improper, 122; prohibitions of,
6; proper and improper, 82, 120;
story of improper, 126; techniques
of improper, 6, 9–17, 20, 26, 30–34,
37–44, 47–49, 60, 93; temporality of
improper, 145. *See also* cemeteries;
death; mass burials

173

174 Index

Burton, Antoinette, 76
Butler, Judith, 26, 28, 93–94, 151n69;
 Frames of War, 37, 48

Campos, General Ramón, 52, 59
Caruth, Cathy, 71
cemeteries, 133; of biopolitics, 134. *See
 also* burial
Césaire, Aimé, 18
Chile, 9, 14–16, 19, 25, 31, 33, 35, 115;
 Operation Television Withdrawal in,
 111. *See also* General Cemetery (Patio
 29)
Cizre, 63–69, 71, 80, 129, 155n11;
 death basements of, 66–70, 76–80,
 101, 129, 134–35. *See also* Turkey
collective movements, 20, 97, 107, 142
colonialism, 18; unreflective
 appropriation of Blackness in histories
 of, 149n41
coloniality: of loss, 16–20; of power, 18
Columbia, 9–10, 15–16, 92, 114. *See
 also* Revolutionary Armed Forces of
 Columbia (FARC); Soacha

Davutoğlu, Ahmet, 59
death, 5, 37; afterlives of, 44; biopolitics
 of, 26–33, 41; as by-product of
 commerce, 17; collective use of
 the memory of, 95; contemporary
 politics of, 20, 29; and disappearance,
 7, 30, 118–19; enchantments of,
 112–17; ignorance of, 42, 125;
 management of the right to, 6, 8,
 139; necropolitics of, 26–33, 44, 65,
 70, 95; political and politicized, 129,
 141; power/knowledge of, 44–50,
 92, 127, 139; privatization of, 40–
 41, 133–34; social, 37; spaces of,
 65–70, 76, 142; and state pensions,
 120, 122; transactions between the
 archive and, 74; unnatural, 38–41.
 See also bodies; burial; enforced
 disappearances; extralegal executions;
 necrosovereignty
death penalty, 30, 153n118
decolonization, 19, 163n26
Deleuze, Gilles, 69, 79
democracy, 9

Derrida, Jacques, 8, 75; "Archive Fever"
 (article), 156n37; *The Death Penalty*
 (seminars), 28
desaparecidos, 52. *See also* enforced
 disappearances
detentions: arbitrary, 10, 13; erasure of
 records of, 43, 51, 119; in periods of
 pressure, 130; refusal to acknowledge,
 54–55; secret centers of, 7, 38, 58;
 torture in, 43, 81–82, 87; unofficial
 public, 56. *See also* enforced
 disappearances; torture
Dotson, Kristie, 56
Drabinski, John, 100, 102
dreams, 103–4, 116, 127; collective
 element of, 106. *See also* nightmares
Dreyfus, Hubert L., 45
Du Bois, W. E. B., 105
Dulitzky, Ariel, 14

enforced disappearances, 6–19, 25, 30–
 38, 48, 50, 81–87, 92, 104–5, 111–13,
 142; enmity, terror, or subversion in
 the case of, 52; epistemic dimensions
 of, 55–58, 105; as executed persons,
 120; experiential temporal lag
 around, 55, 122; as physical and
 literal obliteration, 118–19; reports
 on, 150n55; stories of, 123–28;
 temporalities of, 22, 125, 134. *See
 also* death; detentions
epistemic injustice, 53–54, 60, 97; as
 hermeneutical injustice, 54, 57, 61;
 and knowledges of death, 96, 105; as
 testimonial injustice, 54, 56, 58, 61.
 See also epistemologies; knowledges
epistemologies: of loss, 91–110;
 necrosovereign, 21, 138; resistant,
 11, 101–2, 112. *See also* epistemic
 injustice; knowledges
Erlenbusch-Anderson, Verena, 9, 29, 48
Etkind, Alexander, 18
extralegal executions, 10, 13, 30. *See
 also* death; violence

fables, 22, 112, 114–15, 117, 126, 129–
 44; of disappearance, 124, 126–28;
 founding, 136–43; function of, 123;
 necrosovereign, 121, 123, 128; of

Index

power, 118; spatial organization and, 135. *See also* fabulations
fabulations, 22; and counter-fabulations, 115, 117; critical, 124–25; necrosovereign, 112–17, 119, 123, 126–27, 135; resistances against, 115. *See also* fables
Fanon, Frantz, 140, 163n26. *See also* sociogeny
Ferguson, Kathy, 77, 157n53
Foucault, Michel, 7, 9, 18, 26, 45, 60–61, 75, 140–41, 152n113, 154n18; account of biopolitics of, 150n66; account of resistance of, 108, 115–16, 130; and archive, 119; utopias and heterotopias according to, 131–34; Works: *The Archaeology of Knowledge*, 48; *Discipline and Punish*, 27, 46; *The History of Sexuality*, 26–29, 92–94; "Lives of Infamous Men," 112, 117–19, 123; *Nietzsche, Genealogy, History*, 76, 78; *Security, Territory, Population* (lecture courses), 67, 94; *Society Must Be Defended* (lecture courses), 26, 29–31, 38–40, 49–50, 52–53; *Speech Begins after Death*, 121
freedom, 9
Fricker, Miranda, 53–58. *See also* epistemic injustice

Gendarmerie Intelligence (JİTEM), 103, 116
gender, 114
General Cemetery (Patio 29), 16, 20, 25, 35, 38, 40, 42, 111, 113, 118, 120, 123, 129. *See also* Chile
ghosts, 4–5, 13, 108, 114, 140–43; of the non-spaces, 126, 133
Glissant, Édouard, 17, 37, 99–102, 109
Global North, 18–19, 49
Global South, 15, 19
González, Doña Nena, 111, 113, 121
Göral, Özgür Sevgi, 107
Gordon, Avery, 30–31, 40, 50, 58, 72–73, 78, 104, 106, 108
grief: as collective process, 107; disappearing, 43–61; prolonged, 107, 141; recovery from, 11; regulation of

practices of, 20. *See also* memories; mourning
Guatemala, 14
guerrilla pluralisms, 106, 108

Hantel, Max, 139–40
Hartman, Saidiya, 17, 22, 77, 112–13, 121, 123–25, 127
haunting: haunted archive, 73, 76, 81; haunted memories, 21, 70–73, 105; haunted society, 3, 13–14, 114; haunted spaces, 19, 22, 72–74, 135. *See also* ghosts
Hegel, Georg Wilhelm Friedrich, 16, 36
heterotopias, 131–35; crisis, 132; deviation, 132–33; of mourning, 131–35, 143; necrosovereign, 134; reinvention of spaces as, 142
Hobbes, Thomas, 7
homosexuality, 52. *See also* sexuality
Honig, Bonnie, 36
Huffer, Lynne, 34, 118
human rights organizations, 31, 35, 44, 84

identity: Kurdish, 19; transparent, 100
impasses, 114, 140; epistemic, 11, 99, 143; resistances and, 97–102
infrastructural warfare, 66–67
Inter-American Court of Human Rights, 15
invisibilization, 21, 60, 98, 109
Istanbul: Galatasaray Square, 81–82, 129, 132–34, 141–42. *See also* Turkey

Kırbayır, Berfo, 3, 43, 100–101, 103–4, 109, 138
knowledges, 6, 8; archival disappearances and, 49–54, 109, 117; counter-spaces of nightmare, 131; of death, 44–50, 92, 95–97; impossibility of transparent, 101; mechanisms involved in power and, 46–47, 53–54, 109–10; necro-epistemic, 53–61, 100–106; nightmare, 11–12, 100–110, 112–13, 117, 131, 137–38, 140–44. *See also* archive; epistemic injustice; epistemologies; memories; nightmares
Koopman, Colin, 46

176   Index

Lacquer, Thomas, 10
Lalinde, Fabiola, 104, 106, 109
Latin America, 6, 9, 12, 14–15, 19–20,
  33, 127, 147n8
Latin American Federation of the
  Families of the Disappeared
  (FEDEFAM), 15
laws, 7, 16, 27, 33, 115. *See also*
  sovereignty
Loichot, Valérie, 10, 34
lucidity, 104–5, 109
Lugones, María, 13, 18

Madres de Linea Fundadora, 134–35
Madres de Plaza de Mayo, 12, 19, 31,
  40, 52, 57–58, 84–85, 93, 98, 111–
  13, 119, 122, 126, 130, 134–35, 142,
  145, 161n37. *See also* Buenos Aires
Marriott, David, 138
mass burials, 5, 13, 111, 137. *See also*
  mass graves
mass graves, 11, 25, 30–35, 41, 86–87;
  disqualification of, 59; as emptied of
  remains, 129; inaccessible, 34. *See
  also* mass burials
Maturana, H. R., 139–40
Mbembe, Achille, 7–8, 29, 44, 64–67,
  74–75, 79, 114, 125, 147n4, 155n15
media, 14, 115, 126. *See also* social
  media
Medina, José, 11, 21, 97–99, 105–6,
  108, 159n18
memories, 3, 6; active, 21, 141;
  assemblages of, 68–73; collective,
  11, 21, 59, 68, 74; of death, 95, 141;
  erasure of, 54, 76; of forgetting and
  violence, 135; involuntary, 69–74, 79;
  making, 106–7; mnemonic methods
  of the replacement of, 97–98;
  necropolitics and spatial, 64–68, 73–
  78, 134, 141; opaque, 101; targeting
  the coherence of narratives and, 21;
  transparency of necrosovereign, 109;
  voluntary, 79. *See also* archive; grief;
  knowledges; resistances
Mexico, 115. *See also* Ayotzinapa
Middle Passage, 17, 37. *See also*
  transatlantic slave trade
Mills, Charles, 9

modernization, 18–19; homogenization
  and racialization as the method of, 19.
  See also westernization
motherhood, 19, 58, 112. *See also*
  Madres de Plaza de Mayo; Mothers
  of Soacha; Saturday Mothers
Mothers of Soacha, 19, 51, 112–15,
  119, 123, 142
mountainous zones, 9, 19, 25, 32, 111
mourning: collective, 12, 15; heterotopias
  of, 131–35, 143; houses of, 130–31;
  necrosovereign ways of dying and,
  116, 127; political and politicized,
  129; possibilities of, 67; practices of, 4,
  6, 11–12, 95, 131; prolonged, 12, 22,
  107, 142–43; regulation of practices
  of, 20, 22, 26, 32, 34, 36, 41–44,
  49, 108, 127; spaces of, 6, 9–10, 20,
  122, 135, 137, 142; in the "Western"
  imaginary, 16. *See also* grief

necropolitics, 7–8, 26–33; archive
  of, 77; collective oblivion of, 107;
  death-work of, 72–73, 109, 142;
  rationalities of, 103; space of, 64–
  68, 79–80; spatial methods of,
  155n15; violence of, 79. *See also*
  necrosovereignty; politics
necrosovereignty, 6–12, 32–33, 40, 44–
  49, 59–60, 108–10, 114–20, 125–29,
  140–43; archives of, 78, 109, 114,
  117, 141; assemblages of, 33, 35, 40–
  42, 53, 92, 113, 119–20, 124, 127,
  131, 135–39; as colonial/modern
  power, 19–20; discursive practices
  of, 105; dramaturgy of the real of,
  120–23, 126–28, 132; enchantments
  of, 127–28; erasures of, 64, 72, 123;
  fractured time of, 107; genealogies
  of, 121; haunted spaces of, 135;
  hermeneutical injustices of, 97;
  impossibility of coherent narratives
  in the context of, 11; and knowledge
  production, 21, 44–53; memory
  politics of, 21, 73–74, 97–100;
  mnemonic spatial organization of, 75,
  98; mobilizing death in the context
  of, 96, 116, 131; narrative silences
  of, 98; practices of mourning in the

Index

heterotopias of, 131–35; resistances of death in the context of, 92, 95–97, 141; spatial politics of, 21, 72–80, 100, 131–37, 141; as technology of power, 7–8, 15–17, 47–49, 65, 118, 127; transparency of, 109; utopias of, 132. *See also* death; necropolitics; rebuilding; sovereignty

neoliberalism, 7

Newala Qesaba, 16, 20, 25–31, 34, 37–42, 58–59, 91, 98, 105–9, 116, 118, 129–30, 139, 142. *See also* Turkey

nightmares, 6, 11–12, 22, 91–92, 97–106, 112–16, 127–29; mobilization of, 140. *See also* dreams; knowledges

nongovernmental organizations (NGOs), 14

Ölü ile Diri/Mirî û jî sax (documentary), 3, 33–35, 86–87

opacity, 100–102, 104, 109; of nightmare knowledges, 141; as strategy of resistance, 109

otherness: delineations of subjectivity and, 136; founding fable as shaped by, 138; space of, 136–38, 162n19

Paquette, Elisabeth, 140

Partnoy, Alicia: *The Little School*, 87

Patterson, Orlando, 37, 39

photographs, 82, 121, 130, 145

Pinochet, Augusto, 14

politics: colonial, 6; corporeal, 130; dead-body, 6, 16, 20; and resistance, 6; spatial, 130, 136–37; subjective, 137. *See also* biopolitics; necropolitics; sovereignty

Proust, Marcel: *In Search of Lost Time*, 68–69

Puar, Jasbir, 47

Public Mass Housing Administration (TOKI), 63. *See also* Turkey

Quijano, Aníbal, 18, 149n45. *See also* coloniality

Rabinow, Paul, 45

racialization, 19

racism: ethnic, 29; state, 29–30

rebuilding, 6, 8, 19, 22, 63–80; as construction of condominiums, 25, 63, 69, 71, 75, 109, 129; necrosovereign aim of, 134, 141; resistance against, 131; urban, 21, 68, 80, 129. *See also* bulldozing; necrosovereignty

reinvention, 131, 139, 143; autopoiesis as processes of, 139–42; as counter-spatial movement to the necrosovereign work of rebuilding, 141. *See also* autopoiesis

resistances: death, mourning, and, 129, 141; epistemic, 11, 21–22, 97–103, 106, 109, 112, 140; and impasses, 97–102; modes of, 115, 144; necro-resistances of knowledge, 108–10; power and, 81, 92–97, 108, 129; practices of, 11–12, 15, 20–22, 106–7; relation to necrosovereignty of, 92, 95–97, 141; spaces of, 130, 140, 142. *See also* activism; memories; storytelling; waiting

Revolutionary Armed Forces of Columbia (FARC), 10, 43, 114. *See also* Columbia

rights, 9, 39, 52; distributing resources and, 65

rituals, 10, 40, 46; suspension of the conduct of funerary, 32

Robben, Antonius, 50

Ruin, Hans: *Being with the Dead*, 10, 16, 36, 147n4

Said, Edward, 93, 98

Saturday Mothers, 12–15, 19, 43, 57, 83–86, 91–94, 98, 103–7, 111–15, 119–23, 126, 129–33, 145

Schmitt, Carl, 7, 33

sexuality: discrediting women in terms of, 58; as mechanism of power, 45. *See also* homosexuality

Sharpe, Christina, 17, 37–38

Siirt, 116. *See also* Turkey

silence, 3–4, 42; death does not imply, 128; as epistemic impasses, 99; epistemology of, 99

Silopi, 91. *See also* Turkey

Sjöholm, Cecilia, 36–37

Snorton, Riley, 140

Soacha, 15–16, 43–44, 112, 129. *See also* Columbia
social media, 111. *See also* media
sociogeny, 140
Sophocles. See *Antigone* (Sophocles)
sovereignty, 27–29; authoritarian or exploitative, 115; and biopolitics, 133; Foucauldian formulation of, 30, 38–41; intersections of biopolitics and, 32, 39–41, 67; mechanisms of, 29; space as the "raw material" of, 65–67; traditional theorists of, 33. *See also* biopolitics; laws; necrosovereignty; politics
spaces: and death, 65–68; haunted, 135; of mourning, 6, 9–10, 20, 122, 135, 137, 142; necropolitical, 76–79; necrosovereign, 70, 72–77, 135; temporalities of, 6, 142
Spain, 19, 34
states of exception, regional, 20, 26, 29–30, 148n20, 150n57. *See also* Turkey
storytelling, 115–31, 141, 145; of disappearance, 119, 122–25, 128–29; Foucault on, 118; as mode of counter-conduct, 127–28. *See also* resistances
subjectivity: bodily production of, 96; conception of the overrepresentation of Western, 137; schema for political, 137; transparent, 99–100
Sur, 63, 66–72, 74–80, 129, 134, 136. *See also* Turkey
surveillance, 31, 65

Taussig, Michael, 109
Taylor, Diana, 19, 52, 57, 114
technology: biopolitical, 7–8; necrosovereign, 26; of power, 7–8, 15–17, 27, 45–49, 65, 118, 127
temporalities: of disappearances, 22, 125, 134; necro-epistemic, 107; necrosovereign, 79; nightmare, 103–8; prolonged, 115, 142; of spaces, 6, 142
territorial fragmentation, 65
terrorism, 47–48
Thompson, Kevin, 94
Torres, Nelson Maldonado, 19
torture, 14, 57; detention and, 43, 81–82, 87; public, 27. *See also* detentions; violence

transatlantic slave trade, 34. *See also* Middle Passage
transparency, 109
trash-disposal areas, 5, 15, 19, 25, 31, 34, 59, 91, 104, 109, 129
Truth and Reconciliation committees, 15
Turkey, 13, 15, 19, 33, 114–15, 123; coup d'état (1980) of, 13; map of mass graves in, 4, 150n54; political criminals of, 10. *See also* Cizre; Istanbul; Newala Qesaba; Public Mass Housing Administration (TOKI); Siirt; Silopi; states of exception, regional; Sur

United Nations Human Rights Commission, 183
United Nations International Convention for the Protection of All Persons from Enforced Disappearance, 30
United Nations Working Group on Enforced or Involuntary Disappearances, 33, 54, 147n15
United States, 33; race politics of the, 48
utopia, 131–32

Varela, F. J., 139–40
Verdery, Katherine, 16
violence: erasing, 53; histories of, 53; legitimacy of state-sanctioned, 16, 32, 52; memories of forgetting and, 135; necropolitical, 32, 53, 79; political, 13; sexual, 57. *See also* extralegal executions; torture

waiting, 82, 107. *See also* resistances
Warren, Calvin, 37–38
Washington Post, 43
westernization, 18–19. *See also* modernization
Wyndham, Marivic, 120
Wynter, Sylvia, 17, 22, 131, 136–43, 162n19; account of resistance of, 137–38. *See also* autopoiesis; fables; reinvention

Zurita, Raúl, 4; *Song for His Disappeared Love*, 86, 88